DIVIDED ISLES

Manchester University Press

DIVIDED ISLES

SOLOMON ISLANDS AND THE CHINA SWITCH

EDWARD ACTON
CAVANOUGH

MANCHESTER UNIVERSITY PRESS

Copyright © Edward Acton Cavanough 2024

Published in Australia by La Trobe University Press, 2023

This edition published in the UK
by Manchester University Press
Oxford Road, Manchester, M13 9PL

www.manchesteruniversitypress.co.uk

British Library Cataloguing-in-Publication Data
A catalogue record for this book is available from the British Library

ISBN 978 1 5261 7835 0 hardback

This edition first published 2024

The publisher has no responsibility for the persistence or accuracy of URLs for any
external or third-party internet websites referred to in this book, and does not guarantee
that any content on such websites is, or will remain, accurate or appropriate.

Text design and typesetting by Marilyn de Castro
Photograph on page 13 by Matthew Edwards. All other photographs by the author.
Map by Alan Laver

To the people of Solomon Islands, for your openness,
hospitality and inspiring resilience.

To Steve, Jill and Angus, for a lifetime of belief.

To Emily, for your unwavering love, guidance and support.

CONTENTS

SOLOMON ISLANDS

PAPUA NEW GUINEA

Bougainville

Choiseul

South Pacific
Ocean

Santa Isabel

Buala

Malu'u • Sulufou
Dala • • Bethel
Auki • • Atori

Gizo

New Georgia
Islands

Russell
Islands

Savo
Indispensable Strait

Malaita

Maramasike

Tulaghi

Honiaria

Guadalcanal

Solomon Sea

Kirakira

N

0   200 km

Scale

MILESTONES IN THE HISTORY OF SOLOMON ISLANDS

30,000–15,000 BCE	Earliest human settlement of Solomon Archipelago; introduction of Papuan languages
3000 BCE	Confirmed Austronesian expansion into Solomon Archipelago
1568	Mendaña expedition
c. 1568	Toghavitu eruption on Savo Island
1605	Failed Spanish expeditions
1796	Carteret expedition
1893	British colonial administration declared
1927	Malaita massacre
January 1942	Japanese invasion
August 1942–January 1943	Battle of Guadalcanal
1944–1952	Maasina Rule in Malaita
1975	Country renamed Solomon Islands
1978	Solomon Islands independence established; Peter Kenilorea Snr becomes inaugural prime minister
1983	Solomon Islands extends diplomatic recognition to Taiwan
1998	'The Tensions' begin
2000–2001	Manasseh Sogavare's first prime ministership
2003	RAMSI commences
2006–2007	Second Sogavare prime ministership

2014–2017	Third Sogavare prime ministership
2017	RAMSI formally concludes
April 2019	Fourth Sogavare prime ministership begins
April 2019	Daniel Suidani elected premier of Malaita Province
September 2019	Sogavare government announces the Switch to China
October 2019	Malaitan provincial government issues the Auki Communique
November 2021	Major rioting in Honiara leaves three dead in the worst violence since the conclusion of RAMSI; deployment of Australian-led peacekeeping force
April 2022	Sogavare government signs security agreement with the Chinese government

INTRODUCTION

AT 12.04 P.M. ON THURSDAY, 7 November 2019, I stepped outside a café near the Australian Department of Foreign Affairs and Trade's Canberra office to nervously make a phone call.

'Hi, is this Kate, from *The Guardian*?' I asked. 'It's Ed. I'm calling about the note you sent through just now.'

On 17 October, I'd pitched a story to the paper's Pacific editor, hoping to write about green growth and its consequences in the region. *Can green growth counter Beijing's ambitions in Solomon Islands?* my pitch asked. For months I had been obsessing over what to me appeared a clear strategic liability for Australia and its allies in the Pacific Islands region: poverty. Well, *energy poverty* to be precise. Across the islands, poor rates of electrification had seen a swelling demand for off-grid, local solutions, especially solar for diesel-dependent tourism businesses, that wasn't being met. The region's traditional allies had been slow to step up, and Chinese commercial interests had begun to fill the void. I thought I was onto a winning story.

But as is not uncommon for a freelance journalist writing niche features from quirky corners of the world, the original pitch was met with deathly silence. The rejection was no great loss. I'd been planning to go north to the Solomons anyway, furthering a research initiative on the green-growth issue I'd been piecing together in my other role as a think-tank researcher. So I let the pitch slide. In Canberra to discuss the work, the story was at the back of my mind. After a busy morning of meetings, I grabbed lunch and mindlessly scrolled my phone as I worked my way through an overpriced toasted sandwich and black coffee. As I stared into the glowing screen, the phone buzzed with an incoming email. It was Kate. She rejected my original idea, but had her own request. *The Guardian* wanted to undertake a deep dive on the diplomatic switch from Taiwan to China – to explore, on the ground, how its fallout was affecting everyday people in Solomon Islands. I left my coffee and half-eaten sandwich – cheese, avocado and warmed-through lettuce – stepped outside, composed myself and dialled her number.

A year earlier, I had returned to Australia after nine months travelling across thirty-four countries overland, testing my luck on the road as a freelance reporter. I'd been travelling through a changing world, writing dispatches from the frontlines of those forces of change. I wrote about the fallout of the independence struggle in Timor Leste; the rabid Sinicisation of China's indigenous communities; Mongolia's economic struggles, Afghanistan's unexpected tourism boom and Central Asia's Soviet hangover. After years tethered to a desk, I wanted to try to work out the world – and figure out my own place within it.

But after 242 days of hard travel, I found myself back in Adelaide, my hometown, twenty-seven years old and broke. Knowing that transcontinental adventure was off the cards for a time, I began restlessly searching for opportunities to explore and work in Australia's own region – hunting for projects that felt adventurous enough to punctuate the tedium of my day job, but close enough to home for me not to cut loose and run. I'd been lucky enough to return to my old job, a research position at an Australian think tank, where I conceived a wily plan that would allow me, under the guise of research, to travel into the wilds of the south and central Pacific. For my energy-poverty project, I'd head to Solomon Islands. My first visit had been in April that year. Enamoured, I quickly resolved to get back. I was just trying to figure out how.

Two weeks after Kate's email, I was on a Solomon Airlines flight to Honiara. Landing at Henderson Airport, I relished the ramshackle atmosphere and the smell of the humid air. As I stepped onto the tarmac, the informality felt thrillingly foreign and exotic, despite being just a two-hour flight from Australia. But I was, in the scheme of things, a novice correspondent.

My initial excitement was quickly replaced by nerves, and the magnitude of the assignment dawned on me as I stepped through the slapdash office that serves as passport control.

Over the next fortnight, I'd come face to face with the aftermath of one of the most consequential geopolitical events in Australia's region in my lifetime. I'd travel on rickety boats and old twin-prop planes across five islands, interviewing dissidents, politicians and those whose lives had been upended by a decision that had changed the country forever.

*

Six weeks before I received my commission from *The Guardian*, Solomon Islands' enigmatic four-time prime minister, 65-year-old Manasseh Sogavare, had severed Honiara's thirty-six-year alliance with Taiwan in exchange for a partnership with Beijing. The decision was a major international news event. It terrified security boffins in Canberra, who in Honiara's embrace of China saw Australia's historic Pacific advantage coming unstuck. Further afield, Sogavare's decision was receiving condemnation. It stoked rebukes from the Trump administration and its acolytes, including Senator Marco Rubio, who threatened to cut Honiara off from the global financial system, while US vice president Mike Pence cancelled a meeting with the Solomons' prime minister in protest.

The Switch, as it became known, had inspired endless column inches from commentators writing from afar. But in those early weeks, much of the coverage had explored what the Switch meant not for Solomon Islanders, but for *us:* Australians, Americans, New Zealanders and others outside the region invested in the status quo and fearful of a revanchist China.

There were enough stories about the international fallout of the Switch. My job was to understand how it was playing out on the ground, and how the disparate people of this fragile island nation with a recent history of civil unrest, stretched thinly over a thousand islands and speaking seventy indigenous languages, were accommodating one of its biggest policy shifts since achieving independence in 1978.

From Sogavare's and his supporters' perspective, the decision made sense: to recognise China was to recognise reality. China was already Solomon Islands' largest trading partner, and as the rest of the Pacific cashed in on Beijing's largesse, many felt that it was now Solomon Islands' turn. To Sogavare and his allies, the country's alliance with Taiwan appeared anachronistic, like a throwback to a bygone era when China's economic weight carried less sway. And the Taiwan alliance wasn't even delivering: Taiwan's aid to Solomon Islands was highly publicised and well received by locals, but paled in comparison to the development assistance Solomon Islands received annually from Australia, New Zealand and Japan. What little Taiwanese money did enter the Solomons had, without question, exacerbated the country's corruption challenges, angering Honiara's Western partners, whose focus for years had been on cleaning up government.

But everyday Solomon Islanders were suspicious of Chinese intentions, aware of the risks of debt-trap diplomacy and emotively loyal to the Taiwanese. Some were deeply uncomfortable with embracing China. As this sentiment took root, a roster of Sogavare's opponents – often younger, emerging politicians with their own national ambitions – saw in this anti-Beijing sentiment an opportunity for political advancement and quickly weaponised it for the accrual of power.

The immediate aftermath of the Switch was rocky. There were protests across the country, and although the Sogavare government went to great lengths to reassure the public about the decision, its arguments were met with condemnation. Taiwan, Sogavare said, had been 'useless' to Solomon Islands; by embracing Beijing, a golden era of prosperity would follow. He paired these lofty promises with genuine pledges from China. Within weeks, Beijing had committed funds for a new soccer stadium in Honiara, and a once defunct gold mine was reanimated with a US$500-million infusion of China Rail capital.

But the suspicious origins of these pledges caused consternation, and their focus on Honiara fuelled dissent outside the capital. The economic disparities between the Honiara elite and rural Solomon Islanders had long been the driver of the country's instability.

Opposition to the Switch emerged strongest in Auki, the small and dilapidated capital of Malaita, Solomon Islands' most populous and poorest province. Constituting half the national population, ethnic Malaitans, both those who live on Malaita and those who have settled elsewhere in Solomons, are proud of their identity and have historically resisted central rule – whether from Honiara or from Tulagi during Britain's colonial administration of the archipelago. Malaitan grievances came to the fore during 'the Tensions', a five-year period of civil unrest between 1998 and 2003 that left 200 people dead and led to near complete state failure. In 2003, a fourteen-year-long peacekeeping mission led by Australia – the Regional Assistance Mission to Solomon Islands, or RAMSI – commenced. RAMSI successfully imposed peace, but it was unable to address the economic and cultural determinants of violence in Solomon Island, which have remained close to the surface.

When the Switch was announced, protestors flocked to the streets of Auki, carrying hastily made signs that read 'No Need China'. Elsewhere in the province, Sogavare's MPs were pelted with rocks and abuse as they embarked on a comically unsuccessful roadshow to spruik their prime minister's call.

For the Malaitans, the Switch became totemic of Honiara's constant denial of the province's wishes, and within weeks, these angry islanders grafted an impassioned opposition to China onto their very identity. They had their cause. Now, they needed a champion. And they would find it in an uncharismatic, softly spoken first-time politician: the Malaitan premier, Daniel Suidani.

*

Divided Isles tells the story of Solomon Islands' China Switch, its dramatic internal and regional consequences, the political machinations that led to it, and how a handful of Solomon Islanders have used this transformative, once-in-a-generation political event to accrue and wield political power.

It is the story of Manasseh Sogavare and his fateful decision, and how it transformed the country. It is the story of Daniel Suidani, and how his manipulation of the Switch thrust him from obscurity to global relevance. It is the story of the Malaitan activists who have leveraged this political shift to revive a volatile, albeit improbable, quest for independence for their island. It is the story of a byzantine web of Pacific business elites and their willingness to change the political course of their nation in pursuit of commercial gain. And it is the story of how seemingly powerless islanders have the capacity to radically alter the trajectory of a fragile country and a region essential to Australia's, and the world's, security.

There is a trope among many international observers that the Pacific, with its small countries and brittle economies, is too weak to wield any real influence over global affairs. We see it in much of the coverage of the region, which often portrays countries such as Solomon Islands as little more than chess pieces to be fought over by the US and China. The story to come stands as a rebuttal to this perspective. Because in Solomon Islands – as elsewhere in the Pacific – unassuming individuals have often shown a capacity not only to take advantage of their geopolitical circumstance, but to reshape it to their benefit.

Manasseh Sogavare's decision to embrace China was seismic, sending ripples all the way to Washington, D.C. But it was also deeply personal. He held deep suspicions of Taiwan, dating back to Taipei's shady involvement during the Tensions. He was inherently sceptical of Australian intent. And he was personally eager to leverage a close relationship with China to gain greater concessions from Solomon Islands' traditional Western allies. The decision was cloaked in officialdom and process, but it was Sogavare's call.

Daniel Suidani, the media-savvy Malaitan premier, has been able to skilfully shape the behaviour of Taiwan and even the United States by dangling his province's potential future pro-Taiwan statehood as a temptation, eliciting millions in donations from Washington and Taipei, routinely angering Beijing and strengthening his influence in the process.

That Sogavare and Suidani – two men from a country with next to no material or economic power in a conventional sense – can alter the behaviour of the world's most powerful nations and, in the case of Suidani, shape a media narrative that amplifies his prestige at home and abroad, hints at a deep political sophistication regularly missed by Pacific watchers.

The story of these manoeuvres and the men behind them is important. But power in the Pacific is not exclusive to elected officials. In Malaita, the grassroots rebels who infiltrated the Malaitan government and turned their closely held dreams of independence into something tangible are a key part of this story. Chief among them is the nascent Malaitan separatist organisation Malaita for Democracy, commonly known as M4D, and the men who control it.

Just two days after the Switch, M4D emerged from the ether, initially led by a gruff 35-year-old named Richard Olita. It soon became clear that this new and obscure organisation was a force to be reckoned with, mobilising thousands in Auki to protest the China decision. It was behind large-scale protests elsewhere on the island and orchestrated heated public receptions for Sogavare's allies charged with selling the new China partnership to the masses.

Olita was hired by Premier Suidani, and for years after the Switch, the Malaitan government's manoeuvres mirrored the policy priorities of M4D, placing Malaita Province – which, with over 200,000 residents and an expansive geography, maintains a population and territory larger than most Pacific Island nations – on a dangerous, at times naïve and almost certainly doomed path towards statehood.

*

This book is not an attempt at a comprehensive history of Solomon Islands. But the story of the Switch cannot be told in a historical vacuum. The key personalities involved have their own complex personal histories and operate with an innate understanding of the historical foundations on which they stand.

The Solomon Archipelago is a place of joy and beauty. At the same time, it is host to centuries of grievance and tragedy. Enmities fuelled by ancient internal rivalries, colonial dispossession and exploitation, inadequate reconstruction after the Second World War, uneven economic growth since independence in 1978, and the ethnic tensions that gripped the country between 1998 and 2003 undergird cultural, economic and political discourse in contemporary Solomon Islands. This context cannot be ignored.

Just as Solomon Islands has a long history of disruption, so too does it maintain a tradition of popular resistance to external influence. From the very first moments Solomon Islanders encountered Europeans in the sixteenth century, they fervently voiced their opposition to the outsiders' arrival. Solomon Islanders were not passive during colonial rule, either. Dissent was widespread – particularly in Malaita – inflamed by Solomon Islanders' exploitation as forced labourers on Australian sugar plantations and the often punitive and brutal imposition of colonial law and order. When the Second World War came to the islands, locals were mobilised to help secure an Allied victory. While many remain proud of their contribution, they also know that it wasn't their war: they are acutely aware that their homeland had become the staging ground for someone else's fight. The remnants of that foreign conflict – its destruction of the land, its maiming of Solomon Islanders – are still evident and continue to this day, in the form of unexploded ordnance scattered indiscriminately across the archipelago.

When Solomon Islands finally achieved independence in 1978, this long, often brutal history of imposition wasn't forgotten. It would shape the thinking of the country's early political giants, who would in turn deeply influence the philosophies of future generations of Solomon Islander leaders, including those making decisions today. *Divided Isles* tells this story, too.

When my *Guardian* article was published in December 2019, I assumed my reporting career on Solomon Islands' China pivot might have come to an end. Instead, the story began to gather pace, sustaining international attention even during a global pandemic. As Covid-19 emerged, the story of the country's new relationship with China only became more complex and consequential. Large quantities of Chinese money began entering a country otherwise sealed off from the world. Honiara played host to a new collective of Beijing-backed businesspeople seeking to capitalise on the relationship. The Malaitans who opposed China established secret and illegal diplomatic ties with Taiwan and began flirting with independence. And the country's deepening security relationship with China would bring the United States to the negotiating table, and even influence a national election in my home country of Australia.

Even as the story of the Switch evolved, however, some things on the ground remained stubbornly the same. The impoverished communities I had profiled when investigating energy poverty remained in development limbo. The young were still restless and desperate for opportunities. The cronyism that had long gripped Honiara's elite was as rife as ever.

Returning to Solomon Islands as Covid-19 restrictions were lifted, I saw a country that was in even worse shape than before the pandemic. Unknown numbers had died, often at home, let down by an inadequate healthcare system. Once undisturbed villages now had hand-painted quarantine signs and quickly constructed bamboo fences closing them off from their neighbours, and years of economic progress had been visibly, devastatingly reversed. The Switch continued to dominate headlines. To some international observers, it was all the country was known for. But on the ground, people were just trying to get by.

In *Divided Isles,* I attempt to bring this local reality to the fore. Because the story of Solomon Islands' political intrigue is not just about the men who control the country or the powerful interests that support them. It is not just about foreign powers and their alleged appetite for control and domination of the archipelago. And it is certainly not about *us*, the outsiders looking in with curiosity, good intentions and occasional concern, but whose lives will ultimately not be shaped by the decisions of the powerful in Honiara.

It is a story about the people on the frontline of this profound moment of flux. The people living in often quiet, ancient villages, communities like the one on a modest volcanic clump, thirty kilometres off the coast of Honiara, that would soon come to feel like an island home of my own.

PART I
ISLAND UNIVERSE

Dala Village, Nggela Islands, November 2019.

1

'AFUERA!'

EACH DAWN, 100 BLACK BIRDS WITH red heads and yellow legs settle on a tropical beach in northwest Savo, a volcanic island off the coast of Guadalcanal. In cool white sand they begin to burrow. Protected by palm-leaf fences, the megapodes – endemic to Savo and a handful of neighbouring islands – land in this sanctuary each morning, having descended from the coconut-palm jungle that blankets the nearby volcanic peak, last defiled by an 1830s eruption. The sand, fine and light, is violently kicked in the air as the birds dig holes an arm's length deep to lay a solitary egg. Then, having made their precious deposit, the exhausted megapodes furiously work the sand until the hole is filled. Their eggs secured and the tropical sun now at full strength, the birds fly back towards the thick canopy, waiting for tomorrow's dawn, when they will begin their ritual again.

Wilfred, wiry-framed and grey-bearded, dressed in a tattered old beer-company T-shirt, board shorts and flip-flops he found washed up on the beach, is the custodian of the egg field. A sixty-year-old elder from the neighbouring thatched-roof village of Panueli, he is the megapodes' protector. The eggs, a delicacy in Solomon Islands, are highly sought-after. Around twice the size of a chicken egg and rich in protein, they have become a prized commodity in the markets of Honiara and nearby Tulagi. But their value creates its own problems. Late at night, it is not uncommon for raiders to sneak up on the egg fields. Paddling dugout canoes, they silently come ashore between the waves and capture the eggs Wilfred has left in the ground to hatch so that the flock can be sustained.

Wilfred, custodian of the egg field.

Wilfred's chief responsibility is to ensure the protective bamboo and palm-leaf barricade he has erected remains in place. Sometimes his fences are damaged by wind or waves, but they are always rebuilt. Wilfred has crafted a sanctuary, continuing a tradition that dates back at least half a millennium, to a time when the white, sandy expanse on which the birds now nest was blasted into existence by an event witnessed by the first outsiders to visit this island since the Savoans had themselves settled, countless generations earlier.

In 1568, two Spanish vessels, the *Capitana* and the *Almiranta*, left the Peruvian port town of Callao, now a suburb of modern-day Lima, heading west in search of a land rumoured to have been discovered and exploited by ancient Incan seafarers. The Incans, so the legend went, had brought back 'gold and silver, a throne made of copper, a multitude of black slaves and the skin of an animal like a horse'.[1] Although the Spanish felt entitled to explore and exploit this unknown world, their claim to it was tenuous. In 1513, famed explorer Vasco Núñez de Balboa had become the first European to lay eyes on the Pacific Ocean; after crossing the Isthmus of Panama, he waded into the surf 'up to his middle [and] took possession of it in the name of his sovereign, Ferdinand of Spain'.[2]

This brief swim would inspire a century of Spanish exploration across the endless oceans west of the New World. Seven years later, Ferdinand Magellan sailed between Antarctica and modern-day Chile and continued across an expanse of blue before meeting his death at the hands of indigenous Filipinos in 1521. Subsequent expeditions between 1527 and 1555 led the Spanish to learn of Hawaii, New Guinea and the Marshall Islands, and by 1565, the Spanish, defying local resistance, established a colony in the Philippines. For the Spaniards, the pursuit of this oceanic expanse was driven not so much by an innate desire for exploration or by religious fervour as by a thirst for wealth. The sixteenth century was 'the age of gold' – and to the Spaniards, 'the whole world was yellow'.

As Spanish government and society became settled in sixteenth-century Peru, the rumoured Incan discoveries had become something of a fixation for an emerging generation of ambitious South America–based conquistadors. When Lope García de Castro became governor of Peru in 1564, plans were drawn to, at last, undertake a serious expedition to find this mysterious land of bounty. To lead the mission, the governor appointed his 25-year-old nephew, Álvara de Mendaña de Neyra. Mendaña assembled two ships, procured 150 men including sailors, slaves and friars, and, aided by his second-in-command Hernán Gallego, gathered several months' worth of rations. Having previously traversed South America's Pacific coast, with expertise in shipbuilding and design, and having spent a lifetime at sea,

Gallego, despite his illiteracy, had impressed Mendaña. With so many past expeditions ending in the violent death of captain and crew, Mendaña, an erudite and educated aristocrat but comparably inexperienced seafarer, needed a man of Gallego's stature to survive what would be one of the most daring voyages since the thirteenth-century settlement of New Zealand had brought to an end the Polynesian age of discovery.

The Peruvian ships left on 19 November 1567, and they were lucky to make it far at all. The rumoured Incan expedition was almost certainly fable, and their advisor's claim to know the route the Incans had taken was laughable, yet this advice foolishly guided Mendaña's itinerary. In the definitive account of the expedition, based on the six surviving transcripts from Mendaña's crew, the folly of the journey is noted:

> It is difficult for anyone unacquainted with the ocean miscalled the Pacific to realise the reckless daring of the enterprise. Leaving in the month of November, with the hurricane season approaching; crossing an ocean more than 7000 miles in width, beset with unknown coral reefs in crazy vessels unprotected from the teredo[3] and almost incapable of beating to windward; with the prevailing wind behind them and a 'dead beat' all the way home-ward; depending on provisions that no master, in the worst days of our merchant marine, would have dared to put to sea with the adventurers had a thousand chances to one against ever finding their way home again.[4]

After twenty-six days at sea, Mendaña and Gellego were indeed flailing. The route they'd followed had come to nothing, and the *Capitana* and *Alviranta* had yet to sight land. They were running low on supplies, and mutiny was brewing. So Mendaña and Gallego decided to abandon their original westward route and reorient northwest, towards uncharted equatorial waters. Through January of 1568, the two ships sailed aimlessly, avoiding a cyclone and coral reefs. They then unknowingly drifted south for weeks, until in mid-February they at last saw land 'so mountainous and limitless that they believed it to be a continent'. It was Gallego who first spotted the island they called Isabel, one of the largest in a strip of islands they would eventually name after King Solomon, the biblical monarch known for his wealth. They had just found the Pacific's most expansive archipelago.

The land that Mendaña and Gallego had inadvertently drifted towards may have been vast, but it was by no means vacant, and its inhabitants were by no means passive. Before they made landfall, the Spaniards were visited by a group of locals, who paddled to the ships on canoes and came aboard, grabbing loose items and throwing them overboard for those remaining in the canoes to inspect. In the initial linguistic exchanges between the two parties, the indigenous people appear to have acquired their first Spanish word: *afuera*, loosely translated as 'get outside' or 'go away'. It was a refrain the Spanish explorers would soon hear regularly, shouted at them by Solomon Islanders who 'wished to prevent [the Spanish] from exploring their country'.[5]

Despite this resistance, the Spaniards stepped ashore. At times, they were allowed to conduct their affairs with little interference. But part of the challenge the Spaniards faced was navigating what must have appeared an endless number of tribes, each with a different language, leadership and territory. These tribes were often at war with one another, rendering the establishment of any negotiated co-existence unlikely. Initially, the Spanish had some success. The first chief with whom they made a tentative peace was Bilebenara, who 'had no other end in view but to disarm the hostility of the strangers, and to induce them to leave him alone'.[6] But while the Spanish may have pacified Bilebenara, they soon realised he was at war with a nearby tribe. 'Every petty tribal unit inhabiting a few square miles spoke a dialect that was almost a different language, and was at perpetual enmity with its neighbours', wrote the historians of the Mendaña expedition. As the expedition wore on, the Spanish required more food and resources, which Bilebenara was loath to provide.

During various inland expeditions, the Europeans met tribes 'determined to oppose their advances'. Soon, the Spaniards moved to explore neighbouring islands. Putting his shipbuilding prowess to work, Gallego and his men felled timbers to construct a brigantine, a smaller vessel suited for navigation in shallow waters and over coral reefs. After fifty-four days, the small ship was built. It would spend the next four months exploring the island chain, making important discoveries, but often being aggressively thwarted by hostile locals.

By May, the crew had grown restless. Mendaña put to a vote the question of whether this new island group should be settled; his men rejected the proposal and instead demanded to sail for California. The Spanish, who would be the last Europeans to see these islands for another two centuries, had forgone their opportunity to absorb the newfound archipelago into a growing empire.

Perhaps, had they stayed, they might have succeeded. They would certainly have found gold, of which there is a vast quantity in Guadalcanal, and those discoveries might have provided the Spanish a steppingstone to other nearby riches. But Mendaña's crew decided on a wiser, simpler course. No matter the wealth of the Spanish, no matter their technological prowess or economic lust, they departed, defeated and rejected, unwelcome in a land they had been lucky to set foot in at all.

*

The Mendaña expedition may have failed in its objectives, but it left detailed charts and astute observations of the precolonial Solomon Islands. This is where the documented history of Solomon Islands commences, including the history of an island in the middle of the archipelago known locally as Savo.

When Mendaña, Gallego and their crew sailed past the northwestern edge of 'the volcanic island of Savo a few miles on their starboard hand' in their brigantine, they observed that the volcano was erupting. They noted Savo's 'many inhabitants and bountiful gardens' and presumed it rich in yam, honeycombs, roots and pigs. They happened to be in Savo's vicinity during the island's most volatile and transformative period – a violent time that shaped the island and its culture for generations to come.

The eruption the Spaniards recorded was probably one of several aftershocks that took place in the years after Savo was catastrophically disfigured by an explosion known as Toghavitu; the name is derived from the Savosavo word for 7000 – the number of people who died. On Savo, as elsewhere in Melanesia, history and other essential knowledge – farming techniques, the best fishing spots, how to survive cyclonic conditions – are passed from generation to generation through storytelling. Through these stories, often coded in myth and indecipherable to outsiders, islanders have learned to protect themselves, even from natural disasters like volcanos.

In 1993, Thomas Toba, a geologist working for Solomon Islands' Ministry of Energy, Water and Mineral Resources, gathered anecdotal evidence of past eruptions from Savoans, placing these data-rich tales on record for the first time. Toba interviewed locals from around the island, asking them to recall stories about their island's volcanic history that they had been told growing up. What he discovered was an unbroken chain of stories linking the Savo of the 1990s to the accounts of a handful of Spanish sailors more than 400 years earlier.

Justin Lugha was one of Toba's research participants. He came from Reko, one of the island's larger settlements on the south coast. Today, the village is home to Savo's largest school, its overgrown soccer pitch framed by the distant backdrop of Guadalcanal's mountainous northwest. Lugha recounted the stories of Toghavitu he had heard from elders while growing up.

'It is said that the eruption killed 7000 people,' he told Toba. 'There were gas clouds ... and fire-like appearances in the sky.'

Nicholas Muni, another villager, shared a similar account:

There were two major eruptions on Savo, one was referred to as Toghavitu, which means seven thousand ... There were general signs and indications that the volcano didn't suddenly erupt ... the water level rose and rolled up the crater, destroying all vegetation with associated landslide.

According to some accounts, the crater at the heart of the island even filled with water, allowing these early Savoans, who were direct descendants of the first Papuan émigrés who had landed some 30,000 years prior, to paddle their dugout canoes in the newly formed lake, oblivious to the devastation that was to come. After several days, the inevitable occurred.

Francis Tagusuna of Lemboni village told Toba that the Toghavitu eruption was so violent, it fundamentally altered the geography of Savo:

> Before any eruptions ... Savo Island was very small. Being so small one could just stand over the Paghalula dome [a small mound in the island's east] and look on both sides of the island ... Toghavitu wiped out the early inhabitants of Savo Island. Nothing survived this eruption; all forms of life were utterly devastated, leaving only a dusty, smoky speck protruding from the middle of the ocean.

All that remained were the stories of devastation, held closely by the Savoans who witnessed their families' violent deaths from the nearby villages of Visale and Vila on Guadalcanal. These relatives living on Guadalcanal would later resettle the island of Savo.

Toghavitu forever altered the course of Savo, likely expanding its size and producing fertile expanses of land that led to what observers described as an 'abundance' so great that life in late-twentieth-century Savo was 'undemanding'. The first years after Toghavitu are documented in the notes and sketches of Mandaña's crew from the early months of 1568.

As the dust settled, the surviving Savoan émigrés returned, canoeing over the tranquil, dolphin-filled waters, and began repopulating their ancestral home. The destruction may have been devastating, but it also breathed new life into the island and embedded an indigenous knowledge about the risks of the volcano – a detailed, highly localised intelligence that, centuries later, a new generation of islanders would mobilise for their own survival.

At some point between 1830 and 1840, a second major eruption occurred on Savo. Geologists don't believe it was nearly as destructive as Toghavitu, but accounts passed on through kastom and shared with Toba paint a harrowing scene of the nineteenth-century explosion. As one research subject told Toba:

Tremors and earthquakes caused landslides and slips. Water filled the crater and spilled out through … drainage channels, carrying with it the debris of [Toghavitu]. Later there were minor explosions and increased activity which produced gas clouds that covered the atmosphere above the island, shadowing and covering the face of the sun. There was total darkness over the island.

J.C. Grover, in his 1961 book *A Brief History of Geological and Geophysical Investigations in the British Solomon Islands, 1881–1961*, recorded a second-hand account of the nineteenth-century eruption. Grover writes of Marino Tandabara, of Takamoru village on Guadalcanal, who was told by his grandfather, 'a very old bald-headed man of 80 to 100 years old in 1927', about the day of the eruption:

It started in the evening in a small way at first, but at midnight there were sounds like the continued hooting of a steamer … These became louder and felt as earthquake shocks like repeated thumping about 120 to a minute.

Then came the cataclysmic outburst. The Guadalcanal mountains and all the people standing outside their houses watching the spectacle were lit up as though by daylight, and millions of great fiery rocks red like the moon were thrown up into the sky above the fire of Savo.

At dawn, the Guadalcanal people flocked down from their hilltop villages to the beaches and found the many Savo people who had managed to escape by canoe. Everyone was kind to them and many were relatives … many of them remained for ten years or more, for Savo had been made completely desolate.

The knowledge accrued by Savoans from Toghavitu braced them for a volatile future that was to come. Highly detailed accounts of the sixteenth-century catastrophe were passed down generation to generation, and 200 years later, the Savoan people were ready. The villagers fled to the handful of sheltered sections of the island, where they would be protected from lava flows and ashfall. Although this second eruption was deadly, the number of lives lost was greatly reduced, with perhaps as few as 100 people perishing. Those who made it to Guadalcanal and Nggela held out until it was safe to return. When they did, they found a Savo once again reformed. The second eruption further changed the Savoan landscape, dumping more pumice into the surrounding waters and extending Savo's physical geography for the second time in two centuries, into the undulating clump visible from modern-day Honiara. Viewed from Savo today, the lights of the capital shine brightly.

*

Wilfred, the custodian of the megapode egg field, continues a tradition that his ancestors began soon after the violent period that created this flat, sandy beach. Wilfred is a vessel for this encyclopaedic, story-based knowledge accrued over millennia. This knowledge has been informed by local events, such as the Toghavitu blast and subsequent eruptions, but also by foreign impositions, starting when Mendaña's small, handmade vessel inched past Savo's northwest corner early in 1568, witnessing Wilfred's direct ancestors tending to their yam plantations and farming pigs.

During the subsequent two centuries, the stream of foreign visitors would slow. But then, in the late eighteenth century, a distant world again began to impose itself on the Savoans' island home.

2

JUNGLE ROAD

ALMOST 200 YEARS AFTER MENDAÑA'S brigantine inched past Wilfred's village, Europeans again eyed the archipelago. In 1767, A British navy expedition led by Rear Admiral Philip Carteret sailed past Santa Cruz and Malaita, through the straits around Savo, before venturing further west to chart much of what is now northeast Papua New Guinea. Over the next century, French, Dutch and German vessels navigated the islands, although none managed to establish lasting settlements, dissuaded like the Spanish before them by fierce resistance from local communities. Throughout the nineteenth century, the British established permanent settlements in the archipelago, bringing with them religion and disease and taking countless thousands of able men to work on sugar plantations in the Australian colony of Queensland.

It was not until 1893 that London formalised its colonial acquisition of the Solomon Archipelago, establishing the British Solomon Islands Protectorate after negotiations with Germany for territorial concessions in New Guinea, the southern Solomons and further east, towards Samoa. In May of that year, two British vessels, HMS *Curacao* and HMS *Goldfinch*, were instructed to sail from Australia to the southern Solomons and to 'raise 30 flags starting at Mono Island in the north, continuing throughout the western islands and then on to the main southern islands'. The 'incipient'[1] British Solomon Islands Protectorate was declared in 1893 but had no administrative personnel and no headquarters. For several years, it was more concept than reality, existing primarily in the minds of ambitious

British colonialists but effectively invisible to the thousands of islanders who now, on paper at least, were placed under the protection of the distant and ailing Queen Victoria.

Charles Morris Woodford, a 44-year-old British naturalist and linguist who had first travelled to Guadalcanal a decade earlier to find new curiosities for the British Museum, was eventually tasked with establishing a functioning government. Traders were already frequenting the archipelago, but Woodford was effectively building a colony from scratch: his initial reports noted just forty-four Europeans permanently residing in what would become the protectorate. His first step was to buy the island of Tulagi for £42, which was split between thirty-two islanders on neighbouring Nggela. After establishing its capital on Tulagi – an island 'ideally situated for a small government station ... hilly, well covered in forest, [with] some good springs of fresh water, and ... a well-protected harbour' – Britain consolidated control, eventually extending its rule to Choiseul, Rennell and the Santa Cruz chain southeast towards the New Hebrides (now Vanuatu). Savo, once an isolated outpost at the end of the world, was now just one hour's boat ride from a local outpost of the world's largest empire.

Woodford was in a bind. He had lobbied hard for the declaration of the protectorate but now faced considerable pressure to prove that his project was viable. His receipt of a £1200 grant and salary from British authorities was premised on his capacity to achieve financial sustainability in the protectorate. To achieve this, the highly lucrative labour trade would be continued and expanded. The British began looking across the archipelago for men to satiate the demand. From Savo to Guadalcanal, Nggela to Malaita, Choiseul to Isabel, thousands of men were shipped south to Australian sugar plantations.

Many of these 'blackbirded' Solomon Islanders would never return home, instead being relocated to elsewhere in the Solomons after their period of indentured servitude had concluded or shipped to other places, such as Fiji or the New Hebrides. In Malaita, resistance to the British was fierce and often violent and prompted reprisals. A particularly punitive attack by British personnel on Malaitans in 1927, in which sixty

Malaitans were killed and 200 more imprisoned, quieted the rebellion for a generation.

As the labour trade slowed in the mid-1930s, distant political machinations began to spill over into devastating conflict. In 1931, a revanchist Japanese empire annexed Manchuria in northeastern China, commencing fifteen years of war and occupation that would soon trickle as far south as Savo. By January 1942, Japan had seized control of Tulagi and expelled the British, placing much of the Solomon Archipelago under Tokyo's control. The invasion set the scene for what was to be one of the most pivotal and bloody battles of the Second World War.

By August, the United States, now in a full-blown conflict with Japan for control of countless strategically significant islands across the Pacific, readied for an all-out assault to recapture Guadalcanal. On 7 August 1942, US forces attacked across Guadalcanal and the Nggela Islands, capturing Henderson Airfield, which today serves as Honiara's international airport, and Tulagi, the British capital. The attack prompted the Japanese to direct their warships to a stretch of water between Guadalcanal and Savo, now known as Iron Bottom Sound, to thwart the US advance. At the northern edge of Savo, the first major naval battle in the tussle over the Solomon Islands began. The first Battle of Savo proved to be among the most devastating single engagements for the Allies in the Pacific war, with 1077 Allied servicemen, almost all Australian, killed, compared with fifty-eight for the Japanese, who claimed a comprehensive victory.

As the conflict continued and the Allies' fortunes eventually turned, Savo bore witness to much of the fury. Allied soldiers set up mounted guns around the perimeter of the island, while Savoans, both adults and children, were mobilised to keep watch for passing Japanese boats and submarines. Numerous ships were sunk off the island's beaches, and Japanese and American fighter jets were downed into the heart of Savo's unoccupied jungle interior.

In January 1943, the United States prevailed in the Battle of Guadalcanal. It was a pivotal victory – Guadalcanal was 'Our jungle road to Tokyo', one American general said[2] – and set in motion the fall of Imperial

Japan and American triumph in the Pacific. But as the Americans moved on, the Savoans and their fellow Solomon Islanders were left to pick up the pieces.

The legacy of the conflict is still evident today. When I first visited Savo in 2019, I was told of a pile of scrap metal some children had found covered by overgrowth. The children were removing bits of metal and giving them to their parents to sell to scrappers in Honiara. It quickly became apparent that this curiously located pile of scrap was, in fact, the remnants of a downed Japanese fighter. There are several more scattered in the water just off Wilfred's megapode sanctuary.

The scars of the war weren't only physical. The conflict fundamentally broke any sense of isolation that Savoans and other Solomon Islanders may have been holding on to. Although the country remains remote by international standards, there is a prevailing sense in the Solomons that the world and its problems could at any time show up again. In 1990, as famed travel writer Paul Theroux paddled his way around Savo's circumference, enchanted by its 'pretty huts' and its abundance of fish, oranges, lemons, guavas and megapode eggs, war was looming half a world away. In the deserts of Saudi Arabia, 100,000 US and coalition troops had begun to mobilise in response to Iraqi president Sadam Hussein's illegal invasion of neighbouring Kuwait. Theroux was paddling the Pacific during this time, feeling uniquely detached from the horrors that were emerging in the Middle East.

Sharing a beer with a local, Ataban, Theroux was asked if World War Three was coming.

'We think it will come here,' Ataban told him. 'Everyone is worried.'

Theroux tried to dismiss Ataban's fears: 'Believe me, you are safe here.'

But Ataban wasn't so sure. 'World War Two came here. Right here to this island.'[3]

As the Second World War receded, so too did Britain's grip on its empire. London had conscripted hundreds of thousands of its subjects from across its vast colonial project in the fight against Nazism. But many who had fought under the Union Jack returned home to countries governed by a now diminished colonial power. That injustice fuelled movements for self-rule across the world, and Solomon Islands was no exception. Many Solomon Islanders quickly became frustrated with their treatment after the war. In Guadalcanal, the British refused to allow Solomon Islanders to keep the materials they had used daily during the war – not just weapons, but other surplus items of value that the locals had hoped to salvage, scrap and resell. Meanwhile, British and American servicemen stationed in the islands 'began to make small fortunes [by selling] surplus and salvage materials left behind'.[4]

In Are'are, in central Malaita, a handful of former members of the Solomon Islands Labour Corps, which had been pivotal to the Allied effort, started agitating for independence. They called their movement Maasina Ruru, commonly translated as 'Brother Rule' or 'Marching Rule'. Like postwar independence movements elsewhere in the empire, the Malaitans' asks were simple: after half a century of colonial rule, they wanted a country of their own. They may even have been expecting sympathy in London. By now, Britain's Labour government had begun the process of decolonisation: the partition of India in 1947 would be the start of four decades of colonial disentanglement.

But while London was mismanaging the shift towards independence in the subcontinent, it was brutally punishing dissent in the Solomons. To press their claims, the Malaitans had stopped paying taxes. In 1947, local English officials began rounding up Maasina Ruru supporters. More than 2000 were arrested, and the movement's leaders were imprisoned. By 1950, however, new British colonial leaders were sent to the Solomons, and they released the Maasina Ruru dissenters. Ultimately, the protest was successful: the new colonial administration, now based in Honiara, granted the Malaitans a degree of self-rule, with the establishment of an island council of elected figures.

Through the 1960s and 1970s, similar concessions were made across the archipelago. Recognising the inevitability of the end of empire, even in Solomon Islands, the British allowed the groundwork to be laid for independence. In 1973, the Solomon Islands British Protectorate elected its first Solomon Islander chief minister, thirty-year-old Solomon Mamaloni. By 1975, the country had its current name, dropping the 'British Protectorate' suffix, and in 1978 it became the forty-first British colonial outpost to attain self-rule.

It was clear that the new state would be beset with challenges. Small and economically vulnerable, it would turn quickly to extractive industries, angering traditional landowners throughout the archipelago. Graft and patronage became entrenched, while stable political parties and coalitions struggled to form. The 1952 decision by the British to relocate the capital to Honiara had shifted the economic and political centre of gravity in the island chain. As opportunities for economic advancement outside of Honiara remained rare, young men descended upon this once tiny village to seek work. It led to a rapid growth on the city's outskirts, including the construction of unregulated housing on the fertile hills south of the city. Most of the new arrivals were from Malaita, and much of the new construction was on land traditionally owned by the ethnic Guale people, many of whom had family ties to the land dating back millennia.

By the mid-1990s, growing tensions led to the rise of formal militia. In 1997, the Isatabu Freedom Movement, or Guadalcanal Revolutionary Army, was established. It 'began a campaign of intimidation and violence towards the Malaitan settlers', who responded in turn with the establishment of the Malaita Eagle Force.[5] The violence was modest compared with some nations' civil wars – 200 people are estimated to have been killed between 1998 and 2003. But the Tensions, as they became known, shattered the country. In 2001, the Australian government helped to broker a peace deal between the warring groups, but violence and instability would persist. In the chaos, the then prime minister, Bartholomew Ulufa'alu, was kidnapped at gunpoint by Malaita Eagle Force militia, who forced his resignation. His successor, Manasseh Damukana Sogavare, was forty-five when he became prime minister for the first time in June 2000; his remarkable rise from bureaucratic functionary to prime minister had taken less than a decade.

Sogavare, sceptical of the long history of foreign imposition on his island home, resisted calls to ask the international community for help to maintain security. But by late 2002, a new prime minister was in power. Allan Kemakeza of Savo Island – a man who 'had the look of a policeman – tough, sceptical, ironic, physical, resentful, suspicious, not particularly talkative but very attentive; the sort of man who looks as though he has survived a few fights'.[6] He took an alternative approach, forever shaping the history of his country. After months of pleading by the Solomons government, the Australian government finally, in July 2003, acquiesced to Kemakeza's call for peacekeeping assistance, working with a dozen other Pacific nations to assemble a force of over 2000.

For fourteen years, the Regional Assistance Mission to Solomon Islands, or RAMSI, would remain in place. It was not until 2017 that Sogavare, in his third term as prime minister, oversaw the exit of the Australian-led mission. As we will see, in Sogavare's eyes, the country now, for the first time, was truly able to move on from generations of foreign intervention and stand on its own two feet.

Sogavare would briefly lose power in 2018, before recapturing the prime ministership in April 2019 and quickly beginning a process that would see his country's thirty-six-year alliance with Taiwan upended in favour of a new partnership with Beijing.

*

I first travelled to Savo Island that same month, April 2019, visiting the dozens of villages scattered around its circumference. They were colourfully decorated with pristine gardens, children frolicking in turquoise waters and adults speaking in that distinctive language that has passed on stories and knowledge for generations. The country's complexity and diversity, and the sheer scale of its history, became immediately apparent. On the island, you see countless scenes that look as if they were extracted from the diaries of Álvaro de Mendaña himself. When you walk to the heart of the island's bubbling volcanic crater, you see a turbulent foundation atop which generations of Savoans have navigated with skill, sophistication and ingenuity. When you stare into Wilfred's tired eyes, you see a connection to thousands of years of history, knowledge and resistance to one seemingly unstoppable force of change after another.

As I looked west from Savo's beaches, towards the vast archipelago over the horizon, I came to a humbling realisation. Savo, a community of 5000 carrying a thousand generations of stories, traditions and ancient memories, is just one of 997 islands that constitute the contemporary state of Solomon Islands. Of these, 147 are currently inhabited; each retains its own complex blend of geological, linguistic and anthropological idiosyncrasies no less intricate than Savo's. The first island I had come to know was just one in a vast constellation, a single star in an endless island universe.

PART II
RESTIVE STATE

3

RUNNING AGROUND

IN THE CORNER OF MY ROOM, in a small bungalow overlooking turquoise water, I noticed a scurrying blur. At first all I could see was its black, shiny skin. Then, frightened, it scampered up the wall and wedged itself in a corner, its hundred legs and antennae splaying, at least twelve centimetres long: a Solomon Islands giant centipede.

A few moments earlier, I'd been resting, waiting patiently for the tide to rise before an afternoon swim, working my way through a breezy paperback, its pages sodden after a week of humidity and travel in open-air banana boats. Now, weaponless and unable to confront the critter, I stepped outside to find Richard, the owner of the three-roomed resort where I was staying in this small Central Province village. He had established the resort soon after peace returned to Solomon Islands nineteen years earlier; I was his first guest since the easing of Covid-19 restrictions. He refused to let me tame the centipede. Instead, feeling somewhat emasculated, I was dispatched to the waterfront to wait for my host to do the dirty work. I took a seat on a plastic chair and returned to my paperback. My feet were dangling in azure water filled with schools of mackerel, blue starfish and a rich coral ecosystem. Fresh oysters littered the shore nearby. It was warm, with a biting sun, but the shade of towering mango trees blocked the glare from my eyes. For a moment, all I could hear was the quiet lapping of the waves against the white sand, at a pace just slower than the ticking of a clock.

But then, my ear caught a disturbance. It was coming from across the bay. It sounded like a buzz, at first. Then I could hear drums. Then the bass. Then a melody, accompanied by the roar of a diesel engine. As the sound grew louder, the hollering sharpness of American accents ricocheted across the placid water. Putting on my glasses, I saw a boat filled with day-trippers from Honiara, and guessed that they had travelled ninety minutes across the sound to see the island's famed above-water shipwreck.

In early April 2000, 136 passengers set off for the adventure of a lifetime on a German-built cruiser, the MS *World Discoverer*. The *Discoverer* had sailed in some of the world's most daunting oceans and was the first commercial cruiser to navigate the infamously challenging Northwest Passage.

In command was the 38-year-old German captain, Oliver Kreuss. He'd been working on the vessel for a decade. It was his home. He had even met his wife onboard; she worked as a purser. Kreuss had taken the *Discoverer* around the world countless times, specialising in Antarctic and Arctic cruises. But this time, Kreuss and his passengers were heading to the equator, on a mission to explore the exotic, rarely visited nation of Solomon Islands. Instead of frigid temperatures on the upper deck, they would be able to take advantage of the black-and-white tiled pool as they sailed past volcanic peaks, sandy beaches and quaint island villages, snaking in and out of the country's endless passages, tributaries and bays.

At 4 p.m. on the April afternoon, they were sailing through Sandfly Passage, a thin, deep channel that separates the largest island of the Nggela group from Mbokonimbeti Island to the west. Because of its depth, the passage was popular, but it was poorly charted. As the passengers took in the spectacular green hillsides, the ship firmly struck something beneath the surface. Kreuss realised he'd hit a coral reef. Almost instantly, the boat began to list, and Kreuss radioed for assistance. As the boat started taking on water, he realised he needed to find shallower sea. To the port side of the *Discoverer*, he spotted a sheltered, bright-blue bay and sailed at full speed towards the embankment, aiming for the sand. He had no choice but to beach the vessel, lest it end up fully submerged.

It just so happened that, when Kreuss decided to abandon ship, he navigated his sinking cruiser to one of the Solomon Islands' most idyllic corners. The boat wedged into sand just thirty metres from the same shady mango trees under which I would one day read a tattered paperback. Kreuss and his passengers were shipwrecked in paradise, up close and personal with the pristine wilderness and untouched tribal world the brochures had promised. After escaping the doomed vessel, they found sanctuary and welcome in the village, including from a young Richard, my host at the bungalow.

Ferries from Honiara were sent immediately to rescue the passengers, but Kreuss and his ten crew, Richard tells me, remained in the village for a week, hoping to salvage the beached cruiser. The fractured hull, Kreuss believed, could be repaired. But as Kreuss tried to manage the recovery, he came to a realisation: 'the country was having a civil war'.[1] Just two years earlier, civil strife had broken out between warring factions in the capital. Although Roderick Bay was a good distance from the violence, the entire country was on edge and its economy was in tatters. As soon as the passengers had been ferried to safety, local Solomon Islanders began swimming out to the beached vessel and stealing whatever they could. They stripped it of metal and of useful items – cutlery, crockery, blankets and bottles. Kreuss was helpless. After a few days of waiting, a team of Australians based in Honiara arrived to survey the damage and prepare for a recovery. But the locals didn't allow it. The Australian salvaging company – one of few foreign businesses that hadn't fled Solomon Islands as violence swept the capital – reported rounds of gunfire directed at the crew. They immediately cancelled the mission and left the enormous liner to rust and list by the beachside.

Today, the *World Discoverer* offers an economic lifeline to the villagers of Hararo, who have cashed in on its appeal to tourists. Pieces of the vessel still litter the town. Plastic and metal from the boat have been incorporated into the construction of buildings. Children use bits of the vessel as floating devices and have rigged up a rope swing and flying fox off the ship's upper deck, launching themselves into the water below. The few tourists who come to Solomon Islands often visit Hararo, marvelling at the scale of the wreck and its story.

But the shipwreck also serves as an enduring reminder of the break-down of Solomon Islands at the turn of the century. It is a rusting relic of the Tensions. To Kreuss and his crew, the disruption that forced them to declare the ship a 'total loss' may have seemed to arrive out of nowhere. But the seeds of violence had been sewn much earlier, with a seemingly modest, pragmatic decision by British administrators some half a century before.

The semi-submerged MS World Discoverer *in July 2022.*

*

The 1952 decision to shift the capital of the British Solomon Islands Protec-torate from the five-square-kilometre island of Tulagi, in today's Central Province, to Honiara, was a practical one. The tiny island of Tulagi was simply too small, meaning the colonial capital was unable to grow as Sol-omon Islands' economic development gathered pace in the years after the Second World War. Just to the south of Tulagi, the township of Honiara had more room to move. It had the only viable airstrip in the area, an extended flat oceanfront suitable for development and, like Tulagi, was centrally located in the eastern half of the archipelago, where the bulk of the protectorate's economic and cultural life was centred. The Henderson Airfield had been used by the Allies during the war and was a growing, increasingly interconnected, part of the British Empire.

As the decolonisation movement swept through Britain's colonies in the wake of World War Two, local administrators of the British Solomon Islands Protectorate had to make a series of decisions, ostensibly to ready Solomon Islanders for greater autonomy, if not outright independence. Having relocated the capital, the British began searching for ways to generate local economic activity. The effort was led by economists appointed under the British *Colonial Development and Welfare Act*, who considered various agricultural initiatives aimed at generating local employment and creating an export commodity that would sustain a future independent state. They landed on the idea of establishing oil palm plantations on the northern plains of Guadalcanal, in an area the locals called Tasimboko. There had already been some modest agricultural production in the British protectorate intended for export. Coconut plantations owned by the Lever brothers – whose company would later evolve into Unilever, one of the world's largest conglomerates – were established around Honiara and in the Russell Islands. But the British wanted a scalable and valuable export product. Having found suitable land in Tasimboko, they began negotiating with traditional owners for access.

By 1973, Solomon Islands Plantation Limited (SIPL) and the British government's Commonwealth Development Corporation (CDC) entered into a joint partnership to develop the industry. SIPL would hold 30 per cent of the business, the CDC 68 per cent, and local landowners just 2 per cent, in addition to rents and royalties that would be paid over time. The conglomerate leased the land for ninety-nine years.

But palm oil production, particularly at the scale the British envisaged, is labour-intensive. The local population was too small to realise the administrators' ambitions. So, to staff the plantations, the British began to draw in labour from across the archipelago. Hundreds of families from other islands, especially from Malaita, relocated to Tasimboko, which had by now 'become a magnet for inter-island migration'.[2] Within a few years, this migration had changed the composition of the area and laid the ground for a deepening rivalry between traditional landowners and newer arrivals. Sixty-five per cent of those working for SIPL were Malaitan; fewer than 10 per cent were locals. The crops were, however, successful: soon, palm oil had become the protectorate's largest export commodity, meeting the revenue and employment expectations of the British administrators who had proposed it. Between 1976 and 1998, palm oil and kernels accounted for an average of 11.3 per cent of Solomon Islands' exports[3], reaching close to SBD$100 million (the equivalent of about US$18 million in 2022) at its peak in the mid-1990s. By then, the plantation covered 6300 hectares, an area larger than the island of Manhattan.

Had those 1960s economists from British Colonial Development and Welfare Aid seen the results of their plan, they would likely have been ecstatic. On the surface, it had achieved just what they intended, creating employment and generating a sustainable revenue stream. The crop had even proved resilient to cyclones.

But the scale of the plantation had created unintended consequences. For years, the growing number of SIPL workers in the Tasimboko area had frustrated traditional owners. By shifting the capital city to Honiara, the British had already fomented the displacement of the local Guale people, as a once modestly sized village swelled with new arrivals. Now, in Tasimboko, the establishment of the palm oil plantations was creating a similar dynamic, displacing traditional owners with labourers from elsewhere, especially from Malaita. Alongside these social tensions, the local landowners were growing frustrated with the deal originally struck by the British administrators. Traditional owners owned just 2 per cent of the business, and they now saw this as too small a reward for the considerable social and environmental impacts the plantations were having. This was fuelling deep resentment among the local community, who felt betrayed and belittled by the economic intervention.

The British had their palm oil. But the cost would be severe.

*

Although there were signs of instability in Honiara in the years after independence – a large youth-led riot in 1989, another in 1993 – Solomon Islands, in its early years as an independent state, was generally peaceful. That quietness, however, concealed compounding grievances. There were several recorded incidences of violence between Malaitans and Guale landowners; in 1988, three Guale were murdered by Malaitans in what was claimed to be a revenge attack. This murder inspired the 'indigenous people of Guadalcanal' to petition for compensation for the crime, in one of the first cases of the people of Guadalcanal unifying under a single political or cultural banner. Through the 1990s, several further violent incidents occurred, including rapes.

By 1998, the premier of Guadalcanal, Ezekiel Alebua, who had served as prime minister of Solomon Islands in the late 1980s, saw political utility in helping his constituents to seek SBD$2.5 million compensation for 'Guadalcanal people murdered by immigrants and for the building of Honiara as the national capital on indigenous land'. He took the claims to the national government, now led by Prime Minister Bartholomew Ulufa'alu, and they were rejected. In response, a handful of aggrieved Guale youths took matters into their own hands. The newly established Guadalcanal Revolutionary Army (GRA) began forcibly evicting ethnic Malaitans and, in some cases, killing them. The GRA was a ragtag group, but it was relatively well armed after a successful raid on a police barracks, and it received implicit support from Alebua.

Between 1998 and 1999, the GRA faced minimal organised resistance. The Ulufa'alu administration had been unable to successfully bring the agitators to heel. In response, Malaitans took up arms to protect their compatriots. Hundreds of young men banded together to establish the Malaita Eagle Force (MEF). The MEF also armed itself by raiding a police barracks. Soon, the MEF had entrenched itself in Honiara, establishing roadblocks and controlling much of the city, often in collaboration with the Malaitan-dominated police force.

On 5 June 2000, the MEF forcibly ousted, at gunpoint, Prime Minister Ulufa'alu. A month later, the opposition leader, Manasseh Sogavare, was appointed as Solomon Islands' new prime minister. By August, his government had negotiated a ceasefire between the warring parties. In October, representatives of the Solomon Islands government, the MEF, the Isatabu Freedom Movement (or IFM, a successor to the GRA) and the Guadalcanal provincial government met in the Australian city of Townsville, aiming to strike a peace deal. They signed the Townsville Peace Agreement on 15 October, with both the MEF and IFM pledging to hand over their weapons in exchange for amnesty for their part in the conflict, and with grievances from both sides to be addressed.

During 2001 and 2002, however, the Townsville Agreement failed to achieve its objectives. Some weapons were taken off the streets. But both the MEF and IFM began to splinter; their hardliners formed gangs and smaller militias, and they continued to engage in pitched street fighting and late-night banditry. By now, the lawlessness had seen Honiara all but deserted. The key functions of state were failing and the economy had collapsed: 80 per cent of government revenue had evaporated. And while the violence was concentrated in Honiara and its surrounds, the near collapse of the state had major consequences for every province. Many began seriously flirting with independence. In Western Province and Choiseul, in the country's northwest, discussions commenced about forming a separate political union. In the southeast, in Makira and Temotu, local politicians began making the case to separate. By 2003, Solomon Islands was on the brink of dissolution. Prime Minister Kemakeza had no choice but to look internationally for help.

*

On a sunny winter's afternoon in the Adelaide Hills in mid-2003, Australian foreign minister Alexander Downer was out for lunch with his family when he received a call from Prime Minister John Howard. Howard had just spoken with his Solomon Islander counterpart, and now he relayed the latest request for assistance to his foreign minister. Downer had previously been deeply resistant to intervening in the Solomons dispute, but this time he agreed it was in Australia's interests to get involved.

When the Tensions had begun to unfold, Australia – Solomon Islands' largest and most consequential development partner – did not have a significant history of regional intervention. Since federation in 1901, Australia's military engagements had tended to align with those of its security guarantors – England in the First World War and the United States in the Second World War and its aftermath. As the twentieth century drew to a close, however, simmering tensions to Australia's north began to disrupt this orthodoxy. As early as 1989, conflict in the breakaway Papua New Guinean province of Bougainville, to the west of the Solomon Archipelago, resulted in Australia and New Zealand undertaking a joint peacekeeping operation. In 1999, Australia led a major UN-backed peacekeeping operation in Timor Leste.

In retrospect, the Australian interventions in Bougainville and Timor Leste may suggest that there had already been a shift in Australian thinking about regional intervention with the election of the Howard government in 1996. But in the early months of the Tensions in Solomon Islands, Australia remained steadfastly uninvolved. As late as June 2003, as the government in Honiara teetered, Australia was still officially on the sidelines. Prime Minister Ulufa'alu's requests for assistance in early 2000 had been denied, and Downer was passionately opposed to getting involved, arguing that:

> Sending in Australian troops to occupy the Solomon Islands would be folly in the extreme. It would be difficult to justify to Australian taxpayers. And for how many years would such an occupation have to continue? And what would be the exit strategy? And the real showstopper, however, is that it would not work ... Foreigners do not have the answers for the deep-seated problems affecting the Solomon Islands.[4]

Coups and tensions in the region, Australian policymakers felt, came and went: to intervene every time a rogue Pacific general overthrew a prime minister or a multiparty government caved in on itself would reek of neo-colonialism and would undermine Australia's brand in the region. The 2000 coup d'état in Fiji, which saw the democratically elected administration of Prime Minister Mahendra Chaudhry overthrown by the military, was met with a typically restrained response from Australia. Despite Timor and despite Bougainville, Canberra's reluctance to intervene in the Pacific remained in place. In 2001, however, the will of the Australian government not to undertake such adventurism began to buckle.

As Solomon Islands' civil strife dragged on into 2001, the geopolitical context in which Australia was operating markedly shifted. On 11 September 2001, Howard was in Washington, D.C., scheduled to address the United States Congress. He was among those rushed to safety when the terrorist attacks began, uncertain at the time of the scale of the events that were unfolding. Within days, the Howard government had positioned Australia as America's most steadfast ally in the global 'War on Terror'. This campaign, it would soon become clear, was transnational, directed against no single state or actor. Over time, the War on Terror would evolve into a war not merely against terrorist organisations, or against the governments that harboured them, but against what Western administrations viewed as the *determinants* of terror. The West became deeply suspicious of unstable nations and their potential to serve as breeding grounds for terrorist ideology.

This policy shift, although it was accelerated by the events of September 11, had been happening in Western capitals for two decades. In mid-2001, Mark Duffield's book *Global Governance and the New Wars* crystallised what was now a growing realisation that 'war' and 'development' had merged. By the turn of the century – just as Australia was ramping up its efforts to secure peace in Timor Leste – 'failed' or 'failing' states were being seen in a new light. No longer were they simply a moral challenge for altruistic Western powers to address. Now, Duffield argued, 'the fear of underdevelopment as a source of conflict, criminalised activity and international stability' had turned 'failed states', and even perhaps those who inhabited them, into a threat to the peace and stability Western countries held dear. Duffield's work, published just months before September 11, would quickly take on additional resonance. It was prescient in describing not only America's post–September 11 thinking but Australia's, too.

In the bedlam that followed September 11, Howard's speech to Congress was understandably postponed. He was carried back to Australia by a US Airforce jet, avoiding the shutdown of US airspace. In the air, he became the first leader to invoke the 1951 ANZUS (Australian, New Zealand and United States) Security Treaty, confirming that Australia would join the United States in any military response to the terror attacks. Fifty-nine days after he ostensibly committed the nation to war, Howard's government was re-elected to a third term, overcoming two years of poor polling, after an election campaign focused on national security. Nine months later, in June 2002, Howard returned to Washington with a fresh mandate and a new message for the US Congress.

The honour of speaking to a joint sitting of Congress, where the Senate and House of Representatives convene for a special occasion, is a rarity. Only one Australian prime minister had previously done so, when Bob Hawke joked and charmed his way through a jubilant 1988 address, going so far as to declare: 'There have been few enough times in recent decades when it has been possible to permit ourselves a degree of optimism about the world's future. But this is such a time.'

Fourteen years later, Howard addressed Congress in a fundamentally different global context. 'We stand ready to work in partnership with America to advance the cause of freedom, particularly in our shared Pacific region,' he pledged.

It may seem far-fetched to view Solomon Islands – which in the early 2000s had a population of under 500,000, a collapsed economy and deep internal divisions – as a direct threat to Australian security. But given the deteriorating global security situation, the worry was real. In the weeks after Howard and Downer agreed to Kemakeza's 2003 request for assistance, the Australian government scrambled to organise the challenging logistics and to bring the Australian public with it. Explaining Australia's policy shift in a speech to the Sydney Institute on 1 July 2003, Howard argued that 'a failed state in our region, on our doorstep, will jeopardise our own security'.[5]

While Howard emphasised, appropriately, that Australia's intervention in Solomon Islands was at the request of the Solomon Islands government, he also explicitly placed the intervention, and the dramatic change in Australian policy it represented, within the context of a broader global struggle against instability, a rationalisation that was seen and heard in Solomon Islands.

*

On 24 July 2003, Henderson Airfield was awash with arrivals. Australian soldiers, federal police and military contingents from New Zealand, Fiji, Kiribati, Tonga, Vanuatu and even the tiny nation of Nauru had descended on Honiara. Some 2000 security personnel would arrive during the early phase of the mission, concentrating primarily on bringing stability back to the capital, but also fanning out across the nation.

In early August, Arnon Kekei, a chief of the tiny east Malaitan village of Atori, heard a distant noise unlike anything he'd experienced before. 'I looked over the hill, and we could see a chopper coming down to land,' he recalls. Atori is a port town. Its tiny, broken wharf serves as an entry point to eastern Malaita. On that August morning, an Australian military helicopter had arrived unannounced, with nine Australian soldiers taking control of the wharf at gunpoint.

'They had their guns drawn, looking around, and we were all just looking at them,' Arnon recalls. 'The children were scared, but we were happy they were here.'

The Australians had arrived in Atori to secure a critical piece of infrastructure and a strategic thoroughfare between east and west Malaita. Usually, they were welcomed. Solomon Islanders had been suffering severely during the Tensions. The fighting had led to no obvious outcome, save for economic and political collapse. For Arnon, the presence of the Australians, who established a camp just a few metres from his wharf-side house, was a positive development. The villagers routinely traded meals with the soldiers – 'our kids used to fight over who gets to take the food to the soldiers because they wanted to eat the rations' – and welcomed the Australians into their homes. The Australians, who stayed in Atori for a year, made regular appearances at the local church.

The initial focus of the peacekeeping force was the removal of weapons from the militants. The conditions for this had been struck in the Townsville Peace Agreement but had yet to be realised. Now, the Australian presence inspired the militants to – for the most part – lay down their weapons. Large piles of arms were burnt in ceremonial displays. And although there were a few holdouts among the militant groups, the fighting ended. Within weeks, the Australian intervention had achieved its primary aim. Peace had been restored.

Soon, however, those who were leading the mission recognised that the determinants of the original violence had not yet been addressed. Were the peacekeepers to leave prematurely, they realised, the same unresolved issues that led to the Tensions could easily re-emerge. The mission quickly evolved from peacekeeping – stamping out the violence of the militants – into a much more complicated, nebulous and potentially unachievable endeavour in state building. Although RAMSI remained at its core a peace and security mission, it also began to work intimately with the Solomon Islands government to help improve the capacity of the country's key institutions. But while the peacekeeping component of RAMSI was an unequivocal success, its state-building ambition came under considerable scrutiny. There was, simply, no exit plan. And under RAMSI, Australian officials were effectively in control of large areas of public administration in the Solomon Islands. The police and judiciary were, in essence, Australian-run. It would not be until 2013 that the active peacekeeping operations ended – making RAMSI the longest ever international peacekeeping mission – and not until 2017 that RAMSI was formally dissolved.

Overwhelmingly, Solomon Islanders supported RAMSI. But for some hardliners from across the political spectrum, RAMSI did not achieve what it aimed to and was seen as an undignified foreign intervention in their country. The Malaitans' lingering resentment about their decades of perceived economic exclusion remained unaddressed. The $2.6-billion price tag for the fourteen-year mission also angered many, who questioned where the money had gone, given the country's economic position remained unchanged. And for the most avowed Solomon Islander nationalists, the paternalistic interventions into the apparatus of state by Australian officials had created bitter resentment.

4

———

MANASSEH OF EAST CHOISEUL

ONE DAY, HE WOULD BE STANDING shoulder to shoulder with the US president on the steps of the White House, playing a pivotal role in crafting a region-wide deal with Washington. He would grace a red carpet in front of Beijing's Forbidden City, welcomed as a guest of honour by China's most powerful leader since Mao. He would deliver stinging addresses to the United Nations espousing his nation's sovereign rights, and he would be framed as a dictator-in-waiting – the Pacific's own Fidel – accused of transforming his island nation into an outpost of Chinese totalitarianism. His local opponents would call him a 'paranoid' tyrant, while his supporters would relish his proud nationalism and 'brawler' persona. Those who came face to face with the man would describe him as 'incredibly smart, Machiavellian' and a political 'survivor', able to bend even the most chaotic circumstances to his advantage. But the man Manasseh Sogavare would become is a far cry from his humble beginnings as the poor son of a village preacher from Papua New Guinea.

In 1955, Manasseh Damunuka Sogavare was the last of five sons born to Solomon Islander parents in Oro Province of Papua New Guinea, southeast of the capital, Port Moresby. His parents had come to Papua New Guinea as missionaries. They were devout Seventh-day Adventists, and his father, Loko Sogavare, was a well-known proselytiser who had travelled widely in Oro Province and beyond, into the Papuan highlands. Another of Loko's sons, Moses, would follow in his father's footsteps, spending his life in eastern Papua New Guinea as an award-winning Adventist preacher.[1] Manasseh

Sogavare remains spiritually and emotionally connected to his birthplace. In 2017, during his third prime ministership, he publicly pushed for dual citizenship to be recognised in Solomon Islands, which he said would enable him to retire to Papua New Guinea, where two of his brothers are buried.[2]

As teenagers, Sogavare and his older brother, Jacob, returned to their ancestral island, Choiseul, in Solomon Islands' far northwest. There, Sogavare would complete secondary school in the town of Taginbagara and forge a connection with the community that would eventually send him to parliament.

In 1974, aged nineteen, Sogavare left Choiseul to build a career in the capital, taking up a clerkship at the Honiara Consumers Cooperative shop, where he 'started with simple jobs [such] as cleaning toilets and making tea for expatriate bosses'.[3] He had arrived in Honiara during a period of profound change. The country was in the process of transitioning from its colonial state to full independence. Solomon Mamaloni, a young nationalist, was serving as the first Solomon Islander chief minister of the British Solomon Islands Protectorate. In 1975, the country formally changed its name to Solomon Islands, and by 1978, it had achieved full independence.

As the shackles of colonial rule were at last broken, a 23-year-old Sogavare commenced a career with the Department of Inland Revenue as a low-level functionary. For thirteen years he would serve as a bureaucrat, slowly inching up the departmental ranks to become the Commissioner of Inland Revenue in 1991. In 1993, he was appointed as permanent secretary of the Department of Finance, the most senior role in the department and one of the country's key economic posts.

By now, at the peak of his public service career, Sogavare was nearing forty years of age. If he harboured any political aspirations, he had yet to make them well known. He was respected by government officials and international advisors and showed no evidence of unconventional or radical thinking: he was a stable hand, viewed by Australian aid officials and economic advisors as a reliable – even predictable – administrator.

In the mid-1990s, however, Sogavare began for the first time to openly express political views and to engage more actively in the cut and thrust of political life in Solomon Islands. His political awakening seems to have been prompted by the turbulence of the second Mamaloni government, which was in office from 1989 to 1995. In his position as permanent secretary of the Finance Department, Sogavare witnessed behaviour by the government – corruption, incompetence, backstabbing and nepotism – that he disliked. As inflation spiked and the already fragile economy teetered towards collapse, he began to openly criticise the government. In 1994, Prime Minister Mamaloni sacked him.

Not one to sit idle, Sogavare spent the next two years studying for the first time since high school, completing a Bachelor of Accounting and Economics from the University of the South Pacific. He had begun writing regular opinion pieces in the *Solomon Star*, one of Honiara's most widely read newspapers. As the 1997 election approached, Sogavare successfully nominated for the seat of East Choiseul. Running on a platform that was opposed to the excesses and mismanagement of Mamaloni, over the next three years Sogavare underwent an almost Damascene conversion. Although he entered parliament in August 1997 as an antagonist of Mamaloni, just eighteen months later the two would come together in a marriage of political convenience. The critic would become the student, and the lessons Mamaloni would teach Sogavare – who at forty-three was still something of an ideological blank canvas – would be profoundly consequential.

*

Between 1998 and his death in 2000, Solomon Mamaloni, now as opposition leader, forged an intimate bond with Sogavare, appointing him deputy opposition leader and schooling him on history, politics and a fringe economic philosophy known as 'social credit'.

Originating in the writings of a wealthy British engineer, Clifford Hugh Douglas, social credit is a largely debunked economic theory that, at its core, aspires to democratise economic power in disenfranchised communities and limit the influence of outsiders. In the years following the First World War, Douglas spent his twilight years opining on the inadequacies of the economic status quo in the United Kingdom and Europe. His primary contention was that recessions and downturns occurred when the discrepancy between the price of goods and consumers' incomes was too great. He arrived at this finding after visiting hundreds of businesses in England and noticing workers' wages were considerably less than the prices charged for the goods they produced. This discrepancy was not hard to explain: it is the by-product of the costs of production additional to labour – rents, profits and taxes, to name a few. But to Douglas, it was a profound injustice, and he was determined to solve it.

Through the 1920s and into the 1930s, he elaborated on his philosophy, writing countless papers detailing somewhat utopian solutions to the problem. His key idea was for governments to provide consumers with a 'dividend' – effectively a cash supplement to their incomes – that would make their total purchasing power equal to the total value of production. Social credit differed from traditional socialist arguments that workers should own the means of production; instead, social credit wanted workers to control capital and finance. It also incorporated more libertarian ideals, such as self-determination and a weakened central government, and sought to address the undervaluation of non-financial components of an economy, such as household labour and what Douglas described as 'folk traditions'. Douglas believed that if workers were given a dividend, profit-making providers of credit, such as banks, would have a greatly reduced role in society and the economy, and people would be better compensated for their total contribution to national life.

Douglas' views were initially viewed as economically impractical and empirically questionable. They were rejected by political vehicles of the left, such as the British Labour Party. But as the global economy crashed in the 1930s, his ideas started to seem more attractive. Enmity towards banks and international finance, often tinged with antisemitism, were by then widespread, and social credit's promise to significantly reduce the role of these powerful economic actors attracted wider appeal. Douglas began travelling the world, advising Depression-era politicians. He had the most success in Canada. As depression ravaged the country, one province, Alberta, even elected the world's first social-credit party, which established a government-run bank intended to fund the implementation of Douglas' theories. While Canada became the first testing ground for Douglas' ideas, it was in another postcolonial country that social credit would become entrenched as a political force.

In the summer of 1953, businessman Wilfred Owen – a chemist who had made a fortune in cosmetics and toiletries – became the first leader of the Social Credit Party of New Zealand. Just a year after its formation, the Social Credit Party managed to secure 11 per cent of the popular vote at the 1954 national election. It would take another twelve years before the party managed to secure a seat in parliament, but by the 1970s, the Social Credit Party had become the dominant third party in New Zealand politics. Although its representation in parliament remained modest – at its peak it held just two seats in an eighty-seat house – the party's vote climbed as high as 20.7 per cent in the 1981 election, before fading through the rest of the 1980s. Its success was largely attributed to its charismatic leader, Bruce Beetham, whose career in politics aligned with the rise and fall of social credit as a political force in New Zealand.

For many intellectuals in New Zealand, the Social Credit Party had become an attractive vehicle for progressive ideals. In New Zealand's universities and schools, leading academics and teachers emerged as major proponents of social credit. They introduced their ideas to their students, including a young boarding student from the South Pacific, Solomon Mamaloni.

Born into a comparably wealthy family, Mamaloni was sent to New Zealand to undertake post-secondary education. He studied at Te Aute College, a private boarding school, where he completed a non-degree higher education certificate. It was a formative time for the young Mamaloni. The college had a particular emphasis on Māori culture and history, as well as on leadership and military training; its cadet program saw students trained in weaponry and war tactics. In his biography of Mamaloni, Christopher Chevalier describes Mamaloni's two years as a teenager at Te Aute College as deeply influential. The future prime minister was inspired by the pride and stature of the Māori, who he felt were 'more assertive and less deferential' towards white New Zealanders than Solomon Islanders were to their British colonial rulers. At the college, Mamaloni learned about the 'duplicity, racism and colonial violence' of the British empire and the 'histories of dispossession and resistance in a settler colony'.[4]

Mamaloni's time at Te Aute overlapped with the career of teacher Sam Dwyer, whose son Jeremy would go on to become the deputy leader of the Social Credit Party. Mamaloni also met Bruce Beetham, who invited him to his home.

When Mamaloni returned to Solomon Islands, he quickly became an influential force, rising through the ranks to be elected chief minister in 1973, when he was thirty years old. At his swearing-in ceremony, he wore his Te Aute blazer. When his rival Peter Kenilorea was elected Solomon Islands' first post-independence leader in 1978, Mamaloni became the country's first opposition leader. He almost immediately began promoting social credit ideas, and in 1979 he facilitated the visit of a prominent New Zealand Social Credit Party politician to Honiara. He was particularly critical of Kenilorea's reluctance to remove foreign nationals from key civil posts, and he expressed scepticism about the role being played by big business and centralised control of the economy. He established a new political coalition, the People's Alliance Party. Chevalier observes that the new party 'reflected social credit ideas, including hostility to foreign-controlled banks and economists'. The party unified a diverse coalition and soon became the dominant political force in Solomon Islands, bringing Mamaloni back into power as prime minister in 1981.[5]

As prime minister, Mamaloni began to devolve power from Honiara by allocating more decision making to the provinces. During his first term, he also opened relations with Taiwan – a decision Chevalier suggests came in heated defiance of his own cabinet, who advised in favour of a relationship with the People's Republic of China.[6]

The major policy decisions of Mamaloni's first government were, however, somewhat overshadowed by a volatile diplomatic situation caused by his decision to apprehend a US fishing boat that had encroached on

Solomon Islands' territorial waters. In June 1984, an American tuna-fishing vessel, the *Jeanette Diana*, entered Solomon Islands' maritime zone without permission. The Mamaloni government ordered the vessel be apprehended, which led to a pursuit by the coastguard. During the chase, the coastguard's vessel fired warning shots at the *Jeanette Diana*, prompting its captain to surrender before attempting to flee into international waters. The captain was arrested, and the American ship was seized and put up for sale.

Later, Mamaloni would claim that he had personally ordered the warning shots. Conceding that he had concerns about taking on the Americans, he said that he had comforted himself with a lesson from his time at Te Aute, recalling the words of one of his teachers: "The size of your force is not a determining factor in winning battles; it is what you stand for and the application of human will, stamina and faith that achieves your final goal."[7]

The incident created a diplomatic stand-off between the United States and Solomon Islands. US president Ronald Reagan, who had been lobbied by the American Tuna Association, imposed punitive economic sanctions on Solomon Islands, barring its fish from the lucrative US market. Incensed, Mamaloni decided to play hardball. Five years before, during the Soviet invasion of Afghanistan, the Kenilorea government had blocked any Soviet-flagged ship from docking in Solomon Islands. Now, Mamaloni told the US that, given its sanctions, Honiara would consider reversing its ban on Soviet vessels as retribution. Relations with the US remained sour throughout the rest of the first Mamaloni government, but were repaired by a re-elected Kenilorea government in 1985.

The *Jeanette Diana* affair cemented Mamaloni's reputation. He had stared down the world's most powerful country and asserted Solomon Islands' sovereignty in a way few would have expected from a small, impoverished island nation. Crucially, he had also demonstrated the efficacy of playing the strategic anxieties of major powers against one another in order to empower his ostensibly weak young nation state.

*

By the time Manasseh Sogavare entered parliament in 1997, Mamaloni was three years into his third prime ministership, but his government had begun to disintegrate. Despite the political and economic crisis unfolding around him, an ailing Mamaloni – now beset by gout and kidney pain – had earlier in the year set off on a state visit to Taiwan; at home, angry crowds gathered in front of government ministries, demanding pay cheques that hadn't arrived due to the strained financial state of the government. At the August election, Mamaloni was re-elected to parliament, but he declined to re-nominate for the office of prime minister. Sogavare, meanwhile, took up his seat as the new member for East Choiseul.

Sogavare's departmental experience saw him appointed as minister for finance in the government of the new prime minister, Bartholomew Ulufa'alu. Sogavare had the herculean task of restructuring the country's finances and avoiding insolvency. His job was made all the more difficult by the Asian Financial Crisis, which decimated the regional economy through much of 1997 and 1998. Soon, Sogavare became incensed by what he saw as the 'corruption and cronyism' of an 'authoritarian' Ulufa'alu administration. By July 1998, Ulufa'alu and Sogavare's differences became too great, and Sogavare was dismissed.

At the same time, the opposition was going through its own transition. Opposition leader Danny Philip had been forced to resign after a corruption scandal, and in October 1998, a weakening Mamaloni successfully ran for the opposition leadership. In the turmoil of the change, he appointed a perhaps unexpected second-in-command: Manasseh Sogavare.

Although Sogavare had previously been critical of Mamaloni, the two had a long-standing personal relationship. Mamaloni had known Sogavare when the younger man worked as a Finance Department bureaucrat, and likely viewed Sogavare's economic credentials as a useful asset to offset his own poor reputation for economic management. For Sogavare, siding with Mamaloni also made political sense. The old prime minister was still respected and capable, but – although he was only in his mid-fifties – he was physically depleted. For much of 1998 and 1999, as the Tensions descended on Solomon Islands, Mamaloni conducted his affairs mostly from his home, ceding much of his day-to-day responsibilities and authority to Sogavare. As the country descended into chaos, Sogavare was now a stone's throw from power.

*

It may have begun as an alliance of convenience, but their time together, from October 1998 until Mamaloni's death in January 2000, came to deeply shape Sogavare's political and philosophical views. Mamaloni taught Sogavare about Solomon Islands history, shared his controversial economic philosophies, retold stories of his countless political scrums and conveyed his scepticism of outside influences on their island home.

Sogavare has rarely discussed this formative period of his political life. But a 2017 PhD thesis by American anthropologist Alexis Elizabeth Tucker Sade provides a compelling insight into Mamaloni's influence.[8] The thesis, 'Incorporating the Archipelago: The Imposition and Acculturation of the Solomon Islands State', features long-winded statements by an anonymous 'informant', who shares an identical biography with Manasseh Sogavare; prominent scholars, including Mamaloni's biographer Chevalier and noted historian of Solomon Islands Clive Moore, have said they are certain the informant is Sogavare. Tucker Sade's argument – that Solomon Islands has been shaped and contorted by foreign interference for more than a century, undermining local agency – would undoubtedly have found a supporter in Sogavare.

The thesis begins with an expansive story from the informant. 'You will find this difficult, very hard to believe ... but after the former prime minister [Mamaloni] passed away ... something unbelievable happened,' he says. He goes on to explain that Mamaloni, although deceased, was 'standing before him' one morning when the informant arrived at his office, returned from beyond the grave to offer him guidance. The informant says the pair spent four hours together, the same period of time, Tucker Sade explains, that they had spent together when they first teamed up as political allies.

'When I crossed over,' the informant says, referring to his defection from one side of politics to another, Mamaloni 'held a session with me, four hours, locked door', during which Mamaloni mentored the informant in politics and the 'spirit of nationalism': 'I must convert you,' Mamaloni reportedly said, '... by the end of today you must be a convert.'

This first session together appeared to be extraordinarily influential on the informant. Before, he explains, he was still close to outside forces. 'I was the IMF boy, I was Australia's boy, I was their boy. [Mamaloni] turned all that around overnight ... [Mamaloni] was opposed to the IMF economic agendas, very critical of how aid money is used in the country ... he taught me about what was really going on.'[9] Before, the informant said, he 'didn't ask those questions', believing that foreign donors should be able to spend their aid dollars however they wanted. 'But [Mamaloni] changed that, he said, "No, this is our country, if aid donors want to spend their money here, they spend it where we want it, to drive our development agendas, not theirs,"' the informant told Tucker Sade.

In Mamaloni's formative sessions with Sogavare, he told his junior partner about the nefarious influence of foreign forces in their country, starting with British colonial rule, which Mamaloni believed had left Solomon Islands economically unprepared for independence – 'we came to independence with only timber and coconut'. Mamaloni was also critical of Asian-controlled logging companies and coconut farms operating in the country. Sogavare told Tucker Sade that he had converted to Mamaloni's philosophy wholeheartedly, adopting an 'aggressive nationalist agenda'.

Noting his formerly close and conventional relationship with foreign organisations operating in Solomon Islands, Sogavare told Tucker Sade that the Australians he had previously dealt with were 'baffled' by his new perspective: 'They said, "He changed overnight, he suddenly changed," but I explained that I am not anti-anything, but now I have adopted a serious nationalist agenda.'

It was during these early conversations with Mamaloni that Sogavare's scepticism about Australia's role in Solomon Islands' affairs became entrenched. Mamaloni's own political career, particularly the *Jeanette Diana* affair, had shown that even close diplomatic friends, such as the United

States, would always act firmly in their own interests and were willing to bully smaller countries to get their way. Although Sogavare had maintained close relationships with Australian authorities in his previous roles, he began to view Australia with suspicion. This suspicion deepened as he watched Australia's reaction to the Tensions. The Howard government's initial reluctance to get involved and subsequent about-face struck Sogavare as self-serving. He told Tucker Sade that it was clear Australia only became interested in assisting Solomon Islands when it grew paranoid that the islands might become a safe haven for terrorists after September 11. He believed that the US might eventually have intervened if Australia had remained idle. 'We heard through the grapevine here that George Bush called Howard and said he would go in here if Howard did not,' he said.

Sogavare wasn't entirely against the Australians' involvement. He acknowledged that they had successfully brokered a peace between the warring parties. But he believed Canberra was driven by its own paranoia, rather than by genuine concern for Solomon Islanders. He predicted that Australia's approach would ultimately be unsuccessful, because its ambitions were limited to achieving Australia's interests, rather than fulfilling the longer-term desires of Solomon Islanders:

> The danger with [Australia's approach] ... is that they will go as far as achieving their strategic interests but they will go no more. You see the underlying causes of the crisis are far far deeper. If they were really interested, they would help us, but not one thing that caused the crisis was touched by aid ... We want them to respect us and address the underlying issues for our long-term survival as a country. They are not; right now their actions are their own interest, the economic, commercial, strategic interests.

*

After the death of Mamaloni in January 2000, Sogavare took over as leader of the opposition. By this point, the Tensions had spun well and truly out

of control. Ulufa'alu's government was splintering, and the warring Malaitan and Guadalcanal factions had caused so much unrest that Honiara had
seen an exodus of thousands of residents, including most of the expatriate
community. The country was nearing collapse.

In June 2000, following the kidnapping of Prime Minister Ulufa'alu
by members of the Malaita Eagle Force and Ulufa'alu's forced resignation,
Sogavare was elected prime minister, twenty-three parliamentary votes to
twenty-one. Coming to power with a splintered coalition and at the height
of a period of profound civil unrest, Sogavare's first prime ministership saw
few reforms. Instead, he focused on basic political survival, navigating a
byzantine web of enmities and personalities to retain the support of parliament. He held on for more than eighteen months – but at the next election,
in December 2001, he lost the prime ministership. He retained his seat in
parliament but his party, the People's Progress Party, secured just three of
the fifty seats.

Ousted from the prime ministership, however, Sogavare remained an
active force in the country's affairs. In 2003, when Australia finally agreed
to provide assistance, Sogavare was one of the few vocal critics of the intervention. He was the only member of parliament to vote against it, decrying
the mission as 'neo-colonial' and lamenting that the Solomon Islands parliament had become a 'puppet for overseas agendas'.[10]

His party having been largely wiped out at the 2001 election, Sogavare
needed a new political home. Instead of joining one of the established parties, he contested the next election under an altogether new political banner:
the Solomon Islands Social Credit Party, or the 'Socreds'. Sogavare had by
now abandoned the orthodoxies he had learned as an economics undergraduate and during his time as the 'IMF boy' at the Finance Ministry. His
new party would hew closely to the social credit ideas that had so inspired
Solomon Mamaloni. Enunciating the party's beliefs soon after its launch,
Sogavare said it would be a force to push back against foreign interference.
'It's about time Solomon Islanders take full control of the way things happen
here in the country,' he said. 'Right now, [economic] issues are ... controlled
by foreigners, basically. So we feel that there is a need for another political

party that is preaching a totally different issue altogether.'[11] He claimed that social credit was again gaining traction in Canada, the United Kingdom and other countries, and that he had consulted with some of these foreign social-credit supporters when formulating his new party's manifesto.

'We are advocating for full monetary and financial reform,' he said. These reforms would 'take into account the informal sector' – a reference to the original tenets of C.H. Douglas' social-credit theories – and 'implement a debt-free money system'.[12] Sogavare's chief ambition was to form a government that didn't rely on foreign aid to deliver economic prosperity for Solomon Islanders. He claimed that 'big plans' made by past governments had failed to materialise because they were dependent on the conditional support of donors. By crafting a pure social-credit economy, he promised, the role of international finance in Solomon Islands' affairs would be neutered. Sogavare's deeply ingrained scepticism of foreign interference, inflamed by the RAMSI intervention, was embedded in his new party's DNA. By establishing a social-credit party, a party he believed could win enough seats to catapult him back into the prime ministership, Sogavare was trying to fulfil an ambition his late mentor never could: a Solomon Islands free of foreign interference.

In the April 2006 election, Sogavare's party failed to achieve its lofty goal. It ran candidates in thirty out of fifty seats, but Sogavare was joined in parliament by only one new Social Credit Party member. In the complicated aftermath of the election, however, which saw various candidates vie for the role of prime minister, Sogavare came in third place, with the support of eleven MPs. Snyder Rini, a long-serving MP who had served as the minister for finance and deputy prime minister in the previous government, became the new prime minister. But almost immediately after Rini was declared, and before he could be sworn in, violence gripped Honiara. For days, rumours had been spreading that the election had been rigged, with money from China and Taiwan allegedly lining the pockets of certain MPs to secure their allegiance once in office. The corruption allegations lobbed at outgoing prime minister Kemakeza, who was subsequently convicted, had spread to Rini, who had been his deputy. When

Rini's ascension to the prime ministership was announced by the governor-general, a crowd assembled in front of the parliamentary building grew angry. 'Waku government,' they shouted – *waku* being a racial epithet for the Chinese.[13] The crowd blocked the new prime minister and any MP who had voted for him from leaving the building. Australian and local security forces were called upon but were stoned by the crowd, who then turned on vehicles and property.

A few hundred metres north, on the Point Cruz peninsula, rioters assembled. They began looting businesses and then descended on Honiara's Chinatown, burning down the Pacific Casino Hotel (owned by prominent Chinese businessmen Patrick Leong and Robert Goh) and razing countless other Chinese-owned businesses. The violence was so severe that over 1000 ethnic-Chinese people were forcibly displaced; many sought assistance from the Red Cross, while others decided to leave Solomon Islands altogether, with the Chinese government assisting with an airlift. As the Chinese community fled, young Solomon Islanders were photographed swimming in abandoned beachside pools next to burnt-out buildings. Additional Australian peacekeepers were immediately dispatched from Townsville.

The week of bedlam saw Rini's swearing-in as prime minister delayed. Within days, it was clear his support had evaporated. Facing a certain no-confidence motion, he decided to step down just eight days after his nomination. By 25 April, a new round of negotiations to appoint a prime minister was underway. The two leading candidates were Fred Fono (an ally of Rini) and Job Tausinga. Before the official count, they appeared deadlocked, with twenty-five pledged votes apiece. A stalemate ensued, and Tausinga looked to Sogavare to help secure the numbers. The votes of Sogavare and his single Social Credit Party colleague would be essential to end the standoff. Instead of offering his support to Tausinga, however, Sogavare managed to convince Tausinga and his allies to support *him* as prime minister. 'For the betterment of the nation,' one contemporary wrote, Tausinga 'relinquished his bid for the post of prime minister and offered to support Sogavare.'[14] The deal didn't guarantee Sogavare's ascension, but it positioned him and Fred Fono as the two remaining candidates for the prime ministership. Over the next week, complex negotiations were held involving a broad coalition of parties.

On 4 May, Sogavare once again took the reins of power, winning the prime ministership with twenty-eight votes to twenty-two. At a time of profound chaos, Sogavare had successfully outmanoeuvred his rivals. By capturing the prime ministership from such a weak position, Sogavare demonstrated a unique political nous. He had also honed an ability that would, in the future, be of immense value: he knew how to capitalise on a crisis.

*

When Sogavare first came to the prime ministership in 2000, he did so under the cloud of his predecessor's violent overthrow. Given the instability dominating the country, he was unable to execute any lasting vision. By 2006, his ideological views and policy objectives had crystallised, and he was determined to transform his country.

Given his previous experience, Sogavare would have known that it was crucial to consolidate control of key ministerial and bureaucratic posts. He quickly moved to appoint loyalists to important positions, including the traditionally apolitical posts of attorney-general, solicitor-general, director of public prosecutions, legal draftsman, speaker of the house and governor-general.[15] In some postcolonial Pacific Island states, it is still not uncommon for key positions to be held by foreigners. At the time of Sogavare's appointment as prime minister, for example, the director of public prosecutions, John Cauchi, and the solicitor-general, Nathan Moshinsky, were both Australians. Sogavare quickly voiced concerns about both men; Cauchi resigned not long after and was replaced by a Solomon Islander.

The early weeks of Sogavare's second prime ministership were marred by the arrest of two of his parliamentary allies. His ministers of police and tourism were both apprehended soon after the election, accused of involvement in the riots. Sogavare's reluctance to dismiss them received a direct rebuke from the Australian foreign minister, Alexander Downer, further straining the relationship and prompting a statement from Sogavare: 'The critical comments of Minister Downer ... amount to a serious act of interference with the domestic affairs of Solomon Islands.'[16]

Despite the turmoil, Sogavare was able to execute consequential decisions in these early weeks. He established commissions of inquiry into the riots; their narrow terms of reference caused outrage among the Australian appointees to the commissions and the Australian legal establishment, who saw them as an attempt to absolve the riots' perpetrators of responsibility. During the stoush over the terms of reference, Sogavare came to resent the influence of Australia's high commissioner at the time, Patrick Cole, who regularly spoke out on matters that Sogavare viewed as internal Solomon Islands issues. Sogavare had Cole deported and threatened to revoke permission for RAMSI to continue operating in the country.

During the early weeks of his second prime ministership, Sogavare's scepticism about the usefulness of his country's partnership with Taiwan intensified. His government approached Taiwan, requesting assistance in training and equipping a branch of the Solomons police force for prime ministerial protection. Taiwan initially agreed but then, under pressure from the Australian government not to deliver firearms or firearms training, withdrew its offer of support.[17] This incident stayed with Sogavare; in an interview twelve years later, he cited Taiwan's inability to push back against Australia as evidence of its 'uselessness' to Solomon Islands.

It was clear that Sogavare had unresolvable tensions with the existing legal and police establishment, and that he was frustrated by what he saw as Australia's outsized role in his country's governance. His disdain for international interference was surely increased by the fact that key posts were still held by foreigners, whose motivations he distrusted. As a solution, he appointed a new attorney-general – his personal friend Julian Moti, a Fijian-born lawyer who, ironically, held an Australian passport. Sogavare had attempted to appoint Moti to the position of solicitor-general during his first term as prime minister, but his parliamentary vulnerability had limited his ability to do so. The two had remained close, however, and Moti became a chief legal advisor to the Sogavare administration. Now, Sogavare leveraged the disputes he was having with the legal establishment to displace the incumbent attorney-general, Primo Afeau. During the early months of Sogavare's second term, Afeau had routinely sided with Sogavare's opponents. In August 2006, Sogavare dismissed Afeau and commenced efforts to replace him with Julian Moti.

Moti was already a controversial figure. He had provided questionable legal advice to Mamaloni's administrations; at one point, he had suggested resolving a political stand-off by simply appointing a second prime minister. In 1997, Moti had been arrested in Vanuatu and accused of a horrific child-sex offence. He was put to trial but found not guilty. He then returned to Solomon Islands, where he worked as a private lawyer. He was also a known sceptic of RAMSI. For all these reasons, his rise as an advisor to Sogavare concerned the Australians, who saw in Sogavare's nationalist fervour a weakening of Australian authority. Were Moti to be appointed attorney-general, he would certainly enable Sogavare's impulses and constrain Australian influence over the judiciary, which had served as a powerful check on successive Solomon Islands governments.

In September 2006, Moti was placed under a new legal cloud. The Australian Federal Police revealed that they had fresh evidence related to his alleged offences in Vanuatu and were pursuing his apprehension. Moti was travelling in Papua New Guinea at the time, and Sogavare appointed him attorney-general in absentia. Before he could return to Honiara to assume his post, Moti was arrested in Port Moresby by local authorities at the request of the Australian Federal Police. After being released on bail, he quickly sought sanctuary in the Solomon Islands' high commission and was smuggled out of the country on a Papua New Guinean military aircraft. An inquiry by the Papua New Guinea High Court found that senior advisors to the PNG prime minister, Michael Somare, if not Somare himself, were responsible for Moti's escape back to Solomon Islands.

What proceeded over the coming weeks and months would be viewed, from Sogavare's perspective, as a profound violation of Solomon Islands' sovereignty. After arriving in Solomon Islands, Moti was immediately arrested and detained by Australian RAMSI officials. Although Moti was initially placed under Australian custody, Canberra's requests for his extradition to Australia were denied by the Sogavare government. In a sensational escalation of the standoff, on 21 October Australian authorities raided Sogavare's office, in search of material that would support the legal case against Moti. Sogavare was out of town, attending a meeting of the Pacific Islands Forum, and the AFP had taken advantage of his absence to secure a search warrant from the Solomon Islands Police Force – then led by an Australian. The AFP commissioner, Mick Keelty, later confirmed that Australian personnel were involved in the raid. It is hard to overstate the significance of the Australian raid on Sogavare's personal office. It was interpreted, justifiably, by Sogavare as a profound interference in the sovereign affairs of Solomon Islands. It is hard to imagine any country accepting the raid of their leader's office by a foreign police force. In doing so, the AFP validated many of Sogavare's worst suspicions about Australia's activities in his country.

The Moti affair would dominate much of Sogavare's second term. His continual refusal to permit Moti's extradition to Australia put Honiara's relationship with Canberra in a deep freeze. Eventually, by July 2007 – ten months after his initial nomination – Moti was formally appointed to the position of attorney-general. But his tenure would be short-lived: in parliament, Sogavare's grip on power was waning, thanks largely to his government's souring relations with Australia. Having fended off several no-confidence motions, by December 2007, Sogavare had lost the support of the parliament and was finally ousted. Soon after, the new administration, led by Derek Sikua, dismissed Moti from the position of attorney-general and worked with the Australians to facilitate his extradition. On 27 December 2007, Moti arrived in Australia, and soon began a second trial for a crime of which he had already been acquitted almost a decade earlier.

Had Moti been convicted, perhaps the heavy-handed tactics of the Australians might have been justified. But as soon as he was back on Australian soil, the shaky case against him began to collapse. As early as October 2006 – soon after Moti fled Papua New Guinea – journalist David Marr had raised serious questions about the integrity of the AFP's investigations and the calibre of their evidence. Marr noted that the original court case in Vanuatu had been presided over by some of the most esteemed judges in the Pacific, who had found Moti not guilty due to inconsistencies in the evidence. There were also credible allegations that the evidence had been tampered with, if not fabricated or potentially coerced out of the alleged victim.[18]

When Moti's case was put to an Australian court, it immediately failed. The actions of the Australian Federal Police were admonished by the presiding judge, who cited evidence that the AFP had provided financial incentives for the alleged witness and her family to offer testimony. Judge Mullins ruled that the AFP had broken Solomon Islands deportation laws by not giving Moti the required seven days to lodge an appeal before he was flown to Australia. Much more seriously, the judge expressed outrage at the tactics the AFP had used in soliciting evidence. 'The conduct of the AFP in taking over the financial support of these witnesses who live in Vanuatu is an affront to the public conscience,' the judgement read. 'The assumption by the AFP of the responsibility of providing total living support for the complainant's parents, her brother and their dependants in Vanuatu brings the administration of the justice system into disrepute.'[19]

Judge Mullins stayed the case, refusing to allow it to proceed to trial. This ruling, however, was not a complete vindication for Moti. It didn't declare him innocent of the allegations. In her ruling, the judge acknowledged that as a result of the stay, 'the complainant's allegations will not be dealt with ... and the prosecution will lose the opportunity of endeavouring to prove that the applicant is guilty of the charges'. But she had no choice: the case presented to her was weak, and the way in which its evidence had been gathered was deeply unethical, if not illegal. The allegations against Moti were serious and troubling, but even if the AFP genuinely believed Moti was guilty, its incompetence rendered any prosecution certain to fail.

The stay of Moti's prosecution was a humiliating blow for Australia's credibility in Solomon Islands and a vindication for Sogavare. He had always suspected that the attempts to arrest and extradite Moti were driven purely by politics and designed to undermine his government. For Australia, an extraordinary gamble, one which fundamentally undermined the sovereignty of Solomon Islands, had catastrophically backfired – and it wouldn't soon be forgotten.

Although the Moti affair quickly faded from view in Australia, it remained etched in the mind of Sogavare. He saw it as an attempt by Canberra to undermine Solomon Islands' sovereignty and shape its government to suit Australia's interests. The affair had tarnished Sogavare's second prime ministership and ended any chance he had to enact the ambitious policy manifesto of his new Social Credit Party.

When Moti's prosecution was permanently stayed in December 2009, a jubilant Sogavare, now out of office and serving as opposition leader, spoke to the media in Honiara. 'I am so pleased,' he said, beaming. 'This matter has hung like a dark cloud over me and my government. This decision has vindicated me. It proves that I was right all along.' In 2017, the Australian government issued a formal apology to Julian Moti. The case is now cited as a textbook example of an abuse of process leading to a failed conviction.

*

After Sogavare's ouster in 2007, he returned to the opposition benches and began, once again, calculating a return to the top job. But it would be a long time before he would again assume the prime ministership. With a degree of justification, he was angered that his prime ministership had been undermined by external forces. His souring relationship with Canberra had contributed to his loss of popularity with the public and with his parliamentary colleagues. Australia, through RAMSI and as a leading development partner, remained a crucial supporter of the Solomon Islands economy. Alienating Canberra, many of Sogavare's colleagues worried, would only worsen the country's decade of economic anaemia and civil unrest.

For Australia, Sogavare's removal was welcome. In his successor, Derek Sikua, the new Australian Labor government, led by prime minister Kevin Rudd, saw a more conventional and perhaps malleable partner. But Australia could only momentarily breathe a sigh of relief. As opposition leader, Sogavare would continue to put public pressure on the RAMSI deployment.

His lived experience now re-enforced the ideals he had been exposed to by Mamaloni; his political life imbued him with grievances and enmities that would motivate him through the long opposition years ahead.

By 2008, Sogavare's Social Credit Party was a non-entity, and was dissolved. Although it is common for Solomon Islands parliamentarians to remain independent – in some elections, a majority of elected MPs have had no formal party affiliation – Sogavare had always seen utility in a party structure. A successful party would grant him guaranteed votes and supporters in parliament and provide a framework to advance his reform agenda. Whatever his faults, Sogavare had genuine policy ambitions, and he used his time in opposition to translate his ideological beliefs into policies.

In early 2010, in the lead-up to the elections, Sogavare and eight of his parliamentary colleagues formed a new party, the Ownership, Unity and Responsibility Party (or OUR Party), to be led by Sogavare. It represented a maturation of the platform he had put forward under the Social Credit Party. The party's positions were less radical than those of the Socreds, but they still invoked elements of social-credit philosophy. One of OUR Party's key pledges was to further devolve power to the provinces, giving provincial governments a greater say in how aid was delivered in their jurisdictions. The party promised to boost financial support for rural communities and to restore traditional ownership of land that had been acquired by the British colonial administration.

Even with an agenda tailored to the rural majority, the party performed poorly in the 2010 election, with only three members of parliament elected. Sogavare, undeterred, remained opposition leader for another term, continuing to promote his nationalist vision. By the time Solomon Islands went to the polls again in 2014, he was well positioned to form government. This time, he was eager to learn from the mistakes of his previous prime ministerships, working harder to placate his rivals, shore up support and present a bold vision. His third term saw him launch and win Solomon Islands' bid for the 2023 Pacific Games, a regional sporting tournament. In 2017, he also formally oversaw the end of the RAMSI operation and a security deal with Australia, under which, if there were further unrest, the Solomon Islands prime minister could request, with few strings attached, Australian military assistance to restore law and order.

Sogavare's third prime ministership, however, was soon rocked by a financial crisis, angering the public and undermining his credibility in caucus. Poor fiscal discipline, coupled with a minuscule revenue base, had undermined the government's financial position.

In 2017, Sogavare was summoned to a meeting with the governor-general, Frank Kabui. Although the governor-general is an apolitical figure, they can question the government about its handling of certain affairs and, not unlike the English monarch, offer counsel to the prime minister.

Now, questioned by the governor-general about the government's financial challenges, Sogavare offered him a story. 'In World War Two,' Sogavare is alleged to have said, 'a group of English soldiers buried gold bars somewhere on these islands. When the war finished, the soldiers were in a rush, and placed the bars into the ground. Someday, we will find the gold. Don't worry about the financial situation. Very soon, we will be a rich country.'

5

MAASINA MEN

WITH HIS LOOSE-FITTING SPORTS COAT, schoolboy-like necktie and black-rimmed eyeglasses awkwardly reflecting his computer screen, Daniel Suidani hardly looked like the man standing in the way of China's grand plans for Pacific domination.

It was September 2021, and Suidani, the 51-year-old premier of Solomon Islands' Malaita Province, sat in a drab hotel room in Taipei, recovering from an undisclosed brain treatment paid for by the Taiwanese government, and preparing to be interviewed by Australian journalist Sharri Markson on her provocative Sky News program, *Sharri*.

There was no glittering skyline as his backdrop. Instead, his slumped figure was framed by a pair of beige curtains as rumpled as his jacket. The room was dimly lit. There was no light-ring or studio camera, just a poor internet connection, a hotel lamp and the murky webcam of a battered laptop.

For eighteen months, Markson had been busy promoting the Wuhan lab-leak theory, a controversial, although not disproven, theory about the origins of Covid-19. Now, she had found the time to interview a dishevelled provincial leader from an island few of her viewers would have heard of.

'Solomon Islands,' Markson said as she proudly introduced her scoop, 'has been on the frontlines of an aggressive China. The premier of Solomon Islands' most populous province, Daniel Suidani, *had the courage to say no*.'

*

Two years before, on a hot November morning, I had sat in a wicker chair at Honiara's Heritage Park Hotel, anxiously awaiting Premier Daniel Suidani's arrival. I hadn't known much about Suidani when I arrived in Solomon Islands, but his sensational account of his role in the Switch to China was circulating virulently and I was determined to hear it first-hand.

I'd been waiting in the foyer for an hour when Suidani tapped me on the shoulder and introduced himself. He had been a hard man to track down; turns out, he'd been sipping coconuts by the beach in Vanuatu. 'I've just returned from holiday,' he told me. He was wearing a Cuban hat with 'Vanuatu' stitched on the forehead and a floral Hawaiian shirt. His eyes were slightly jaundiced, and his teeth were stained red with betel nut. He looked more like a middle-aged vagabond than a revolutionary. He answered my questions in a soft voice, speaking cautiously, as if worried that someone would overhear us.

'I received a call in the middle of the night,' Suidani began, 'giving me an offer to support the Switch.'

The unknown caller – who Suidani claims without evidence was a local proxy for China – asked to meet with him.

'They were offering an amount of money, telling me on the phone, "If you'll join us, there's a package here." But I refused ... I am taking a very bold stand against the Switch,' he said.

It was a story the premier had been spruiking at every opportunity. With his unverifiable account of high-stakes international corruption, Suidani had made himself a central character in one of the biggest political events in his country's young history. As we spoke, I realised that the premier, although just months into his job, was no novice politician. He had recognised sooner than most that Solomon Islands was now divided into two camps. One, led by Sogavare and composed mainly of MPs and elites in the capital, supported the pivot to Beijing. The other was composed of a large majority of everyday Solomon Islanders, who saw in China a communist, irreligious menace and were looking for a leader. Suidani, with Machiavellian savvy, had quickly claimed that mantle.

Over the next two years, Suidani's status continued to rise. He was profiled by *The Australian* and *The Sydney Morning Herald*, featured on Australian TV in a *60 Minutes* story about China's 'takeover' of the Pacific, and became a fixture on right-wing news channels such as Sky News Australia. He also became a darling to a small group of academics, who saw Suidani as an important bulwark against Beijing. As his international profile grew, the premier and his team had skilfully shaped the glowing coverage to bolster his power at home. By mid-2021, he had become a political titan, and one of the most influential men in the Pacific. Dubbed the 'Father of Malaita', he was carried through adoring crowds on a ceremonial throne, balanced on his subjects' shoulders. He had the ability to mobilise masses of supporters and to quash any political opposition, whether in Auki or in Honiara.

*

A former schoolteacher and construction manager, Suidani emerged from relative obscurity in June 2019. He was a new player on the political scene in Solomon Islands, but he stood on the shoulders of generations of Malaitan nationalist leaders. Malaitan resistance to external rule predates British colonialism. When the Mendaña expedition came to the island, it received significant pushback from the locals. Stories of this encounter are still told on the island today.

'When Mendaña came here,' one Malaitan told me, 'he looked over to the land, and saw two enormous men breaking trees with their bare hands. They were giants of Malaita. The Spanish were too scared to settle here, so they never came on land.'

The documented history is less colourful, but the first Spanish contact with the Malaitans was indeed hostile. In early April of 1568, Mendaña's crew spotted land in the distance across the channel, and Mendaña dispatched the hastily constructed brigantine to investigate. By May, the Spanish were attempting to chart the island they named Malaita, having misunderstood a local fisherman (the indigenous name for the island was in fact Mala; Malaita means 'of Mala'). They sailed the length of the island's south, before arriving at the Maramasike Passage, which they believed to be a river. The passage separates 'Big Malaita', the main island, from 'Marama-sike', or 'Small Malaita'. While anchored near an island the locals called Uru, the Spanish were attacked by a flotilla of twenty-five canoes; at another rest-ing point, they were accosted by a volley of arrows. The Spanish returned fire, killing numerous Malaitans. The Malaitans' resistance to the Spanish approaches eventually forced the brigantine to leave, never to return.

Clive Moore, in his book *Making Mala,* notes that 'Like many of these early exploratory visits to Pacific islands, two aspects stand out: the defen-sive violence of the visitors and lingering after-effects, such as disease.'[1] Some historians believe, based on oral tradition, that these first encounters, while brief, introduced foreign diseases to the island.

As with the other major islands in the Solomon Archipelago, Malaita maintains a rich indigenous history – a tapestry of traditions and languages reflecting thousands of years of human settlement. Unlike some pockets of the archipelago, where Papuan languages remain, the seventeen languages spoken today on Malaita have Austronesian origins, suggesting settlement in Malaita occurred between 5000 and 4000 years ago.

The first Malaitans had come a long way, although they may have done so during periods when the sea level was considerably lower. Only on the clearest day can one faintly see any of Malaita's neighbouring islands, such the Nggela Islands or Isabel. It is separated from Guadalcanal by 100 kilo-metres of what is known as the Indispensable Strait, a hostile passage that is too far today for even adventurous traditional fishermen to cross in dugout canoes; it was likely more accessible to ancient seafarers known for covering vast distances in traditional seacraft.

Until the British began visiting the island in the mid-nineteenth cen-tury, the Malaitans had remained remarkably isolated from the outside world, although they were connected through trade and commerce with neighbouring islands. The population, split between the inland highlanders (*wane i tolo,* or 'bushpeople') and coastal dwellers (*wane i asi,* the 'saltwater people'), had swelled to potentially more than 100,000. In the nineteenth century, most of the population lived inland, although some lived not just by the sea, but *on* the sea. Characteristic of Malaita are its pristine lagoons –

Lau in the northeast and LangaLanga in the west – in which, over decades, Malaitans fleeing persecution, conflict and overpopulation built artificial islands on which they settled.

Lau Lagoon

Malaitans were visited occasionally by European and American whalers and other merchant vessels during the eighteenth century, and even hosted a number of castaways, but regular engagement with the outside world didn't begin until the middle of the nineteenth century. In 1850, a British naval vessel, the HMS *Havannah*, spent three days at Port Adam, on Maramasike's east coast. A hesitant group of locals emerged in canoes and exchanged local produce for 'red cloth, tomahawks, knives and bottles'.[2] During the nineteenth century, inter-island raiding parties – groups of armed men who would slink quietly into villages, killing men and stealing goods and women – were common across the archipelago. The Malaitans had become skilled at fending off these raids, but they certainly would have been anxious about interactions with unannounced outsiders.

By the 1870s, British settlement across Australia, New Zealand and Fiji had expanded considerably. Populations were growing; so too was the demand for produce and a desire by colonial administrators to export cash crops such as sugar and wheat. For these industries to thrive, the British needed labour. Soon, some Malaitans were being forcibly taken into schooners and dispatched against their will across what must have felt like unimaginably vast distances. Some Malaitans may have gone voluntarily, seeing an opportunity to accrue wealth and the luxury goods the European traders were known for, but it is unclear whether this was common. Across much of the Pacific during this period, the thirst for labour led to unequivocal cases of kidnapping and enslavement. Between 1870 and 1910, Malaitans became integral to the British colonial economies of Oceania. During these years, 9,428 Malaitans went to Queensland and 5,149 to Fiji. By 1910, more than 15,000 Malaitans had been taken from their homeland to work on British plantations.

During the twentieth century, more Malaitan labourers began departing voluntarily for the colonies, hoping to make money and support their families. Whether they went voluntarily or not, many Malaitan labourers were subject to appalling conditions, including rates of pay as low as £6 a year, long, arduous days and uncertain prospects of ever returning home.[3]

Interactions between the British and Malaita were formalised as the colonial administration matured in Tulagi. Among the colonial administrators charged with establishing functional government in Malaita was the Australian-born William Robert Bell. A Boer War veteran and trained accountant, Bell's first interactions with the Malaitans came during his participation in the labour trade, between 1905 and 1911. When the First World War broke out, he remained in the Solomons with a medical exemption and in 1915 was dispatched to Malaita as its district officer, with responsibility for overseeing the island's anaemic British-run plantations. Bell would spend the next twelve years 'pacifying Malaita, using the constabulary as his main weapon'.[4]

By the mid-1920s, he was also in charge of collecting a new tax that had been levied on all subjects of the British Solomon Islands Protectorate. In 1923, the colonial administration began imposing a 'head tax', a levy of £1 to be paid by every man in the protectorate. In Malaita, this equated to up to 23,000 men, many of whom were forced to sell what little they had, including indigenous currency such as shells and pig's teeth, to meet the fee.

On 5 October 1927, Bell and his colleague, a cadet named Kenneth Lillies, were collecting taxes in East Kwaio, on the eastern side of Malaita, when they came under attack by the local community. The two administrators, as well as thirteen police officers travelling with them for protection, were killed. Bell's death was caused by a brutal beating to the skull with the butt of a rifle. When news of the deaths reached Tulagi, the British were determined to exact revenge. A force of 128 men, many of them indigenous Malaitan police, were sent on two naval vessels to eastern Malaita, where they embarked on a punitive expedition of unprecedented scale. They killed over 200 indigenous Kwaio and captured 198, at least thirty of whom would die in prison over the subsequent two years. The incident became known as the Malaitan Massacre and was the most violent engagement between Europeans and indigenous Solomon Islanders before the Second World War. Today, Malaitans still discuss the incident; it has left a scar on the people of Kwaio especially, and to other Malaitans became representative of the injustices inflicted on their island.

When the Second World War reached the Solomons in 1942, the Malaitans became intimately involved. Their role as a supply of labour for the British continued, and they worked with American and Australian forces as part of the Solomon Islands Labour Corps. Few Malaitans saw direct fighting, but they were integral to the war effort. These few years of engagement with outsiders other than the British have been described as a period of 'enlightenment', during which Malaitans saw a weakened Britain lose control over the Solomons to the Japanese and be rescued by the Americans. Some saw the many black Americans who fought side by side with white soldiers as indicative of a more equal culture, in which dark-skinned subjects weren't automatically deemed inferior to their colonial masters. As the war wound down, these experiences gave rise to a new organisation that would aim to advance Malaitan national identity, pursue greater Malaitan autonomy and even wrest control of the island from the British altogether: Maasina Ruru, or Marching Rule.

Maasina Ruru was founded by a handful of tribal leaders, but its message spread rapidly. Soon, the movement began to proliferate across the island chain, reshaping Malaitan society and putting pressure on British rule. The movement promised 'abundance, wealth and independence from the British administration' and worked to establish a network of allied local authorities. The Maasina Ruru leadership was 'assisted by influential men and chiefs, each of whom was responsible for a defined district'.[5] The proxies acted as 'messengers, police, or terroristic strong-men as needs arose'. Maasina Ruru restructured village life in Malaita. The movement began to act as a de-facto local government, asking Malaitans not to pay taxes to the British administrators and instead to contribute to Maasina Ruru. The movement also encouraged highlanders and more isolated villagers to relocate to coastal settlements, enabling a new scale of agricultural and economic activity and creating larger settlements on the coast. Soon, the movement spread to neighbouring islands – Santa Isabel, San Cristobal and northern areas of Guadalcanal. Inspired adherents from these islands would embark on days-long canoe trips to Malaita to hear directly from the group's leadership. In 1947, the British arrested the group's leaders; by 1951, civil disobedience in Malaita in response to the arrests forced administrators in Tulagi to acquiesce. The Malaitans were permitted to establish a local governing council – the first such decision-making body to include indigenous islanders in the protectorate. It was a long way short of autonomy or independence, but it represented a marked step forward. It also inspired others in the archipelago to agitate for change. Today, Malaitans remain proud of the impact Maasina Ruru had on advancing the cause of independence in Solomon Islands. And the determination to ward off foreign rule, so powerfully illustrated by the Maasina Ruru leadership, has remained central to many Malaitan nationalists' identity.

*

Malaita's long history of resistance to and scepticism of external influence continued after Solomon Islands emerged as an independent state in 1978.

There were hopes that, with independence, economic progress would inevitably follow. Instead, it stalled.

'Malaita is exactly the same as it was forty years ago,' one East Fataleka elder told me late in 2022. 'Nothing has changed'. As Malaitan economic development stalled, Malaitans themselves continued to leave the island. Thousands would relocate to Guadalcanal, especially in and around Honiara, looking for work. By the mid-1990s, many key institutions, such as the Royal Solomon Islands Police Force, were staffed predominately by Malaitans, who had largely displaced the indigenous Guale people from the outskirts of the capital. It was this dynamic that led to the Tensions, and the political and economic fall-out still shapes life in Solomon Islands today.

*

When Suidani emerged as the premier of Malaita in 2019, he was acutely aware of this long history. His instinctive capacity to pay homage to the past struggles, and his understanding of the contemporary and historical grievances of his people, appeared politically deft – but he was lucky to have reached a position of power at all.

As in national politics, the political party structure at the provincial level is weak and malleable. Instead of voters supporting the agenda of a particular political party, provincial elections tend to focus on hyper-local issues. In Malaita, the provincial assembly is composed of thirty-three members, each representing just a few thousand constituents. The young population of Solomon Islands means that there are often fewer than 1000 registered voters in each electorate, meaning candidates can campaign on a face-to-face and deeply personal level.

In 2019, a new candidate in Ward 5 of Fataleka Constituency, a mountainous, isolated district in Malaita's northeast, put his hand up for election. His name was Daniel Suidani. Forty-eight years old, Suidani had spent his career serving his community as a schoolteacher, far from the complicated world of Malaitan provincial politics. For more than a decade, he taught at schools across the island, before eventually leaving the classroom for a more lucrative career in the road-construction industry. Throughout Malaita, roads are in a constant state of disrepair. Unsealed and often poorly constructed, the few thoroughfares that link the most remote communities often deteriorate in the wet season, as Isuzu trucks carrying dozens of passengers and tonnes of cargo tear up road surfaces, transforming dusty bitumen tracks into muddy, almost impossibly damaged arterials. When the wet season lifts, a roster of road-maintenance crews is contracted to patch up the damage, funded by aid agencies, international NGOs and both the Malaitan and national governments. Suidani eventually established a small contracting firm working largely on road repairs. His business expanded beyond Malaita to the capital, where his firm won a contract to build the road that leads from Mendaña Avenue – Honiara's main thoroughfare – to Parliament House. The project was beset with delays and built on an incredibly steep incline, and many viewed it as a failure – but it brought Suidani's name to broader public attention for the first time.

By 2019, Suidani, now a well-known figure in his remote highland community, decided to embark on another career change and nominated as an independent for the Ward 5 provincial constituency seat of Fataleka. Travelling village to village by pick-up truck and jeep, Suidani courted just enough voters to prevail: he was elected by a razor-thin margin of just nine votes, 310 to 301. He then headed to Auki to participate in the complex negotiations that lead to the formation of a new provincial government. At both the national and provincial levels, new administrations are generally not formed until at least several days after the election. Rarely does a single political party command an outright majority; instead, new coalitions are negotiated by all the elected MPs, who horse-trade ministries, projects and even the premiership in a complex, often secretive series of discussions that can take weeks.

In the negotiations following the June 2019 election in which Suidani was first elected, one of the sticking points was who would assume the office of premier. There was growing resentment in some constituencies that they had never had a member of their own serve as the head of the provincial government. This was particularly the case for the constituency of Fataleka, whose newly elected representatives pushed for one of them to be given the premiership. Eventually, a new coalition was formed, the Malaita Alliance for Rural Advancement, or MARA. Reflecting a remarkably quick rise from relative obscurity to national prominence, Daniel Suidani – a compromise candidate and political cleanskin – was appointed to lead this coalition for the next four years.

The centrality of Malaita Province to the national affairs of Solomon Islands meant that Suidani now held one of the country's most high-profile seats. He quickly realised the scale of the challenge he faced. He was in charge of a delicate coalition and responsible for the interests of some 200,000 Malaitans, many of whom had been left bitter and jaded by decades of poor governance, corruption and economic disenfranchisement.

Suidani needed help. He needed a team of advisors. And, perhaps most importantly, he needed an issue through which he could assert his authority. He wouldn't have to wait long.

PART III
THE SWITCH

6

DEVIL'S NIGHT

FIVE MONTHS BEFORE SUIDANI'S APPOINTMENT as premier, there had been a similarly complicated series of negotiations in Honiara for the position of prime minister. The national election was held in April 2019, but it would be several weeks before Manasseh Sogavare emerged victorious and once again assumed control of his nation.

The election had seen a complex mesh of political parties win seats: there was, as usual, no clear majority. The prime ministership would fall to whoever could most deftly negotiate one of the most diverse parliaments in the country's history. Only eighteen months earlier, Sogavare had been removed from the prime ministership following a vote of no confidence. He had not revived his OUR Party for the 2019 poll, instead running as an independent. The election saw twenty-one out of fifty seats won by independent candidates. Two parties – the internationalist Solomon Islands Democratic Party, led by Matthew Wale, and the Kadere Party of Solomon Islands, typically an advocate of industry – secured eight seats each, with eleven smaller parties making up the remainder of the count.

Such a cluttered result favoured Sogavare. He had been in this situation before, scrambling in the aftermaths of the 2006 and 2014 elections to secure alliances with the often diverse and disunified MPs. Unlike in other Westminster countries, Solomon Islands elections rarely see two leaders pitted against each other to secure a popular mandate. Instead, individual MPs campaign on their personal mandates, often detached from any identifiable party philosophy or tradition. Sogavare understood the objectives and aspirations of these individual MPs, pledging local projects and initiatives to secure their support. Selecting a prime minister isn't as simple as holding a vote on the floor of parliament. Before this can occur, political groupings must be formed, which then nominate their candidates for prime minister. These candidates are then approved by the governor-general, who asks parliament to hold a vote. After the 2019 election, as these parliamentary negotiations were taking place, Sogavare was integral in negotiating the establishment of a new political grouping, the Democratic Coalition Government for Advancement or DCGA, which quickly coalesced around Sogavare as their candidate for prime minister. He also re-registered the OUR Party.

Meanwhile, Matthew Wale's Solomon Islands Democratic Party, with eight MPs, forged a new grouping of its own, called the Grand Coalition. The 51-year-old Wale, who had represented the Malaitan capital city of Auki in parliament for over a decade, aspired to the prime ministership, but he now emerged as the Grand Coalition's second choice. Instead, the coalition nominated a first-time MP representing East Malaita Province, Peter Kenilorea Jnr. Forty-seven years old, Kenilorea was the son and namesake of Solomon Islands' first prime minister, and he entered parliament with a unique degree of gravitas and a wealth of experience. For two decades, he had represented Solomon Islands at the United Nations in New York, developing an internationalist, democratic worldview and fostering a reputation as one of Solomon Islands' brightest political talents. After returning from New York, Kenilorea Jnr was appointed permanent secretary of Solomon Islands' Ministry of Foreign Affairs – the top bureaucratic position in the ministry. In this role, he famously negotiated the security treaty with the Australian government that enabled the Solomon Islands' prime minister to request security assistance from Canberra if the need were to arise. Kenilorea Jnr was popular with everyday Solomon Islanders. Many were nostalgic for his father, and others were attracted by his success on the global stage, his approachable demeanour and his savvy social media presence. Initially, Kenilorea Jnr was endorsed by the Grand Coalition to run for the prime ministership – but after days of behind-the-scenes wrangling, he was replaced by the more senior Wale.

As the day of the vote for prime minister neared, Wale sought to legally contest Sogavare's candidacy. He contended that, given the late registration of Sogavare's OUR Party, Sogavare was ineligible for nomination. Wale requested a delay to the parliamentary vote, which was rejected by the governor-general, Sir Frank Kabui. Wale's protest was also dismissed by the High Court, who noted that Sogavare's late party registration was allowable under a loophole in the country's poorly worded electoral laws. On 24 April, Wale led his coalition in a walk-out of parliament, in a final attempt to delegitimise Sogavare's appointment. With Wale's MPs boycotting the vote, Sogavare was unanimously elected. As had become common after new prime ministerial appointments, Sogavare's ascension was met with widespread protests and looting in the capital, in a prelude to what would be a tumultuous term of parliament.

The immediate policy objectives of Sogavare's new coalition were unclear. Rarely are the agreements forged in the heat of post-election negotiations disclosed, and the 2019 election was no different. Prior to the poll, the prime minister had not foreshadowed any radical changes to the country's foreign policy. But the relationship with Taiwan had emerged as an election issue during the campaign, with several high-profile incumbents pledging to reconsider it if they formed government. The prime minister before the election, Rick Hou, who had replaced Sogavare in 2017, had pledged in March to reassess the relationship with Taiwan just days after receiving an anxious Taiwanese delegation, who had been dispatched to Honiara to gauge the strength of the government's support. Other high-profile candidates, including another former prime minister, Gordon Darcy Lilo, had also been advocating for a Switch. 'Sooner or later, when we see our country hasn't been able to grow out of [the Taiwan] relationship,' Lilo was reported to have said while campaigning, 'we are at liberty to review our relations and to explore other avenues.'[1]

James Batley, Australia's high commissioner to Solomon Islands from 1997 to 1999 and leader of the RAMSI mission from 2004 to 2006, was in Honiara for the April election as an observer. On polling day, he told *The Australian* newspaper that the issue of Taiwan's recognition regularly came up on the campaign trail. 'It is an issue that's in the wind here. I think there is a sense that this is an issue that the next government will at the very least have to consider actively. But as to where it goes, I really couldn't tell you,' he said. 'It's not the first time the issue has been raised in the Solomons. At the moment there is the sense that China is a rising power in the Pacific … and certainly some educated Solomon Islanders are saying let's consider this, let's look at this, should we switch?'[2]

It is certain that the issue would have been discussed during Sogavare's negotiations to secure the prime ministership. In addition to the MPs who had openly discussed it during the campaign, there were others within Sogavare's emerging alliance who had political and personal interests in the Switch. One of them was Jamie Vokia, a first-term MP from the Northeast Guadalcanal constituency. Vokia only just managed to secure his seat, defeating popular former prime minister Derek Sikua by fewer than 200 votes in what was viewed as a shock result. The constituency is adjacent to Gold Ridge, one of Solomon Islands' largest gold deposits, and prior to the campaign, there had been rumours of Chinese interest in reanimating a mine at the site. It was an idea that had Vokia's backing.

When Sogavare returned to office, he was determined to remain in power and to achieve a lasting, tangible legacy. A new partnership with China could help him to achieve this, while placating those in the new DCGA coalition who had been championing a partnership with Beijing. On 20 May 2019, less than four weeks after Sogavare returned to office, DCGA MPs began briefing journalists about their intentions to push Sogavare towards abandoning Taiwan. The *Solomon Times* reported that MPs had delivered Sogavare an ultimatum: that he facilitate the Switch to China within sixty days or face another no-confidence motion.[3] These MPs, it was reported, had been promised major investment in infrastructure in their constituencies by Chinese intermediaries, but only if ties with Taiwan were abandoned. Sogavare now established a formal process to investigate the merits of such a Switch, creating a 'bipartisan' taskforce that would, over the coming months, consider the merits of switching diplomatic recognition from Taipei to Beijing.

Sogavare may not have been the driving force behind the push for the Switch, but the arguments for it found fertile ground in his philosophy and his political ambitions. In July, with the taskforce process well underway, Sogavare was interviewed by Australian academic Graeme Smith, in one of the few meaningful on-the-record discussions he has given to foreign reporters or researchers since 2019.

The interview was brief, but it was dominated by the issue of Taiwan. Sogavare was unequivocal in expressing his scepticism about the utility of Honiara's partnership with Taipei. 'To be honest, when it comes to economics and politics, Taiwan is completely useless to us,' he said, when Smith asked him about the growing chatter about a potential Switch. Sogavare expressed frustration with Taiwan's inability to push back against pressure from Solomon Islands' traditional partners, such as Australia. He cited the 2006 incident from his second prime ministership, when he had sent forty Royal Solomon Islands Police Force members to Taiwan to receive specialist training. Sogavare alleged that Australian foreign minister Alexander Downer travelled to Taiwan and personally lobbied Taipei to abandon the program. 'The police training is ours' was how Sogavare paraphrased Australia's position. There is no record of Alexander Downer travelling to Taiwan at the time Sogavare alleges, but Australia did have concerns about Taiwan's methods in Solomon Islands, particularly regarding its direct payments to politicians. For Sogavare, Australia's perceived interference in the Taiwan–Solomons relationship demonstrated how weak a partner Taiwan was. As an astute political operator, and a mentee of Solomon Mamaloni, Sogavare knew instinctively that a partnership with China would give him more leverage – both at home and abroad.

He cited Fiji's ability to leverage its partnership with China for strategic advantage as a model he wanted to emulate. Some months later, when his interview with Smith was released, Sogavare claimed it was meant to be off the record and that Smith had recorded it under false pretences. Sogavare had, nevertheless, revealed his true position, ultimately undermining any sense of objectivity in the diplomatic review process he had established.

The leadership of the taskforce was given to John Moffat Fugui, who was a veteran Honiara MP and the education minister. Within weeks, Fugui had gathered a committee of six other MPs for a fact-finding mission across the Pacific Islands region. The taskforce would visit Vanuatu, Fiji, Samoa, Tonga and Papua New Guinea, to witness up close the development benefits a relationship with China might bring. 'We will use their countries as case studies to see the kind of development relations they have, the kind of assistance they get, the conditionalities or lack of conditionalities they might have, the kind of governance,' he told Reuters on 25 June 2019.

At the time, Fugui was playing a straight bat regarding the outcome of his report. Prior to the tour of neighbouring countries, the taskforce's deliberations had been confined to Solomon Islands. Their investigations had been informed by domestic stakeholders, including businesses who would benefit from a normalisation of relations with Beijing. But until June, the taskforce's work had been somewhat academic: weighing up the economic and political risks associated with the Switch. Only by leaving Honiara could the taskforce broaden the scope of its inquiry and meet firsthand with Chinese officials. No external participants were invited on the tour; the delegation would consist of Fugui and the six other MPs on the taskforce Jamie Vokia, Rex Ramofafia, Chachabule Amoi, Rollen Seleso and Titus Fika – plus two government officials, Bernard Bata'anisia and McFadden Arounisaka.[4] Local reporters questioned the composition of the delegation, noting that certain participants had already made their mind up regarding the Switch.[5]

For four weeks, the taskforce travelled the region, speaking to government ministers and visiting Chinese-funded projects. During the tour, the delegation did not meet bilaterally with any of their Pacific Island counterparts. Instead, all meetings occurred with a Chinese official in the room, according to Transparency Solomon Islands, an anti-corruption NGO and a branch of the global group Transparency International.[6]

In early August, while the taskforce was in Port Moresby, it was announced that it would visit China itself, accompanied by a ministerial delegation consisting of much of Sogavare's cabinet. They would travel to

Beijing at the invitation of – and at the expense of – the Chinese People's Association for Friendship with Foreign Countries (CAFFC), an entity that is alleged to be routinely involved in courting elites in developing countries.[7] The taskforce and the delegation toured Beijing between 15 and 19 August. It was reported that the ministerial delegation was intended to be kept under wraps: 'the latest trip was intended to have been a secret, but was however leaked to social media which caused much outcry', a 'government insider' told the *Island Sun* on the eve of the trip. As the story broke, Sogavare denied that the visit was supposed to have been kept secret. In publicising the visit, he argued, his government was engaging in the highest degree of transparency, and had informed the Taiwanese about the trip.[8]

News of the trip was met with an icy response by Taiwan. By now, it was becoming clear to officials in Taipei, as well as those on the ground in Solomon Islands, that the relationship would soon be ended. But for the Taiwanese, Honiara was an ally they could not afford to lose. When President Tsai Ing-wen had been elected in a landslide in 2016, she had pledged that Taiwan's gradual retreat from the international stage would be reversed. But the first few years of her presidency had instead coincided with the loss of an increasing number of allies. Between 2016 and 2018, four countries – São Tomé & Príncipe and Burkina Faso in Africa; Panama and the Dominican Republic in Latin America – had switched to Beijing, ceasing all diplomatic relations with Taipei. As Taiwan's allies dwindled, its relationships in the Pacific took on a new importance. In mid-2019, Taiwan still enjoyed formal ties with six Pacific nations: Marshall Islands, Nauru, Palau, Tuvalu, Kiribati and Solomon Islands. By far, Solomon Islands was the most crucial of these relationships. It was Taiwan's largest partner in the Pacific, and unlike some other nations, which had oscillated between support for Beijing and Taipei in the past, Honiara had remained committed to the Taiwan relationship since Solomon Mamaloni had thrust it upon his reluctant cabinet in 1983. Now, Sogavare's cabinet was taking tourist pictures in Beijing and dining with bureaucrats and businesspeople. For Taiwan's foreign minister, Joseph Wu, Honiara's rapid shift was a significant threat, not only to Taiwan's prestige, but also to the viability of his position as foreign minister. As the Solomons delegation travelled through Beijing, he flew to the tiny island nation of Palau, one of Taipei's strongest allies in the Pacific, and issued a stern warning to Solomon Islands about the dangers of their approach. 'Very often, the Chinese will say that they can come with a huge amount of investment, business opportunities, people are going to get wealthier,' he said. 'But ... it takes only two or three years to realise that those promises are empty promises.'[9]

Less than a month after the Solomon Islands delegation returned to Honiara, the taskforce, headed by Fugui, delivered its report. On 16 September, their findings, which had been accepted by the government, were released to the media. Their recommendations were unanimous. Solomon Islands must 'normalise diplomatic relations with the PRC' and do so by mid-September 2019. The report criticised the status quo, arguing that, if the government did decide to 'remain with the ROC [Taiwan]', the 'ROC has to increase its bilateral assistance to Solomon Islands'. It also noted the futility of Solomon Islands' long-held policy of assisting Taiwan to achieve legitimacy through membership of the United Nations. The report was blunt: 'Our continued support for ROC UN membership will not succeed.' It went on:

> Solomon Islands international relations and diplomacy is at a crossroad. We have to make adjustments. Our diplomatic relations must be pragmatic, useful and relevant now and in the future. Prospects for reunification between PRC and ROC will affect our relations with ROC. Globally, only sixteen countries recognize ROC. Solomon Islands is the only Melanesian country amongst them. In the last two years, four countries have switched diplomatic recognition from ROC to PRC. The challenge for Solomon Islands is to maintain space and momentum in this diplomatic manoeuvring between ROC and PRC. The challenge for Solomon Islands, therefore, is to maintain its international engagement and diplomacy, relevant and pragmatic, as far as the question of PRC and ROC is concerned. On the reaction from traditional donors as a result of the switch, there will be some impact on

the country and hence the need to review and enhance our engagement with our traditional donors.[10]

The report was matter-of-fact when considering the limitations of
engagement with Taiwan. All countries that recognise Taiwan understand
the fundamental constraints on the extent of this relationship, and the fact
that Taiwan's role in the world is severely limited. The report enunciated
this dispassionately. But this contrasted to the enthusiasm it showed when
outlining the benefits of switching to Beijing. 'Normalising diplomatic ties
with the PRC', the report stated, 'will open up many frontiers for Solomon
Islands never seen in the forty years of Solomon Islands independence.' It
spruiked China's international record, arguing that Beijing's seat on the UN
Security Council would benefit Solomon Islands' interests in areas including climate change, trade and development. The taskforce argued that
'it is important that developing countries such as Solomon Islands work
alongside China to enhance and promote multilateralism in the global
environment'. The report recognised that Solomon Islands' 'traditional
donors' – presumably including Australia and New Zealand, although these
countries were not mentioned by name – would be aggrieved by the Switch.
It found that there would be 'some impact' on these traditional relationships, but that ultimately, the decision would strengthen Solomon Islands'
negotiating position.

'China will provide us with an opportunity to leverage, engage and
maximize fully and constructively with our diplomatic partners', it said.

*

In making a case for the Switch, Fugui's committee was not recommending
anything out of step with much of the international community. Although
concerns over China's presence in the Pacific had been growing, particularly
in Canberra and Washington, Honiara understood that its partnership with
Taiwan made it an outlier. Australia itself had controversially recognised
China before most other Western nations did, on 21 December 1972. Just one

day later, New Zealand did the same. Earlier that year, US president Richard Nixon had made his famous visit to China, commencing a process that led to the normalisation of ties between the United States and the People's Republic of China in 1979. Over the next four decades, the vast majority of the global community followed suit. From this perspective, Solomon Islands' decision to abandon Taiwan wasn't unusual or unwarranted. If the rest of the world could benefit from formal relations with what would soon be the world's largest economy, why couldn't Solomon Islands? Even opponents of the Switch recognised this reality. The world had changed dramatically since Mamaloni had first established ties with Taiwan in 1983. Many Solomon Islanders, understandably, felt they were stuck in the past.

Irrespective of whether the ultimate decision to switch from Taiwan to China was the right one, the murky process that led to such a major policy shift created discomfort in Solomon Islands. When Fugui's report was handed down, suspicions were raised about its language, which at times appeared to echo talking points from Beijing. More concerningly for those anxious about China was the emphasis on the need for the Switch to happen quickly. The first recommendation of Fugui's report stood out:

Normalize diplomatic relations with the PRC and sign the Joint Communique to establish diplomatic relations by mid-September 2019. This must happen before the 1st October 2019, to coincide with the commemoration of the 70th Anniversary of the founding of PRC.

After thirty-six years of diplomatic relations with Taiwan, the committee was recommending that recognition of Beijing be extended within a fortnight, before the seventieth anniversary of China's founding – an event that was clearly important to Beijing but had no relevance to Solomon Islands. Opposition figures suspected that deals had been done while the delegation was in Beijing to ensure the Switch occurred by this deadline. The *Island Sun* newspaper reported rumours that Chinese authorities had been pushing Solomon Islands to proceed at pace by warning that should the October deadline be missed, China might walk away from the deal.

Some opponents of the Switch suspected that this haste wasn't being driven by senior Chinese leaders so much as by influential ethnic-Chinese businesspeople in Solomon Islands who saw a commercial advantage in normalising ties with Beijing promptly. The influence of the Chinese business community in Honiara is unique. Ethnic-Chinese residents of Solomon Islands constitute less than 2 per cent of the population but play a much larger economic role. The community's origins date back to the late nineteenth century, when Cantonese merchants from southeast China, predominately from the Guangdong region west of Hong Kong, settled throughout the South Pacific, establishing a commercial presence that has carried on to this day. Solomon Islands' key industries – logging, construction and mining – are dominated by a relatively small number of business elites, many of whom maintain ties to mid-level commercial entities in mainland China. Even before the Switch, China was already Solomon Islands' largest trading partner by far, despite the lack of formal diplomatic ties. Within Solomon Islands, there was a sense that, if relations were normalised, these commercial relationships would become more streamlined. While much of the international concern over the Switch focused on the potential for high-level political interference, local business figures and mid-level businesspeople in China played a much more influential role in shaping the taskforce's approach.

Wherever the pressure to move quickly was coming from, in agreeing to the 1 October deadline, Sogavare had made an irreparable strategic error. While in the past, some countries had oscillated between Beijing and Taipei, it was unlikely that the Solomons' Switch to Beijing would be temporary. It would be a permanent shift, and would certainly lead to greater political, economic and cultural entanglement between the two countries, which would be hard to undo. This meant that Honiara had one chance to execute a deal with Beijing and to extract whatever concessions it could. The Switch presented a one-off opportunity for Solomon Islands. Although Beijing reportedly played hardball during negotiations, Solomon Islands had the upper hand. Beijing's need to be recognised by every UN member state is well understood. A patient, strategic Sogavare government would have recognised this and secured economic support on a scale that Taiwan, or any other donor country, would not have been willing to offer.

But as the proposed date for the Switch approached, it became evident that whatever deals had been negotiated behind the scenes would not be made public. Fugui's report had made clear that, if Solomon Islands continued its relationship with Taiwan, it would expect additional Taiwanese development assistance. But the report made no such demands of the Chinese, instead outlining broad, general benefits that would likely accrue if the Switch occurred. As Sogavare rushed to ink the deal before the mid-September deadline, whatever more specific concessions he had managed to extract from Beijing would remain a secret.

*

In a final attempt to avert the Switch, Taipei had dispatched a senior delegation to Honiara on 15 September, a few days before the decision was made public. It was led by Taiwan's deputy foreign minister, Dr Szu Shein Hsu, who frantically worked to lobby parliamentarians and members of Sogavare's cabinet. At a press conference in Honiara, Dr Hsu leveraged growing anxiety about China's 'debt-trap diplomacy' to try to dissuade the Sogavare government from executing the Switch. 'I heard there is a saying that the Chinese government would like to provide US$500 million ... How is Solomon Islands going to pay for that debt?' he asked. But Dr Hsu's last-minute gambit would prove fruitless, and Taipei began preparing for the inevitable.

On 16 September, upon hearing that Sogavare's cabinet had agreed to the recommendations of the Fugui report, Taiwan pre-emptively moved to cut ties first, issuing a statement 'terminat[ing] diplomatic relations with immediate effect to uphold national dignity'. Taiwan's Ministry of Foreign Affairs chastised Sogavare for his management of the process. Despite Sogavare having assured Taiwan that a decision would only be made after four inquiries into the Switch had been held, he had decided to terminate ties with Taipei 'based solely on a highly biased ... report, which is full of fabrications and blatant misinformation.[11] Sogavare had 'not only broken his own public promise, but also disregarded the fruits of the thirty-six years of cooperation between Taiwan and Solomon Islands ... Taiwan believes that the majority of the Solomon Islanders will find the decision unacceptable since it completely lacks credibility'. The Taiwanese accused China of buying off 'a small number of politicians' to ensure the Switch occurred prior to 1 October, and of seeking to undermine Tsai Ingwen and her staunchly anti-Beijing party in the Taiwanese elections due to be held the following year. For Taiwanese foreign minister Joseph Wu, the decision by Honiara was a profound personal setback. It was worsened when, just one week later, Kiribati followed Solomon Islands' lead, normalising ties with China and expelling Taiwan's diplomats.

Taiwan's practical contribution to Solomon Islands, however, had been declining for some time. When the Switch was officially announced in September 2019, Taiwan was Solomon Islands' eighth largest bilateral supporter. In the years before, when relations were better, Taiwan had been more generous. But compared to other countries including Australia, New Zealand and Japan, Taiwan's aid and development assistance to Solomon Islands was modest.[12] What Taiwan had done effectively, however, was to strategically integrate its aid contribution into the political and economic life of Solomon Islands. Taiwan had directly funded the controversial Constituency Development Funds, or CDFs, which gave each member of parliament a cash sum to spend in their electorate as they pleased. On a generous reading, CDFs permitted MPs to cut through bureaucratic red tape and directly support important community-based initiatives. In practice, CDFs had become campaign slush funds: in the weeks leading up to polling day, MPs would often use their CDFs to buy basic goods – ranging from food to solar panels – for communities whose votes they needed to win. The annual value of CDFs varied, but, since the program was established in 2000, each of the country's fifty constituencies has received approximately SBD$66,000,000, or around US$10 million. The CDFs had come under intense scrutiny and had undermined Taiwan's reputation as a responsible donor. The Australian government saw Taipei's financing of the scheme as facilitating the very type of political corruption that RAMSI's focus on 'capacity building' was trying to stamp out.

Taiwan had also ingratiated itself by establishing highly visible development programs and cultivating a narrative that spruiked Taiwan and Solomon Islands' shared values and history. Across the Solomons, Taiwanese-funded agricultural programs had been effective and popular. They had established piggeries and provided practical advice to farmers, improving harvests and yields. Taiwan had also engaged closely with local civil-society groups, working to integrate itself into the community.

Taiwan's tolerance of Christianity and its successful transition to democracy, however, resonated in the Solomons, a deeply religious nation. Many in the Solomons were fearful of mainland China's communist system of government, its non-theist traditions and its active persecution of religious minorities. More tangentially, Taiwan had long argued that it was itself a 'Pacific nation'. It was from the island of Taiwan that, 5000 years ago, the Austronesian wave of Pacific immigration began. Taipei, seeking to integrate itself into the Pacific family, had worked assiduously to connect this prehistory to the present.

But this history counted for little when it came to altering the views held by Sogavare and his cabinet supporters. On 17 September, Taiwan's ambassador to Solomon Islands, Oliver Liao, stood in front of a crowd of local supporters, staff and his own deputy foreign minister, Dr Hsu, for a sombre ceremony. 'It is a sad day that we have to lower this flag that had been flying in Solomon Islands for thirty-six years,' Liao began. The ceremony had an air of informality, as if it had been hastily arranged. Liao was wearing a Hawaiian T-shirt:

> As the head of mission of the embassy here, I just wanted to thank you for your staunch support and friendship. Although your government made a decision not in our favour, I'm fully aware we have a lot of friends in our society here. All along, I've always known that we have more than 80 per cent of your populace continue to stand for Taiwan. I know that it was also very difficult for many members

of your government to try and stand up bravely to try and support our friendship and our relations, because of the way the vote was conducted. Anyway, our friendship continues, especially our friendship with the civil society. Over the past few years, in my tenure … I have been so deeply touched by your support and your friendship. We really love you, and hopefully in the future our paths may cross over again.

In February 2020, Moffat Fugui and Jamie Vokia, the two key pro-Beijing voices in the taskforce, were both dismissed from parliament after their elections were found to have been tainted by bribery.[13] Vokia's dismissal would commence a years-long legal process, during which he would fail to clear his name. Fugui had more luck. In May 2021, as Honiara's presence in Beijing became formalised, Fugui was appointed Solomon Islands' first ambassador to China.

7

ESCAPE FROM ADELIUA

AS THE POLITICAL RAMIFICATIONS BEGAN in Taipei, on the ground in Solomon Islands, Taiwan's aid workers had more practical concerns. After years of integrating themselves into Solomon Islands society, they had been recalled to Taiwan almost overnight. Across the country, they didn't even have time to pack up the equipment and documents associated with their projects.

Six years before the Switch, Taiwan had established one of its most effective development programs. In fields near the Fiu River, nestled between the small grass landing strip that serves as the gateway to Malaita and to the provincial capital, Auki, the Taiwanese had established Adeliua Farm, an agricultural initiative that aimed to stimulate local employment, introduce new farming techniques and teach communities how to harness their environment for agricultural production. After it was established, Adeliua Farm expanded to include a piggery, which reared animals to be distributed across Malaita and provided practical training for local farmers who had not raised animals in the past. Adeliua was a popular project. The fruits of the initiative were seen at the Auki Market, where better-quality produce and more diverse products, often grown on Adeliua Farm itself, began to fill the shelves. When Taiwan announced the termination of its ties with Solomon Islands, the Taiwanese staff at Adeliua had no choice but to immediately travel back to Honiara. Along with the rest of Taiwan's staff in Solomon Islands, they would soon be flown to Brisbane to plan their next moves.

Six weeks later, I visited the farm. The piggery was closed, its gate locked, although some pigs remained. It was a Saturday. My guide, a local schoolteacher named Sam, who had taken it upon himself to show me around his community, said there would usually be more people at the farm on the weekend. Worried about the pigs dying, a local chief had taken custody of them. Six weeks after the Switch, no one in the community knew if more funding would be coming to sustain the project.

The piggery was a few hundred metres away from the main farm. As I walked down the road, an older man appeared from a nearby property. He wore a tattered black-and-white chequered shirt, had few teeth and carried a rusty machete over one shoulder.

'Did you allow the Chinese to come to our country?' he jokingly asked. 'Because we already have enough friends.'

Stephen Donga was a 71-year-old former schoolteacher who had retired to a small farm near Adeliua. 'I try my best to support the farm, but I am weak now,' he said.

'Are you worried about this farm, now that the Taiwanese have left?' I asked.

'I should worry,' he said. 'What about you people in Australia? Do you mind helping us continue with the farm? Taiwan don't like us now because of our government.'

Stephen Donga

I kept walking down the road towards the main farm. When I got there, a shirtless, balding, middle-aged man with betel-nut-stained teeth was listlessly wandering the fields.

'Do you work here?' I asked. The man approached the barbed-wire fence that separated the thin gravel road from the farm.

'I do. I'm Misak,' he said.

We talked about what had happened since the Switch. Misak had been a labourer at the farm. He didn't know if he still had his job, but he continued to turn up to the property each day, tending to the crops and equipment. Behind him, an open-air shed covered discarded equipment: boxes, tools and a small trailer with Chinese writing scrawled on one side. Misak went over to the shed and grabbed a machete and a fresh pineapple. He sliced it up and shared it with me and Sam through the fence. Misak was worried about the future of his job, but he was confident that the Taiwanese funding would be replaced by funds from another donor, or by support from the government.

Misak, the operator of the Taiwanese-funded Adeliua Farm.

*

During my first meeting with Daniel Suidani, he had lamented the overnight abandonment of Adeliua Farm and the uncertainty it had thrust upon workers such as Misak. 'Being the leader of the province ... I should have been told,' Suidani told me.

Elsewhere in Solomon Islands, other families were coming to grips with similar consequences of the Switch. One of Taiwan's most popular initiatives had been its scholarship program. Although there are two universities in Solomon Islands, many of the country's brightest students hope to study abroad, where they can often pursue a more diverse, comprehensive and technically robust education in specialist fields such as engineering or medicine. Taiwan had funded scholarships throughout its thirty-six-year relationship with Solomon Islands. Two generations of the country's most promising students had been educated in Taiwan's prestigious universities. But when the Switch occurred, existing scholarships, affecting 106 Solomon Islander students, were immediately in doubt. Within days, Taiwan confirmed that current scholarships would be terminated: the students would be allowed to remain in Taiwan, but they would only be able to continue their studies if they funded them themselves.

Front page of the Island Sun *newspaper,*
publishing the pleas of the students in Taiwan.

In the gift shop of the Honiara National Museum, Patricia Luilamo, a 52-year-old single mother, was one of the parents scrambling to work out a plan. Her daughter Georgia had just one year left of her degree in international relations and had called Patricia, distraught. In November 2019, Patricia told me that she hadn't been sleeping since the Switch, as she tried to figure out how she could possibly afford to fund the rest of Georgia's university education. The cost of keeping Georgia in university, Patricia said, was around AU$2000 per semester, a sum that was close to unachievable on her modest government salary running the gift shop. But Patricia had told her daughter not to worry. She would find the money, somehow.

Patricia Luilamo

Almost three years later, in July 2022, when I returned to Solomon Islands after Covid-19 restrictions were lifted, I went back to the gift shop to see Patricia. Had she managed to support Georgia's final year, I asked her. She had, but only through extraordinary determination and innovation.

'I didn't have enough money with my salary, so I had to come up with other options,' she said. 'I held a fundraiser, raising awareness about what was happening and trying to get some support. But it didn't provide enough for more than one term. So, I had to find another way to make an income. I decided to rent a small plot of land outside of Honiara off a friend, and I went there and planted as many watermelons as I could. After a few months,

I hired a couple of boys to help me collect the watermelons and bring them back into town to sell.'

Georgia Luilamo ended up completing her education, thanks to the extraordinary resilience of her mother. When I first met Patricia in 2019, she was devastated. Three years later, she was simply angry. The Switch had upended her life.

*

Within days of the announcement of the Switch, Chinese interests had flooded Honiara and other parts of the Solomon Islands, in some cases trying to formalise partnerships with individuals with whom they had been engaging for years.

A delegation from the China Sam Enterprise Group Limited, or Sam Group – an opaque Chinese conglomerate with business interests in 'energy and chemical, military industry, international trade, port affairs, investment, film and other fields' and overtly proud of its connection to the Chinese Communist Party – soon descended on Tulagi to make an offer to the provincial government. Sam Group had plans to secure exclusive development rights to the small island. A few weeks earlier, during Sogavare's first official visit to China following the Switch, senior executives from Sam Group had met with him.

Accounts of Sogavare's meetings with Sam Group differ. According to a press release issued by Sam Group in October 2019, which has since been deleted, several Sam Group executives met with Sogavare at their Beijing headquarters. The press released stressed that a 'strategic cooperation agreement', under which Sam Group would participate in 'investment, trade, infrastructure, agriculture, fishery, communications and tourism', had been signed. Weeks after the meeting, once the political complications of the Switch had grown, Sogavare, under questioning in parliament, denied that any such agreement had been signed. He said that Sam Group's account was simply false, and that he had not met with them in Beijing. He had informally met with Sam Group in Guangdong, in China's south,

Sogavare said, later in the state visit. What is indisputable is that a meeting took place at some point during the trip: Sogavare and a Sam Group executive were photographed together in an image released by the Sam Group.

Throughout 2019, the premier of Central Province, Stanley Manetiva, a genial politician in his mid-fifties known to give away dugout canoes as gifts to constituents, had been warmly engaging with Sam Group representatives. They met in the provincial government headquarters; the dilapidated fibro buildings reflected the province's financial troubles. The air-conditioning was loud, the meeting room was echoey and the chairs were plastic. The paint was stripping and the corrugated-iron roof was rusted.

In mid-September 2019, meeting in a hotel in Honiara, Manetiva and representatives from the Sam Group, having worked on their relationship for months, signed a memorandum of understanding. It was soon leaked, sending shockwaves to Western capitals wary of Solomon Islands' new relationship with China, and it caused concerns across the archipelago. What the well-mannered, and certainly naïve, Manetiva had signed on to was a sweeping pledge that would see Sam Group 'lease the entire island of Tulagi', granting the state-owned enterprise 'wide-ranging powers to the Chinese conglomerate to develop infrastructure on Tulagi and surrounding islands', Reuters reported at the time. Given Tulagi's strategic significance, Western officials feared the agreement could grant deep-water port access to China in the heart of the archipelago.

With the Tulagi agreement emerging just weeks after the Switch, commentators critical of Sogavare's China pivot pounced on the news. For many, it represented the worst-case scenario: that Solomon Islands was already falling under China's spell. The incident was dubbed the 'Tulagi Turning Point' by Alan Tidwell, a respected academic, who asked:

> How long will it be before Tulagi begins to take on features like those found on the faux-island bases in the South China Sea? Will China build an airfield on Tulagi? China's J-10 fighter aircraft could use Tulagi, as they've done in the Paracel Islands, which arguably brings the coast of Queensland into range.[1]

Although Tidwell reassured his readers that a Chinese J-10 wouldn't be able to make sorties on Queensland from Tulagi without refuelling, his point was clear: the Tulagi lease represented a direct threat to Australia. Tidwell's analysis was among the most explicit, but other commentary followed similar lines. Journalists began asking Australian officials about the possibility of a military base in Tulagi, and the officials expressed 'genuine concerns', particularly given the 'susceptibility of the country's government to inducements from Beijing', *The Australian* reported on 17 October.

*

For Stanley Manetiva, the Tulagi lease saga was deeply hurtful, embarrassing and politically consequential. In the years after the incident, the premier lost his authority and was eventually deposed after being accused of corruption in the wake of the leasing scandal. He had since quietly drifted away from politics.

For two years after the Switch, I had been trying to reach Manetiva for an interview. Although he had given a handful of interviews to international journalists, he had become more reserved and suspicious in the wake of the Sam Group incident. After three years of engagement on Facebook, he agreed to meet with me while we were both in Honiara. Early on a Saturday morning, I caught a taxi to the Pacific Casino, a sprawling hotel on the city's eastern fringe, to meet him. I walked upstairs to the Rainbow Restaurant, which at 10 a.m. was empty of any patrons. For thirty minutes, I nervously waited for the former premier to arrive. The door swung open, and in came the six-foot-four politician, clad in a Brisbane Broncos rugby league shirt, cargo shorts and blue flip-flops. In between the incessant ringing of the phone, we discussed his fall from office and the incident that had catapulted him from the near anonymity of provincial island politics to the pages of *The New York Times*.

I began by asking Manetiva why he'd become so publicly quiet; why he'd drifted into the shadows.

'I'm in the outside now ... I want the people to make their own judgement' about the government that had replaced his, he said.

Manetiva hadn't always planned to enter politics. He was quite content as a high school teacher, working across Central Province with a home base in the provincial capital. He did, however, idolise his father. An MP who served six terms in the Central Province Assembly, Manetiva Snr had encouraged his son to enter the provincial assembly. In 2006, on his first attempt, Stanley succeeded his father in his Tulagi-based constituency, and by 2014, he had won the support of enough colleagues to be appointed premier – achieving a position his father never had. For Manetiva, his time in office would not be governed by any single policy objective or philosophy, but by principle: 'My one rule was to always tell the truth,' he said.

The job was the honour of his life. But with it came an unusual cast of suitors. In 2014, when Manetiva was first appointed premier of Central Province, he received an invitation. A Chinese businessman based in Honiara had reached out to him with an offer of a fully funded visit to mainland China. The trip was to be paid for by a company Manetiva had never heard of – 'China Sam', as he called it – who would wine and dine him and his provincial secretary, who headed up Central Province's fledgling bureaucracy from a ramshackle shed in Tulagi.

'We were invited, and we met all these big companies. I go to that company, we go to that company, we go to that company, then we have a meeting with the head of Sam Group,' he recalled.

'Did China Sam invite any other premiers to China during this period?' I asked.

'No no no, they want to have a relationship with Central Province, because of the strategic location.'

In 2016, after a tumultuous assembly session in which his supporters began to form new coalitions, Manetiva was removed as premier. To move on, he had decided to travel abroad to complete an undergraduate degree. But after completing his degree, he returned home, was re-elected to his seat in 2019 and again secured the numbers to reclaim the premiership. Almost immediately, the phone started ringing, and on the line was a familiar voice.

'When I came back from studies, they had access to me, and they called me,' he said, referring to Sam Group.

'This was before the Switch?' I asked. 'And they wanted to talk about the Tulagi project?'

'Yes. They contacted me ... they wanted to talk about this project. It was still the same.'

In the months before the Switch, Sam Group 'middle men', as Manetiva called them, continued to engage his government. After the Switch, Manetiva was invited to a meeting in Honiara with Sam Group officials. It was at this meeting that he was handed a large document, which he had assumed was a memorandum of understanding regarding ongoing engagement between the Sam Group and his provincial government. Initially, Manetiva didn't see any reason to be concerned. The signing of an MOU in Solomon Islands, and elsewhere in the Pacific, is so common and often so inconsequential that the very act of publicising MOUs is often mocked by Pacific-watchers and development professionals. MOUs come and go, typically with much fanfare but very little follow-through. For Manetiva, the Sam Group approach didn't seem any different from other such engagements.

'In any government formalities, when you meet people, you sign a document,' he said – so he signed it, in keeping with convention. 'They actually wanted to trick me,' Manetiva soon realised. 'They told me to sign, then they gave me all the documents. At the time, it was very lucky that I didn't have the stamp with me.'

Manetiva was referring to the formal provincial stamp that he would imprint on all official documents, in addition to his signature, to give the document full authority. On this occasion, he had forgotten to bring the stamp with him to Honiara, leaving it on his desk in Tulagi. The Sam Group representatives had to improvise.

'They told me to sign, and then they'd bring all the documents over to the province. Then I'd stamp, and then I'd email them,' he said. 'But when I came back to the office, I read again, and then I realised that I don't want to put the stamp on it, so I told the permanent secretary to shelve the project.'

The document that leaked to the media, and which would come to signify just how vulnerable Solomon Islands was in its new relationship with China, did not have the stamp Manetiva referred to. But it did have his signature. The premier was shocked by how significant the story came to be. And it would cost him dearly. Soon after the incident, he began fielding allegations from his political rivals that he was corrupt, and that he was using the provincial government funds for personal endeavours. 'Every dollar spent has to be checked, how would this even be possible?' Manetiva protests. He would soon be removed from office for a second time.

Manetiva was cagey about whether he personally supported the Switch or not. He said that, even if he did, his opinion was irrelevant, given the lack of power he had as a provincial government leader. His willingness to travel to China on the dime of a foreign company did, however, suggest at least an open mind to Chinese investment in his province. It also demonstrated the long-term tactics that commercial interests such as the Sam Group had been putting into practice for several years leading up to the Switch. The group's tactics may have been audacious, but they misunderstood where power really lies in such foreign-investment decisions in Solomon Islands. Although their engagement with Manetiva from early on in his premiership suggested a sophisticated strategy, it ignored the fundamental and unavoidable constraints placed upon provincial leaders such as Manetiva. Even if it were his intention to lease the entirety of Tulagi – his island home, his local constituency and the place where his revered father had made his career – Manetiva simply did not have the legal authority to do so. Without the permission of tribal leaders and the national government, Sam Group's strategy was never likely to be successful.

After days of frenzied media speculation about the deal, Solomon Islands' attorney-general John Muria Jnr (whose father had also been attorney-general), formally voided the document that had been signed between Manetiva and the Sam Group. The project was dead. But its impact on how the Switch was perceived, especially among foreign hawks who had been outspoken about the Chinese threat in Honiara, could not be reversed.

For Manetiva, the damage to his reputation was severe. But he is comforted by his own belief that he did nothing wrong. 'I always have a principle that I want to tell the truth. I don't want to hide it,' he told me, as dishes clanged and waitresses giggled behind the counter of the empty Rainbow Restaurant. 'But I always believe ... the truth always comes behind. Falsehoods ... are the frontline. I believe the truth will come out, that's what I believe.'

8

THE GAMES

WHEN I WAS FIRST SENT TO SOLOMON ISLANDS on assignment for *The Guardian,* my mind was focused on the thrill of having been dispatched to the wilds of the South Pacific to cover arguably the region's geopolitical event of the decade. But for a freelance reporter, such foreign visits are a break-even proposition. Long gone are the days of a roving reporter being on a healthy salary paid by cashed-up, profit-making media machines. Instead, those of us travelling to report on the world are often doing it on a shoestring, stretching razor-thin budgets as far as they can go just to get to wherever the story needs to be told.

Because of this economic necessity, lofty ideals are occasionally disturbed by an unexpected opportunity to cover a far less meaningful story, so long as it pays the bills. After a few days in Solomon Islands, one of these unexpected opportunities fell into my lap. My trip happened to co-incide with Prince Charles' three-day tour of the country. Only twice in the nation's history had a royal visited Solomon Islands – in 1959, when Prince Philip briefly passed through, and in 2012, when his grandson, Prince William, had followed. Now, in November 2019, Charles was in the country to launch a new marine-conservation initiative.

The tour came at the height of his brother Prince Andrew's sordid sex-abuse scandal. Having befriended notorious predator Jeffrey Epstein, Prince Andrew was alleged to have been involved in soliciting sex from minors trafficked by his disgraced acquaintance. Photos of the prince with his alleged victims had been widely circulating for months. So on 16 November,

Prince Andrew sat down with the BBC to try to mitigate the fallout. His interview couldn't have been more disastrous. Amid his numerous denials, the prince also offered a preposterous alibi aimed at debunking a victim's claim that he had sweated on her. Due to his traumatic experience in the Falklands War, Prince Andrew said, he had developed a rare condition that prevented him from sweating. Predictably, the UK tabloids soon dipped into their archives and found images of the prince sweating profusely soon after his service ended. In the middle of this firestorm, Prince Charles was en route to Solomon Islands, perhaps simply to get away from it all. On the hunt for some extra cash, I gleefully jumped at the suggestion from my editor that I find the prince and ask him what the world wanted to know: could his brother perspire?

I raced back from Auki to Honiara, buying a ticket on the rusting twenty-seat Twin Otter turbo-prop plane that makes the thirty-minute flight daily from Malaita to Guadalcanal. After rocking through the air at 5000 feet, I landed and headed to Parliament House. The prince had arrived that morning and was to deliver an address to MPs. I hadn't prepared for the eventuality of having to report from Parliament House: I didn't have a press pass and assumed I'd be rebuffed by security. But when I stepped out of the cab by the front gates, I tidied my shirt, stood up straight and walked towards the entrance with purpose.

'Edward Cavanough from *The Guardian*,' I confidently said, knowing full well I was yet to even have a story published in the newspaper I was claiming an association with.

To my surprise, the gate swung open, and I was ushered by a security guard down the sloping road towards the front door of parliament without any resistance. Assembled was a small cluster of local reporters. Cameras and microphones in hand, they were preparing for Prince Charles to appear, hoping to get a quick photo before the future king would be whisked into a waiting car with a cadre of advisors, on to his next engagement. To my disappointment – and my editor's – we were sternly told by security that the prince would not be taking any questions. Soon after, the bi-fold doors swung open, and out stepped the tan-suited prince, who briefly smiled and waved to me as I took my photos, but remained at a safe, question-free distance.

The prince's next engagement was his most important in the country, and it would be among the more significant public events in Solomon Islands since independence. He was scheduled to deliver a public address to thousands at Honiara's largest public sporting ground, the Lawson Tama Stadium. The stadium is modest: its few small stands surround a soccer pitch, buttressed against a steep embankment. Most spectators assemble on the grassy hill to watch soccer matches. Built in the mid-1960s, the stadium, named after a prominent Australian businessman, is ageing and decaying, its inadequacies so great that few international sporting events are held there. But in a city with next to no public infrastructure, the stadium was the only suitable location for the prince's public event. As a large crowd gathered on the hillside and the few small spectator stands filled, Prince Charles took to the microphone.

'*Mi hapi visiting place blong yu-fela*' – I'm pleased to be here – he said, to rapturous applause.

*

Covering Prince Charles' trip, and seeing up close the pomp, ceremony and excesses that went along with a royal visit, I did wonder what his perceptions of the place must have been. All that elegance – the pressed tan suit, the Rolls Royce, the jewellery – looked absurd when contrasted with the dereliction of Honiara. I wondered what this city looked like to a future king. His motorcade may have been bulletproof, but it still had to travel the same pot-holed road into town as everyone else. He would have had to stay in the same dated hotels that, while a luxury for a modestly compensated freelance journalist, must have been somewhat of a step down for a royal. As he drove around Honiara from engagement to engagement, Charles would have seen what everyone else sees, albeit through tinted windows: rubbish strewn across the streetscape; broken windows and boarded-up buildings; dust plumes kicking up behind old cars on poorly maintained roads; spiked security walls enveloping most private businesses and public buildings. A stone's throw from Honiara are some of the world's most pristine environments, but the city is among the most confronting in the Pacific. It is a city that has been broken time and time again, whose inhabitants struggle every day to keep ahead economically. And it shows.

The dilapidated state of public infrastructure had been both an embarrassment and a roadblock to progress for Solomon Islands, and for Manasseh Sogavare. It was a poor reflection on an otherwise striking and culturally vivid country, and it limited Honiara's capacity to play host to economically stimulating events. Frustrated after his first two relatively unsuccessful prime ministerships, Sogavare, after assuming the leadership for the third time in 2014, had turned his attention to a major initiative aimed at providing the impetus for a nation-building frenzy. He wanted a project that would secure his legacy. He wanted a project that would signal to the region – maybe even the world – that the dark old days of Solomon Islands were a distant memory; that the country, once languishing, had now arrived. Sogavare was going to host the Pacific Games.

First held in 1963, the Pacific Games, formerly the South Pacific Games, have become a central feature of the Pacific's regional integration. Each of the Pacific Islands' twenty-two countries, territories and associated states are involved. Even the smallest, such as Nauru, Niue and Tokelau, field modest teams. Accredited internationally, the games also provide a unique opportunity for Pacific Island athletes from these smaller nations to perform at an international level against the larger Pacific countries, such as Fiji and Papua New Guinea. But as with all major sporting meets, hosting the games is a complex and costly endeavour. The need to accommodate thousands of athletes and their support crews, and to provide facilities for the thirty-two sporting events that constitute the games, places considerable strain on small, often fragile island economies. This has seen hosting of the games rotate between a handful of countries. Fiji has hosted three times, as have Papua New Guinea, New Caledonia, Samoa and French Polynesia. Guam, the US territory in the western Pacific, has hosted twice. Not all countries have the capacity to host the games. Tuvalu, for example, has a population of just 1200 people, concentrated on a tiny atoll, which cannot physically host an event on this scale.

But Solomon Islands, among the larger of the Pacific nations, is different. Its inability to host the games was not the result of geographical limitations, or of its modest population. Instead, it symbolised the country's decades of economic malaise and social turmoil. The last time Solomon Islands played host to any moderately significant international sporting event was when it held the Mini Pacific Games, a scaled-down, amateur version of the larger event, in 1981, when Sogavare was still a functionary at the Inland Revenue Commission. In 2008, when Beijing hosted the Summer Olympics, it was billed as modern China's emergence – a statement, witnessed by the world, of China's progress. In the Pacific Games, Sogavare saw an opportunity to send a similar message.

The contest to host the 2023 Pacific Games was initially between Fiji and French Polynesia. As the wealthiest independent state in the Pacific, and the second largest by population after Papua New Guinea, Fiji was well equipped to host the event. French Polynesia, still a colonial asset of France, also had the resources to host the games. But before formalising its entry into the contest, Fiji withdrew, leaving French Polynesia without a clear competitor.

In May 2016, two years into his third prime ministership and almost a year after Fiji had withdrawn from contention, Sogavare made an unexpected announcement: Solomon Islands would enter the race for the 2023 games. The bid would be a long shot. Not only had French Polynesia hosted the games before; it also had the support of the games' governing body, the Pacific Games Council, which would select the host. '[French Polynesia] has certainly laid down a marker and they will be difficult to beat,' the council's executive director, Andrew Minogue, told media in mid-2015. Minogue's clear support for French Polynesia was the main reason Fiji had withdrawn its bid. *Papeete 2023* seemed like a done deal.

Undeterred, Sogavare went all-out in pursuit of the games. Soon after announcing his intentions, he took leave from parliamentary duties to fly to Vanuatu and meet with the Pacific Games Council to argue Honiara's case.

Despite the obvious deficits in the Solomon Islands bid – its lack of suitable infrastructure prominent among them – Sogavare had a plan. He told the Pacific Games Council that, if successful, Solomon Islands would build a new national stadium and a host of other sporting arenas. There would be no scenes of spectators crammed onto a grassy hillside next to an ailing 1960s stadium. Instead, the Pacific's finest athletes would compete in a world-class stadium, with a capacity to host 12,000 spectators. The city's existing infrastructure would be spruced up, and the athletes would be housed in a brand-new village on the edge of town.

The council was impressed. '[Solomon Islands] have put a solid bid proposal together … it will be interesting to see,' said Minogue before the vote.[1]

On the day of the decision, which was held in Vanuatu, Sogavare and his team engaged in a last-minute round of furious lobbying. The jurors – one representative from each of the twenty-two participating nations – retired to vote. The announcement shocked the region. Solomon Islands had prevailed; Honiara had won by a single vote. Sogavare had pulled off an extraordinary coup. He had placed his personal credibility on the line, and his prime ministerial visit had been just enough to convince the voting council members that Solomon Islands was serious.

But now the prime minister was in a bind. Conditional to the games' success was his administration's ability to deliver one of the largest public works efforts in his country's history. Historically beset by financial troubles, the Solomon Islands government would require ample assistance to achieve this mammoth task. The price of failure would be extraordinary: the prime minister's legacy now depended on the games' success. He had seven years to pull it off.

*

In December 2017, eighteen months after Sogavare successfully secured the games, he was again deposed from power. His successor was Rick Houenipwela – generally known as Rick Hou – a genial economist and former Reserve Bank governor who earned a reputation as a straight shooter after refusing bribes during the Tensions. Hou was now responsible for preparing for the games. In early 2018, his parliament ushered in the *Pacific Games 2023 Act*, which established a new agency, the National Hosting Authority (NHA). Its mandate was to plan for the games, including the commissioning of major infrastructure works.

With a staff of just two full-time and three part-time employees, the NHA met for the first time in December 2018. In its first three months, it moved quickly to pursue international support for the centrepiece infrastructure project, a new national stadium, to be constructed on the grounds of the prestigious King George VI High School. The NHA knew where to turn for support. During the first few months of 2019, the issue of Taiwan's recognition had started to be discussed in the context of the looming election. The Taiwanese were by now feeling vulnerable. Although few candidates were openly campaigning for a Switch, a shift to China was on the agenda for the next term of parliament. In response, the Taiwanese ambassador to Solomon Islands made it clear that Taipei would be willing to fund and manage construction of the stadium. Taiwan established a memorandum of understanding with Rick Hou's government just days before the April 2019 election.

But after the election, with Sogavare once again in the prime minister's chair, he moved to consolidate control of the NHA. Two of his senior and trusted advisors, prime ministerial secretary Jimmie Rodgers and his deputy, Christian Nieng, were given responsibility for running the NHA during Sogavare's fourth prime ministership. For Sogavare, ensuring that the Pacific Games proceeded successfully and on time became a central objective. Hosting the games had been his idea, and he was determined to deliver. In July 2019, despite murmurs about a potential shift to Beijing circulating Honiara, Sogavare's government formalised the deal struck between his predecessor's administration and Taiwan.

Almost immediately, however, the legitimacy of this arrangement was called into question. Sogavare had by now established the committee processes that would eventually lead to the Switch. He had publicly criticised Taiwan and the relationship's utility to Solomon Islands. Despite Taiwan's promise to build a stadium, no ground would be broken before the Switch occurred, three months after the ink was set.

Two weeks after the Switch was announced, Sogavare flew to Beijing, in a trip filled with pomp and ceremony, to flesh out the details of the new relationship. Although the precise outcomes of these negotiations would never be released, some indications trickled out. One of the first announcements after Sogavare returned to Honiara was China's commitment to support the new National Stadium. Beijing had pledged AU$74 million to build the 12,000-seat stadium Sogavare coveted.[2] The groundbreaking ceremony would have to wait until March 2021. Then, Sogavare, the Chinese ambassador and representatives from the state-owned construction firm awarded the tender were present. A beaming Sogavare grabbed two shovels and tossed the soil, declaring the 2023 Pacific Games Stadium Project underway.[3]

9

RIVERS OF GOLD

WHEN, IN LATE 1568, ALVERADO MENDAÑA'S Spanish brigantine first set off from the north coast of Isabel to explore more of the archipelago, the conquistador had one aim in mind: finding gold. It was, after all, the pursuit of wealth that had inspired the young Spaniard to embark on such a dangerous journey; he hoped to explore and occupy a fantastical land of wealth and enshrine his place in history. In those first weeks in the archipelago, Mendaña had yet to find what he was searching for. The archipelago was richly endowed, yes: it was teeming with fruits and timber, potential slaves and minerals. But in the expedition's first weeks on Isabel, they had seen no traces of gold. After sailing south past Savo Island, Mendaña and his crew saw for the first time the island of Guadalcanal. Mountainous and forested, with expansive tracts of flat, fertile land on its northern coast, the island appealed to the Spaniards. The brigantine first attempted to land at 'the islet of Tandai', a small clump of land just off what is now Point Cruz, but were, as was becoming routine on this first voyage, accosted by locals whom one sailor decried as 'miscreants'.[1]

Mendaña's men would inch east along the Guadalcanal coastline, regularly being met with such resistance. After several days, they anchored at the mouth of the Matepono River, about thirty kilometres east of what is now Honiara. Mendaña dispatched a party of twenty-two men, led by Alfred Nuñez, to trek inland and 'prospect the stream beds for alluvial gold'.[2] Nuñez's party was 'continually assailed by the natives with arrows and stones'. Just two attempts were made to pan for gold, but 'in both cases, the current was too strong for the washing dish, and the annoyance from the natives was too persistent for careful experiment'. Nuñez did, however return to Mendaña with positive news. There were, he said 'indications of gold' on Guadalcanal. But Nuñez's fleeting glimpse of the mineral would be as close as the Spaniards ever got to realising their dream. Mendaña's mission soon faltered. The Spanish were never to return.

*

The story of Nuñez's tentative proclamation of gold on Guadalcanal didn't go unnoticed by those who colonised the archipelago some 250 years later. In the two decades before Japan's successful invasion of the archipelago, British prospectors had turned their attention to the area, albeit unsuccessfully. But the British focused primarily on the development of an agricultural export economy, a logging industry, and the labour trade between its regional possessions, rather than on mining. Only in 1983 would the area identified by Nuñez as containing gold be developed. That year, Amoco, a major US oil and minerals firm, was awarded a tender by the Mamaloni government for what had by now been named 'Gold Ridge'. But prospecting did not identify significant quantities of gold, and the mine proved unprofitable. Through the 1980s and 1990s, a number of companies floated in and out, none of them successfully capitalising on what many now knew was under the surface. It would not be until 1997, when the mine was acquired by Ross Mining, an Australian firm, that the fruits of Gold Ridge would be harvested.

Through 1998 and 1999, Ross Mining established an open-pit mine at Gold Ridge, producing 210,000 ounces of gold. Two years in, Ross Mining's early success saw it acquired by a larger firm, Delta Gold. For Delta, the acquisition was terribly timed. Just a month after Delta purchased Gold Ridge, the violence in Honiara became so bad that the company was forced to recoup its investment costs through a political-risk insurer, which in turn acquired Gold Ridge in its own right. Once the RAMSI intervention had stabilised the political situation, the insurer tendered the mine again. In 2005, Australian Gold purchased Gold Ridge and began to redevelop operations, before it, in turn, was purchased by Allied Gold. Prospecting by Allied Gold showed the site to be promising, but the mine's operational life was predicted at the time to be 'just eight years, with potential to extend mine life to 12–15 years'.[3]

To fully realise this potential, Allied sought outside investment from the International Finance Corporation. For the IFC, an organisation dedicated to investing in emerging economies to enhance development, Gold Ridge, despite its tumultuous history, had promise. 'At full production,' the IFC argued, 'the project can be expected to account for as much as 20 per cent of Solomon Islands' GDP'.[4] The IFC claimed that the project would raise considerable government revenue, facilitate new housing initiatives for local landowners and create at least 500 jobs for Solomon Islanders. To achieve this outcome, the IFC pledged US$30 million.

By the end of 2010, production recommenced. Soon, four open-pit mines were in operation. Then, once again, the owner of the mine, Allied Gold, was absorbed by another, larger operator: the Australian company St Barbara Limited. At a price of AU$1.025 per share, St Barbara purchased Allied Gold for AU$556 million. It was a sizeable investment that allowed St Barbara to expand into both Solomon Islands and Papua New Guinea, where Allied Gold also had operations. Again, however, the new owners of Gold Ridge hit trouble. St Barbara's official company history tells the story:

> In the Solomon Islands, torrential rain and flooding led to the suspension of operations at Gold Ridge in April 2014. Force majeure notices were issued under certain mining and supply agreements when it became clear that production could not be resumed due to factors outside the operator's control. The Gold Ridge Project was sold to a Solomon Islands company associated with local landowners in May 2015.[5]

What St Barbara's official account omits is that the sale to local landowners was completed for the measly sum of AU$100. The company, recognising Gold Ridge was bereft of opportunity and loaded with risk, decided to offload its asset for an extraordinary loss, the only condition being that all legal liabilities were transferred to the local owners. Four centuries after Nuñez had his first tantalising glimpse of gold on Guadalcanal, the story of Gold Ridge appeared to be over.

But despite its tumultuous history, there was always a desire to see Gold Ridge's promise fulfilled. After the 2019 election that saw Sogavare return to power, a handful of MPs in his new government were among those lobbying for the mine's reopening. One, Jamie Vokia, represented the communities where Gold Ridge is located. Another was Bradley Tovosia, the newly appointed minister for mines, who was also one of the MPs lobbying for the Switch. As the Switch neared, speculation about the future of Gold Ridge intensified. The mine did present a genuine opportunity for Solomon Islands and for the communities near it. Many of these landowners held a stake in the mine and would benefit financially should its production resume.

On 20 October 2019, less than one month after the Switch, Sogavare announced that Gold Ridge would indeed be reanimated, thanks to an investment of US$825 million by the Chinese firm Wanguo International Mining. The firm had contracted China State Railway Group to complete the physical infrastructure required to get the mine operational. They would 'build roads, bridges, mining facilities and a hydropower station', said the Chinese ambassador, while additional works on a new deep-water port near Honiara would also commence. 'This is not only a new beginning for the Gold Ridge mine, but also a very important early harvest of the friendly co-operation between China and Solomon Islands, which established diplomatic relations just thirty-five days ago,' the ambassador said.[6]

Immediately, the scale of the investment stoked concern. Australian mining analyst Peter Strahan told the Australian Broadcasting Corporation that the agreement was 'way over the top', considering how low-grade the mine's output was. These thoughts were echoed by some Solomons opposition politicians, who decried the lack of transparency around the deal.

Within days of its largest geopolitical decision since independence, the Sogavare government had permitted the largest private investment in the country's history. Hundreds of millions of dollars would flow through a project that had proved unviable for the better part of a century. This 'early harvest', as the Chinese ambassador had described it, was meant to signify a new beginning. Instead, it became a totem of the lack of transparency that defined the Switch and its aftermath.

*

The concerns about the reanimation of the mine were informed by a lengthy history of proved and alleged corruption throughout all levels of government, public administration and business in Solomon Islands. For decades, concerns about the corrupting influence of foreign money on Solomon Islands' political elite had been expressed. The growth of extractive industries – mainly logging – had seen countless examples of corrupt influence, enabling foreign businesses to fell and export lucrative old-growth timber, with little benefits delivered to local landowners. Mining and prospecting licences were often attained through shady deals with ministers and senior bureaucrats, or through strong-arming of the local communities upon whose land the extraction would occur.

At the political level, corruption in Solomon Islands has been relatively overt, particularly through the Constituency Development Funds (CDFs). Established in the early 2000s and ostensibly designed to direct aid spending to local communities, CDFs quickly became a means for MPs to line their pockets and buy votes come election time. Of course, much corruption occurs behind closed doors and is hard to verify. But Ruth Liloqula, the head of Transparency Solomons, is one of the few locals who has been able to expose and identify the nature of corruption in her country. From a small office in Honiara's Hyundai Mall, Liloqula – four-foot-ten and impeccably dressed – leads a team of just four people, working under intense scrutiny, to seek and publicise the truth. She is the face of Solomon Islands' anti-corruption movement, appearing regularly on local and international news, often calling out corrupt politicians and bureaucrats by name. In Honiara, Liloqula's message is amplified by half a dozen billboards that explain how corruption takes root and why it should be eradicated. Liloqula keeps no papers in her office, ever concerned about a raid.

Corruption of the CDFs, she says, is largely driven by the scheme's inadequate governance and poor oversight. The funds are held in bank accounts specific to each constituency and can be released with the signature of just two individuals: the MP and their personally appointed constituency officer. While constituency officers are technically public servants, they are chosen by the MP, sometimes from outside the public sector. 'Often, these constituency officers are not qualified. Sometimes they are the MP's wife,' says Liloqula, who has evidence of three MPs appointing their spouses as co-signatories of a CDF.

Unsurprisingly, MPs in Solomon Islands deny any involvement in corruption. What is obvious, however, is that many have become fabulously wealthy since joining parliament, and few bother to conceal their riches. Some MPs' children have emerged as larger-than-life figures in Honiara's small club scene, partying each weekend at venues such as Club HP with the young expatriate community, picking up the tab to impress their visiting friends and driving the most expensive cars in the country. In Malaita, one jaded, impoverished islander told me that there was a saying in Solomon Islands: 'If you want to be a millionaire, become an MP.'

The main driver of this excess is, according to Liloqula, the misallocation of CDFs. Liloqula isn't alone in her condemnation. In 2022, the permanent secretary of Solomon Islands' Ministry for Rural Development called out parliamentarians for using CDF money for pet projects in Honiara, rather than in their constituencies.[7]

The Switch, Liloqula argues, became a vehicle for further foreign interference. She and Transparency Solomons stress that they were not against the Switch per se: like many other groups, they acknowledge the reality that most countries recognise Beijing, and that Honiara was likely, at some stage, to join them. 'But we were not ready for the Switch,' she tells me, arguing that the few entities responsible for monitoring and addressing corruption in the country are ill-equipped to manage the pressures that would now intensify as Chinese commercial interests flooded Honiara looking for access. In Liloqula's view, the CDFs have always been a driver of corruption, but the new relationship with China has made things worse.

In the months preceding the Switch, even those in favour of normalising ties with China recognised that Taiwan's funding of the CDFs would need to be replaced. While Taiwan didn't exclusively fund the CDFs, its support accounted for around one-quarter of the scheme. In Solomon Islands' 2015 budget, for example, the CDF program totalled SBD$260 million, with SBD$70 million of that flowing from a Taiwanese grant. For MPs eager to switch to China, filling this funding gap was a major priority. After his trip to Beijing to iron out the details of the new relationship, Sogavare told the media in Honiara that while China would continue to support the country's rural development, it would not be directly providing cash grants to the CDF program. Instead, China would offer its support to specific projects – 'up to three projects' in each constituency.[8]

To observers critical of the CDF program, this appeared an improvement. It seemed designed to placate concerns that the Switch would fuel corruption; instead, Sogavare was promising, it provided an opportunity to clean up a program long known for being rorted. As ties between Honiara and Beijing matured through 2020 and 2021, however, the integrity of this initial pledge became questionable. Projects were not flowing as promised, a situation exacerbated by Covid-19 travel restrictions, and the CDF hole needed to be filled. In early 2021, Solomon Islands' budget papers revealed that, contrary to Sogavare's statement, China had tipped in US$11.3 million directly to the CDF program.[9] MPs now had exclusive access to substantial pools of Chinese cash.

The CDFs afford enormous power to incumbent politicians, enabling them to buy votes and then, from their seats of power, to accumulate even more riches by other means. Liloqula says that since the Switch, this is occurring on a grander scale than ever before. Without a financial dividend, she contends, MPs would be much more willing to support an alternative leader.

The Gold Ridge project, in Liloqula's view, was rife with issues, and exemplified how the normalisation of corruption had allowed poor projects to become established in Solomon Islands. China's extraordinary investment pledge of US$865 million – equivalent to around two-thirds of Solomons' annual GDP – was cause for alarm. Investment on this scale was unprecedented in Solomon Islands. The structure of the deal was such that Solomon Islands was unlikely to see any significant local economic benefit.

'I used to work on Gold Ridge,' says Liloqula, who trained as a scientist. 'When I was there, [the mine] would pay SBD$43 million in tax to the Solomon Islands government every year ... now, it will pay no tax.' Local landowners were given a promise of 10 per cent royalties from the proceeds of the mine. But whether that royalty reflected the true value of the minerals being extracted is questionable. The composition of the Gold Ridge deposit is such that it does not allow for the direct extraction of 'nugget gold'; instead, it requires large volumes of composite rock to be processed in order to extract valuable metals. Experts have noted that Gold Ridge is a 'relatively low-grade project with modest return', even questioning whether it is in fact viable.[10] The processing of the composite rock will not occur in Solomon Islands, but in China, where the metals would then be used in China's domestic supply chain. As well as gold, the Gold Ridge deposit also has traces of rare-earth elements, such as cobalt, which are becoming highly sought fter in the global race to manufacture technology that will enable decarbonisation. The value, in essence, is being created offshore, not at home, adding to uncertainty as to whether the 10 per cent royalty would constitute the true value of the gold, or only the value of the low-grade deposits that are shipped offshore.

The fact that the Gold Ridge investment was announced almost immediately after the Switch suggested that it was likely included in the deal struck between Beijing and Honiara. China Rail's pledge to establish rail and ports infrastructure to facilitate the project means a state-owned Chinese entity will own and operate pivotal infrastructure on the island of Guadalcanal. Because of the lack of transparency around the Switch, one can only speculate as to whether these details were demanded of the Solomons government during negotiations.

For many Solomon Islanders, allegations that corruption had influenced the Switch came as no surprise. The perception of corruption at the highest level of government has created an ecosystem through which it trickles down to lower tiers of public administration, all the way to the basic government services that locals interact with regularly. One of the clearest, and perhaps most shameful, examples of grassroots corruption in the Solomons is the manipulation by low-ranking local public servants of Australia's Seasonal Worker Program. This program allows Solomon Islanders to work for up to three years in regional Australia. Often, these workers fill labour shortages in fruit and vegetable picking, but many work in other sectors, including meatpacking, construction and bespoke industries such as leather manufacturing. The Seasonal Worker Program is an essential driver of economic activity in the Solomons. Each year, thousands of islanders head to Australia, lured by the promise of jobs that pay up to AU$30 per hour – about twenty-five times the Solomon Islands' minimum wage of SBD$8, or AU$1.50 per hour. Solomons' seasonal workers in Australia and New Zealand remit tens of millions of dollars each year to their families. Over the course of their time abroad, they often save enough money to send children through school, start a small business or build their own house once they return home. The program has transformed the lives of thousands of families in Solomon Islands. But despite its virtues, it is also rife with problems and open to exploitation.

To qualify for the scheme, Solomon Islanders must meet a wide range of criteria. They're required to pass English language tests and police and medical checks and must usually apply for the program in person in Honiara. For most of the lowest-income individuals in Solomon Islands, these criteria are impossible to meet financially. In many communities, children from subsistence families do not attend school, because their parents have no formal income and are unable to pay the SBD$500 school fees expected each term. Many younger Solomon Islanders therefore speak no English, which effectively disqualifies the most disadvantaged Solomon Islanders from the Seasonal Worker Program. Travelling to Honiara is also prohibitively expensive for the most impoverished Solomon Islander families. In and around Honiara, many young men have participated in the Seasonal Worker Program. By contrast, in some of the most remote villages I have visited, especially those on the east coast of Malaita, not a single member of the community had participated in the scheme. Those who do have enough funds to attempt to qualify soon find themselves subject to low-level corruption from the some of the authorities administering the scheme. Police are alleged to prioritise checks for those who pay a little extra; the same goes for health professionals undertaking medical checks, and officials processing visas for successful applicants. In 2021, the *Solomon Times* published one applicant's account of their experience:

> I was asked by an officer to pay some money to fast track some required documents, they called me on my phone and said if I want the document fast then I need to pay. I was very upset because when I went for the interview, everything went well, when I was shortlisted and asked to do physical tests, I was very happy because I knew my chance is high. Those that handled the recruitment part were very professional and very helpful. The problem started when we deal with other people to get clearance and other documents, it became too much for me. I was asked to pay money everywhere I go, people who want their things done fast have to pay. When I was called to give some money, I was very angry, I told the guy off and he said 'Ok good luck lo iu' [*Good luck to you*].[11]

Many of those profiteering from the scheme are intermediary 'agents' who are paid a fee for each successful applicant by businesses in Australia and New Zealand, as well as by the hopeful applicants themselves. Agents who play the game and pay extra to those who demand it are more likely to see their applicants succeed. Ruth Liloqula says that Transparency Solomons has investigated the issue, and that the corruption of the Seasonal Worker Program is well known. But she says that no authority has made any serious attempt to stop it – neither the Solomon Islands government, nor the donors responsible for the program.

That the Seasonal Worker Program, a key initiative of the Australian and New Zealand governments, has found itself subject to such widespread corruption, speaks to the endemic nature of the problem in Solomon Islands. Many of the most serious allegations of corruption, such as those involving direct payments to MPs supporting the Switch, are challenging to prove. Honiara is awash with speculation about corruption, and it can be hard to distinguish between legitimate misdeeds and unsubstantiated innuendo. Low-level corruption such as that seen in the Seasonal Worker Program, however, is widely discussed by everyday Solomon Islanders. It is all the evidence they need to know that their system – a system that has received billions of dollars in donor capital, designed to improve the quality of governance in the country – remains fundamentally broken.

PART IV
REBELLION

10

'NO NEED CHINA!'

IT WAS EARLY ON A SATURDAY MORNING in November 2019, just a few weeks after the Switch, that I first made my way from Honiara to the Malaitan capital, Auki. I had roped in my brother Angus to keep me company, promising him an island adventure that would shake him up after his years of relative opulence in the heart of Europe.

Angus, a 34-year-old Australian diplomat, was fresh from an extended posting in Berlin. For four years he'd called that cosmopolitan city home. I'd visited once, at the end of my year on the road. Dishevelled and exhausted after travelling some 16,000 kilometres overland from southern Australia to the German capital, I found the comfort of Angus' lifestyle a shock. For an Australian diplomat, a posting to Berlin is surely one of the most desirable. The work is important and the job interesting, and the living quarters – each diplomat was granted an expansive apartment in Berlin's central *Mitte* district – were enviable. His posting having come to an end, and having relished our previous opportunities to travel together, Angus had decided to keep me company as I travelled the Solomons on assignment.

We met around midday at the Coral Sea Resort and Casino. Angus, who'd made no real preparations for the trip, put his faith in me to guide our brief adventure. Within an hour of his arrival, we were traipsing around the gritty Point Cruz terminal area, on the hunt for a ride to Malaita Province.

Like so many of the bureaucratic processes in the Solomons, catching transport around the country requires patience and creativity. Rarely are ticket offices clearly marked. Instead, you need to ask endless questions of locals – security guards sitting idly, port workers loading sacks of rice into banana boats – to find out which boat is the right one and when it will depart. Soon, Angus and I found ourselves boarding the *Fair Glory*, a rusting hulk of a thing crammed to the brim with humanity.

Over 500 Solomon Islanders, mostly Malaitans going home, had packed themselves onto this ageing Taiwanese ferry. As it began to lumber along, Angus and I searched for a seat. Eventually, we found a small vacant spot and parked ourselves on the hard, grated outer deck for the six-hour crossing. Next to us sat an extraordinarily overweight schoolteacher named Paul, who was returning home.

Paul had few possessions with him, save for a bag of lime strapped to his chest to aid his betel-nut chewing. Solomon Islanders use ground coral to grate against their gums, creating micro-abrasions that ensure the intoxicants of the betel nut enter the bloodstream more readily. The chewing of the betel nut – which appears to be almost universal among Solomon Islander men, especially outside Honiara – creates a dark red dye that stains the teeth and gums: 'Solomon's lipstick', as some villagers call it. As Paul detailed the various medical ailments that had prompted his visit to Honiara, he regularly reached into his little pouch, withdrew a chunk of betel nut and rubbed it vigorously into his raw gums, before chewing away. Soon, he entered a deep slumber. For the next six hours, my brother and I rocked across the Indispensable Strait, serenaded by a cacophony of lapping waves, the engines of diesel ferries and Paul's tremendous, baritone snoring.

When the Switch was announced, modest protests had emerged in Honiara, but they were immediately overshadowed by an intense display of anger in Malaita's provincial capital. Just three days after the announcement, a large crowd, consisting mostly of young men, descended on Auki's main road, situated between its bustling central market and its port. Auki is a small town of just 7000 people. Its dusty main road runs for a few hundred metres, hemmed in on one side by the ocean and on the other by a dozen or so small retail outlets selling the most basic items for survival: noodles, rice, cans of tuna and bottled water. At times, Auki can feel entirely asleep.

Arrive in the town on a Sunday afternoon and you will be hard-pressed to find anyone on the streets at all.

But on that September morning of 2019, Auki was alive. Up to 2000 men, some carrying signs that read 'No Need China' and chanting the same slogan, descended on the sleepy township to make an unequivocal statement: Malaita rejected Sogavare's Switch. The protests were not violent. No one was hurt, no property was damaged. It was a legitimate democratic expression that, unlike some protests in Honiara, never descended into rioting. But its coordination and scale were suggestive of the emergence of a powerful campaign of dissent against the new relationship with Beijing.

In the weeks after the Switch, after I'd been commissioned by *The Guardian* to investigate what the fallout had been on the ground, I had focused my attention on the rumblings that were emerging in Malaita. In the early local coverage of the unrest in Auki, one name kept coming up: Richard Olita. Described by various outlets as the secretary of a previously unknown organisation called Malaita for Democracy, or M4D, Olita had been flagged as one of those responsible for the burgeoning protest movement in the province. I was determined to find him.

Sign left over from initial protests after the Switch in Tulagi, November 2019.

*

Angus and I arrived in Auki late on a Friday night. After a restless sleep in a cheap, unairconditioned hotel, we spent the next morning walking the streets to get a sense of the mood. Some six weeks after the protests, evidence of them was still around. Many of the signs that the protestors had carried were still leaning against shopfronts or littered on the ground. Local Malaitans were willing to publicly voice their opposition to the Switch. I spoke to a number of people in the market and on the streets, usually men, who remained more favourable towards the Taiwanese, with whom they'd become familiar through the programs Taipei had supported just outside of town.

'The young people, they don't want China, they want Taiwan,' John Oka, a fifty-something shopper told me. It was a sentiment echoed by a young man named David, who ran a betel-nut stand near the market with a 'No Need China' sign leaning against it. He was angry that the prime minister hadn't consulted the Malaitans, or anyone else in provincial areas, before the Switch.

The voices of those on the ground were important, but I remained focused on finding Olita. After asking a handful of local residents if they knew him, Angus and I were soon directed to a small second-floor office that overlooked Auki's main strip. Inside, in a room stuffed full of handmade signs and banners, was the man I had been looking for.

Richard Olita, thirty-five years old and bearded, with a rotund belly and a laugh to match, welcomed me warmly into his small office. He'd rented this room to help run the new organisation and to give himself, as M4D's secretary, an air of legitimacy. He pulled two plastic chairs from under a desk and placed them on the deck, which overlooked Auki Harbour.

M4D had emerged, seemingly from nowhere, after the Switch. The protests had turned a once unknown entity into a powerful force and a household name. Photographs of the protests showed people carrying M4D signs, and the organisation appeared to be leading the most vocal resistance to the Switch. But in the early weeks after the Switch, M4D was still a mysterious entity. Who controlled it and what was motivating them? What were the group's aims? And how did it become so influential so quickly?

The origins of M4D are unclear. Some have suggested it emerged immediately after the Switch, others that it had appeared just before. In any case, while it seemed at first to be a relatively directionless protest group, with a vague aim of advancing 'democracy' and improving living standards, it found in the Switch a unique opportunity. The organisation had been founded by Knoxley Atu, a former militant and participant in the Tensions. But Atu, in M4D's earliest days, was keeping a low profile. It was Richard Olita who was emerging as the public face of the organisation.

Olita had not previously had a public profile, but his nationalistic impulses can be traced to his involvement in the Tensions. In 2000, aged sixteen, he left home for Honiara to assist his fellow Malaitans in their struggle. By that point in the Tensions, central Honiara had become something of a Malaitan exclave, with Malaita Eagle Force militia and the Malaitan-dominated police force maintaining control of the city. Olita, although young, wanted to help in any way he could. 'I was cooking rice for the militants in the bunkers ... During the fighting was not a good time,' he recalled. 'And that is when I first saw Sogavare ... he even came to the bunkers.'

Sogavare was still opposition leader, and shortly after would ascend to power after the Malaita Eagle Force coup topped Bartholomew Ulufa'alu.

For Olita and his former comrades in the MEF, the disdain for Sogavare was deeply personal. They felt aggrieved and wanted to undermine his leadership. This was also true of Knoxley Atu, the mysterious and, until 2021, largely behind-the-scenes leader of M4D. Atu had been an active member of the MEF and was possessed by a deep mistrust, even a hatred, of Sogavare, born out of the 2000 coup and a belief that Sogavare had subsequently refused to facilitate better outcomes for Malaita Province.

Olita had spent the April 2019 election campaign working for Matthew Wale, the national opposition leader. But this experience, Olita argued, gave him a detailed insight into how elections really work in Solomon Islands. He described the mechanics of how money is used to secure votes. Many MPs use their election funds to pay key figures in communities for information about the appetites of local voters. They also cover travel costs, which are expensive in rural communities, to get voters to the polls, and truck their proxies around to spread their message. Then there is the more blatant vote-buying: direct promises to chiefs or other key figures to deliver projects, or even just cash handouts in exchange for their support. It is a game that overwhelmingly favours incumbents. Over time, fewer outsiders have been elected to Solomon Islands' parliament at each national election, because they rarely have the resources to compete against sitting MPs.

Olita's anger was real. But it was clear that M4D was not an organic, emotive response to corruption and disenfranchisement. It had more weight than that, and appeared to be more considered in achieving its goals. In the Switch, M4D found an issue around which it could coalesce a supporter base, with a view to building a powerful case for the group's ultimate goal – a Malaitan state.

'Our main goal is independence. We want to run things for ourselves. [M4D] is now going very strong thanks to the China issue ... when the China issue came through, we [saw] it as an opportunity,' Olita explained.

'Manasseh Sogavare didn't campaign on a platform. The political party was formed after the election. What he did, when he wanted to become prime minister, he told everyone else to resign from their parties to join the OUR Party ... Maybe we can call it "OUR Communist Party" now,' Olita said, erupting into laughter.

'We have seen what Sogavare has done in the past. Every time he comes into the prime minister's post, there will be friction and fighting. Every time he comes into power there is a riot.'

As part of Olita's strategy in the early days after the Switch, M4D had been pushing Premier Suidani to continue engaging with Taiwan. 'Maybe it is a sister relationship at the start, but as time goes on, we're going to work on strengthening ties.' Olita said that Premier Suidani and his advisor Celsus Talifilu were planning a visit to Taiwan. Olita and his new protest organisation appeared to have a seat at the decision-making table in Auki, and they had demonstrated a capacity to mobilise thousands at short notice if required. But there was no guarantee this support could be sustained. Olita and Atu knew that, to advance their dream, they needed an issue on which they could pin the failures of the fourth Sogavare administration; an issue with which they could mobilise their supporters into action and build the case for a new Malaita.

Richard Olita in Auki, November 2019.

They would find it in the suspicions, fears and frustrations many everyday Solomon Islanders held about China, and the thousands of Chinese people living and working in their country.

When you arrive in Honiara, your first port of call might be one of the hundreds of small retailers on Mendaña Avenue, the main road the runs through the heart of town. One of the first things you will notice is that, almost without exception, these small stores – usually selling everything from canned goods to plastic toys to pharmaceuticals – are staffed and run predominately by ethnic-Chinese. Although many of these stores employ indigenous Solomon Islanders, the shops have become illustrative of the dominance that ethnic-Chinese Solomon Islanders maintain over daily economic life in the country.

Chinese immigration to Solomon Islands began as early as the late nineteenth century, albeit in very small numbers. Initially, the few dozen Chinese who came to the British Protectorate of Solomon Islands had come as labourers, following the precedent set in other British colonies and protectorates around the Pacific. Until the 1930s, most of the Chinese living and working in the protectorate would end up returning home or using the Solomons as a 'back door' to Australia. But by the 1930s, the number of Chinese had increased to around 200; in Tulagi, the capital of the British protectorate, a small Chinatown that even featured Chinese restaurants had sprung up. Although the Chinese population in the protectorate remained small over the coming decades, the Chinese who were there began to work harder to establish themselves, seeking British passports and, in some cases, even joining the Coastwatchers, the famed Solomon Islander scouts who worked closely with the Allies during World War Two.

As the country began its path towards independence in the 1960s and 1970s, the Chinese community made further efforts to assimilate: many converted to Christianity; others built schools. Even more began to invest. A Chinatown of 'wooden red, green and blue trade stores with tin roofs and crossed-frame railing verandas'[1] sprang up in Honiara, and similar communities developed in Gizo, in Western Province, and in Auki. These traders often started simply, selling basic supplies and servicing their own communities with the tastes of their homeland. Their children, however, went further. Some leveraged their parents' relative wealth into new ventures in logging, hardware, importing and other trades. When independence came, many Chinese left Solomon Islands, fearing that their place in the newly independent country would not be as secure as it had been under British rule. For those who remained, however, the exodus of almost half their community created new opportunities to consolidate control over even more businesses. Many then used this wealth to become the country's first hoteliers, publicans and restaurateurs.

There have been subsequent waves of Chinese immigration. New immigrants in the 1980s, 1990s and 2000s – 'refugees of the ideology' that now governed mainland China – came to the islands with the explicit intention of establishing businesses. Many of these newer migrants – ethnic-Chinese from mainland China, Malaysia and more rarely Taiwan – made less effort to assimilate into Solomon Islands culture or to learn the language and serve as model employers, and it is towards these more recent arrivals that much of the animosity by indigenous Solomon Islanders is directed. Many are given the title *waku,* a derivative of a Cantonese word that loosely translates to 'outsiders', which is commonly used as a derogatory racial slur towards all foreigners, not just ethnic-Chinese.

Although there is some resentment that the Chinese community controls most of the retail sector in urban Solomon Islands, these Chinese-owned businesses provide an important service. They are usually much cheaper than locally run stores, as some Chinese business owners collaboratively procure stock from abroad, leveraging their networks to run effective cartels and undercutting prospective competitors on basic products such as rice. For aspiring Solomon Islander retailers, this might be frustrating, but for most locals, these Chinese-run businesses provide employment and cheap goods and have become part of the fabric of the country.

Where frustration has been more evident is in the perceived corruption and damage caused by Asian companies involved in extractive industries. Through the 1980s and 1990s, companies from Malaysia, South Korea and Japan came to dominate the local logging industry, which, in such a young country, operated under little oversight. Logging became a lucrative business: hundreds of millions of Solomon dollars' worth of timber was exported every year by the mid-1990s, and corruption became endemic. Logging companies became adept at buying off politicians and coercing local communities, who owned the land, into allowing projects that were ultimately exploitative. It didn't take long before Solomon Islanders noticed that, while several politicians and logging interests were becoming extremely wealthy, the communities promised the world had seen little material benefit.

Resentment about the role that Chinese and other Asian interests were playing in the country burst to the surface in 2006, in the aftermath of a national election in which Snyder Rini secured the prime ministership. The announcement of his victory was met with protests on the steps of Parliament House in Honiara. The crowd was angered because Rini had been deputy prime minister in the previous government, under which allegations of Chinese and Taiwanese interference had fuelled popular discontent. After a standoff between the protestors and police, the firing of tear gas triggered the assembled mob to violence. Quickly, the crowd descended on Chinatown, where they looted and destroyed many buildings owned by newer Chinese immigrants. The protestors demanded Rini's resignation, which he offered; meanwhile, Sogavare was jostling for the numbers to take over. What is clear from the 2006 riots is that they were likely designed, and perhaps even led, by a particular large group of individuals. The rioting wasn't indiscriminate: it targeted 'new Chinese' businesses and even the house of a former advisor to the previous government, leaving many of the 'Old Chinese' businesses untouched. As Clive Moore notes:

> There is not much doubt that there was an attempt at organisation of the riots. There seems to have been a core of about 30–40 agitators who led the crowd, and identifiable individuals were also responsible for setting most buildings alight. There was prior knowledge of the riot among some Solomon Islanders.[2]

The 2006 riots were the worst violence Solomon Islands had seen since the RAMSI peacekeeping mission was established. It certainly illustrated an undercurrent of resentment among disenfranchised Solomon Islanders towards Chinese and other Asian businesses. But more than that, it demonstrated the capacity for this resentment to be exploited by skilled political actors – individuals who would benefit from the chaos of protest and riot, and groups who saw political advantage in reminding Solomon Islanders about the injustice of China's economic dominance.

*

The M4D leadership's primary goal may have been to achieve independence. But this alone didn't make it stand out. Many Malaitan populists have advanced this idea, as have agitators in other provinces across Solomon Islands since independence. What differentiated M4D was that, in addition to its broad aspirations for an independent Malaita, the organisation had much more immediate and specific aims, and was willing to stoke the anti-China sentiments of its community to advance its ultimate objectives.

In the weeks after the Switch, M4D began piecing together a manifesto that it hoped would shape the Malaitan policy agenda. Although in retrospect the Malaitan provincial government's opposition to the Switch may have looked ironclad from the outset, in fact, the Suidani government's response to the Switch was muted in the weeks after it was announced. Suidani was, after all, a new premier and a political novice. Although he was a genuine critic of the Switch, he had few ideas, let alone implementable policies, to push back against it at first. Celsus Talifilu didn't join Suidani's office as an advisor until a month after the Switch. M4D saw a vacuum and worked to fill it. Their protest in Auki had demonstrated they had power, and they wanted to leverage that power into a policy commitment that Suidani's young administration would be bound by.

In the two weeks after the Switch, M4D crafted a list of demands, which focused primarily on barring Chinese investment in Malaita and maintaining some sort of relationship with the Taiwanese. Boldly, the organisation gave the provincial government a deadline to respond to its demands for action. I asked Olita about M4D's tactics. 'We were looking at the Chinese businesses. We don't want Chinese businesses here. We want them closed down and locals [to] run the shops.'

'How could you make that happen?' I asked.

'Simple. Every year, you need to renew your [business] licence. The provincial government can say, "Sorry, we cannot renew your licence." [Then], we will find local businessmen, Malaitan businessmen, and ask how much money they have, and then get them to take over the stores. [The Chinese] can go back to Honiara, maybe other provinces. Maybe if the Taiwanese ran the shops, we would let them stay.'

In October 2019, Suidani responded to M4D's campaign. He called a meeting of the provincial assembly members, tribal leaders from across the province, and urged them to coalesce around a unified policy agenda that, he hoped, would temper M4D and help the province to move into this new period of Solomons history with a single voice. The meetings took place between 15 and 17 October. Present were M4D members, including Olita, who pressed home their objectives.

On 17 October, Suidani's office issued a document, the *Malaita Provincial Government Auki Communique*. Four pages long, in thirty-three points it outlined Malaita's development priorities in the wake of the Switch. Points two and three noted M4D's involvement in the shaping of the document:

> The MPG [Malaitan Provincial Government] is aware of the deadline for the Malaita for Democracy (M4D) submission is due today ... The MPG after gathering information from these engagements expressed itself in the following terms outlined in this Communique as the way forward to addressing the issues raised by M4D in its submission and the long outstanding developmental issues faced by Malaita Province.

The document went on to detail an expansive list of grievances and aspirations. It 'observed the need for Malaita to be free from unwarranted interference', and that the island had been subject to 'systemic neglect ... since the colonial period through to the independence era today'. It blamed a 'lack of political will and oversight at the national level' for a 'lack of a cohesive and coordinated structure to forge forward movement in the development of Malaita and the Malaita Outer Islands', and subtly blamed this inaction for 'the abuse of Malaitan and Malaita Outer Island labour and resources for other agendas'.

The communique also detailed the MPG's objections to various types of development, including logging above 400 metres sea level, and condemned 'any development that disempowers, impoverishes or violates' the Malaitan people.

Two clauses in the communique particularly stood out and would receive considerable attention across Solomon Islands and internationally. They were clause seven:

> MPG acknowledges the freedom of religion as a fundamental right and further observes the entrenched Christian faith and belief in God by Malaitan peoples, and therefore rejects the Chinese Communist Party – CCP and its formal systems based on atheist ideology.

And clause twenty-five:

MPG strongly resolves to put in place a Moratorium on Business
Licenses to new investors connected directly or indirectly with the
Chinese Communist Party.

The Auki Communique had, in effect, banned Chinese-run businesses
from operating in the province. It was precisely what M4D had been calling
for, and it now formed the centrepiece of the Malaitan government's plan
for the months and years that were to come.

The communique immediately caused concern for the dozens of Chinese business owners in Auki. Some closed their doors and others moved
to Honiara, as Olita had hoped they would. But the rest of the plan he had
described, to effectively nationalise these small retailers and hand them
over to indigenous Malaitan operators, did not occur, and would have vio-
lated Solomon Islands' law.

When I spoke to Premier Suidani two weeks after the signing of the
Auki Communique, we discussed the complexities of implementing the
new policy. I was curious how, given its modest resources, the Malaitan
provincial government would be able to determine whether a business
entering the province was linked to the CCP. He demurred, stating only
that 'Chinese people can use local people to penetrate our systems'. He confirmed, on the record, that he agreed that existing Chinese shop owners
should leave Malaita, and that his business licensing authority gave his government the power to make them do so.

Many elements of the Auki Communique were understandable. Malaita's history has been shaped by foreign interference in the form of coerced
labour, colonial tax-usurpation and the exploitation of natural assets.
I could sympathise with the desire to affirm, resolutely, that the province would no longer be exploited in this fashion. But the communique
went further, effectively restricting business activity on the basis of race,
unsubtly playing off the deeply held suspicions and prejudices that many
Solomon Islanders hold towards Waku. It created an enemy not just of the

Chinese Communist Party, but of Chinese people.

Suidani's unequivocal endorsement of this policy bound him and his government to a challenging, consequential mission: to stop all Chinese investment in the sprawling island. Within months, Suidani began standing in the way of projects that had even the slightest association with Chinese businesses. In 2020, the World Bank put out to tender the reconstruction of the Fiu Bridge, a crossing on the Fiu River on the road from Auki to its airport. The bid was won by an ethnic-Chinese-run construction firm. Suidani, seeing his first opportunity to demonstrate his commitment to the communique, refused to allow the project to proceed. The interference won him political credit in the short term, but it meant the bridge would not be built, leaving Malaitans to rely on a rickety, dangerous bridge. It was the price to be paid for the stance Suidani had committed to.

The Auki Communique also noted one undeniable but underexamined reality of politics in Malaita. Clauses ten through twelve, under the heading 'DEEP DISUNITIES', noted the historical divisions within Malaita Province. 'MPG acknowledges the disunities that exist amongst Malaitans and Malaita Outer Islanders in terms of individual, tribal and regional ideologies and priorities,' the document said. 'MPG noted that these disunities are often taken advantage of to paralyse inclusive and effective collective actions towards moving forward, resulting in stagnation or regression.'

The political calculus that Suidani and M4D had made was that taking a bold stance against China, and therefore a bold stance against the Sogavare government's Switch, would help to overcome these 'deep disunities'. It would take some three years before they would know if their gambit had worked.

After Olita and I spoke at his office, he asked if I wanted to see Ozi Beach, Malaita's nicest white-sand swimming area, a few kilometres from town. I agreed, and we walked through the town's outer communities, on dirt paths and past Ozi Lake, to a small beach hut selling iceblocks and Sol-Brew beers. As we drank and watched the sunset, Olita appeared satisfied with what he had achieved in a matter of months. He said he had received an offer to move on from M4D and work directly for the premier in his office. It was a job he intended to take.

'What do you think will happen from here?' I asked. 'How do you think the Sogavare government will react to the communique?'

Olita, chewing his betel nut and sipping quietly on his SolBrew, couldn't be sure. He only knew one thing, he said:

'Interesting days are coming.'

11

WUHAN WINDOW

SINCE JANUARY 2020, I'D REMAINED largely confined to my hometown. As Covid-19 closed international borders, my world, like everyone else's, became much smaller. In the early months of the pandemic, the unknown nature of Covid-19 justifiably caused anxiety among policymakers and health professionals. It was not yet clear just how deadly the disease was, or how rapidly it would evolve and mutate, or whether a vaccine would be possible. The economic effects in Australia were unprecedented but were quickly handled by authorities, and for me, the pandemic soon transformed from an imminent threat to a surreal period during which my life slowed down, shrank, but remained comfortable and sheltered from the worst of the pandemic. I had a full-time job. I could work remotely, from the comfort of home. Although I could see and sense the extraordinary moment the world was facing, I remained mostly detached from it. The closest I got to the economic consequences were the scenes I saw from my home window. Working from Adelaide's west end, I witnessed lines of international students, who weren't provided any financial support by the Australian government, snaking past my building, queuing to receive charitable support from a nearby food bank.

The pandemic did test Australia. Its governments began plans for temporary morgues in city parks and restricted daily activities, at times even limiting outdoor exercise. Years since the disease emerged, it is still testing Australia. But Australia's world-class health system offered a degree of hope that, were the outbreak to rapidly spread, most of us would be okay.

Solomon Islanders, however, were confronted with an altogether more existential challenge.

During a 2019 visit to Solomons, working on the initiative to alleviate energy poverty, I had travelled briefly with a solar technician. After several challenging days working in Savo and the neighbouring Nggela Islands, he had a mild asthma attack – not severe enough to panic, but requiring medical attention and medication he wasn't in possession of. We decided to travel by banana boat to the nearest hospital, in Tulagi, some forty-five minutes away by sea.

We'd been to Tulagi previously on the same trip. Now, we discovered that the fibro walls and rusting roofs we'd encountered in government buildings and private homes were also present in the small hospital in the centre of town. Entering the hospital, we were confronted with a difficult scene. Many windows were shattered. Patients were wailing in pain out in the open, as a skeleton crew of nurses with bare feet tried to respond to childbirth, injuries and severe illnesses with equipment that looked like it would be at home in a nineteenth-century field hospital. The storehouse, fortunately, was well supplied: my colleague was able to buy the medicine he needed to control his asthma symptoms. But our visit to the hospital provided a window into the state of healthcare in Solomon Islands.

Tulagi is not a distant outpost. It was the British capital until the 1970s and is one of the largest townships in the country outside of Honiara. The acute lack of healthcare begs questions about the economic legacy of Solomon Islands' lengthy colonial history and the efficacy of the billions of investment dollars extended by donor partners over recent decades. The same can be said of Honiara's National Referral Hospital (NRH), the country's largest health facility. The hospital routinely runs out of basic supplies, sometimes including life-saving medications such as antibiotics. A young Australian doctor I once spoke to over a cold coconut at Palm Sugar Café in Honiara, who had been volunteering at the hospital, spoke about how traumatic it had been when she first arrived, seeing patients in their mid-twenties losing their lives to basic infections and preventable illnesses. In 2022, when a 7.3 magnitude earthquake struck Honiara and a tsunami warning was issued, the administrators of the beachfront NRH had no plan for evacuating patients, reflecting an organisational deficit that compounds problems caused by lack of staff and equipment. When donations reach the hospital, they sometimes do so with little advanced planning. In 2022, the Chinese government gifted the NRH a dialysis machine – the first in the country. The donation was warmly received and enthusiastically covered in the local press. But it came with no staff, training or ongoing capacity to manage the machine. On Malaita, the healthcare situation is even more dire. The one major clinic, the Kilu'ufi Hospital, just outside Auki, is a small, rust-covered facility with only two dozen beds, serving a population of over 200,000 people.

It was in this context that, at the outset of 2020, policymakers in Solomon Islands were faced with a dire choice. Covid-19 emerged in China in late November 2019, just two months after the Switch had kick-started a deepening of relations between China and Solomon Islands. As the virus spread, the threat to vulnerable countries in the Pacific became very real. In the earliest stages of the pandemic, it was the global elite who seemed to be most rapidly spreading the illness. Australians returning from skiing holidays in Aspen and politicians undertaking junkets in Geneva were among the earliest vectors for what would rapidly become a global pandemic. For the first three months of 2020, Solomon Islands did not record a case. It was a similar story across much of the Pacific. But what was clear was that, if Covid-19 did come to their shores, the ailing health system, coupled with the public's over-reliance on traditional medicine and scepticism of vaccines, would leave the country particularly vulnerable.

For Daniel Suidani and his advisor Talifilu, the fear of Covid-19 spreading across their ill-equipped province was real. They also worried that, given the growing hostility between Auki and Honiara, the flow of assistance from Honiara might slow. 'We knew at the time the government was not happy with Malaita,' says Talifilu, 'so we needed to be supported.'

At the start of the pandemic, governments across the world scrambled to secure enough personal protective equipment, basic medications such as paracetamol and antibiotics, and more advanced technology, especially ventilators. As governments competed for life-saving materials, low-income, sub-national jurisdictions such as Malaita were left fighting for the scraps. They didn't have enough surgical masks, nurses or doctors, let alone beds or ventilators to service their often immunocompromised population. These concerns forced the Malaitan government to get creative.

By now, Taiwan's former representatives to Solomon Islands were getting settled into new roles back in Taiwan or in other posts, as the reality of the Switch sank in. Oliver Liao, the last Taiwanese ambassador to Solomon Islands, had returned to Taipei, chastened and distressed by the events that had led to the Switch. Those who saw Liao earlier in 2019 believe he was confident the Switch would not occur. He had relayed this confidence back to Taiwan, which made the eventual Switch deeply embarrassing for him.

Liao's second-in-charge, Oliver Weng, was appointed to a new role in Brisbane at Taiwan's Economic Exchange Office – a de-facto consulate. Weng remained in close contact with his loyal associates in Solomon Islands, working assiduously to maintain ties with them. One of those associates was his close friend Leliana Firisua, Solomon Islands' former ambassador to Israel. '[Felisua] has a long, long relationship with Taiwan ... he was the only one in Solomon Islands that the Taiwanese trusted,' says Talifilu.

In the months since the Switch, Felisua had continued to talk to Weng, discussing potential ways for the Taiwanese government to keep a line of communication and engagement open with Solomon Islanders. In those early weeks, a broad coalition had emerged that was frustrated by the Switch and its impacts, many of which the government was unprepared for. The Malaitan government had, in late February 2020, considered asking Taiwan for Covid-19 assistance, but knew that it would be challenging to navigate the delivery of any goods. Another senior figure, Sogavare's recently ousted deputy prime minister, John Maneniaru, was also angered by the Switch and eager to maintain a relationship with Taipei. In October 2019, just after the Switch, Maneniaru had been replaced as deputy prime minister by Manasseh Maelanga after expressing concerns about the government's new foreign policy direction. But Maneniaru also had a personal interest in the issue: one of his children was studying in Taiwan on a scholarship.

Felisua had been in conversations with Maneniaru after the Switch and pledged to assist his child.

Now, Felisua organised a meeting in Brisbane with Oliver Weng, Maneniaru and Suidani. The meeting was scheduled for early March 2020, just weeks before Solomon Islands' borders closed. Joining Felisua, Suidani and Maneniaru were Celsus Talifilu and Peter Kenilorea Jnr, the eloquent internationalist who had returned to Solomon Islands in 2016 with a clear ambition to follow in his father's footsteps and serve as prime minister. He was worried about the relationship with China and the corrupt way in which he believed it had emerged. He preferred the status quo and would not rule out, if he were ever to form government, switching back to Taiwan.

The five men travelled to Brisbane, where they met with Weng to discuss their interests and their requests of Taiwan. Oliver Weng denies having met these individuals in Brisbane, although two of the participants independently confirmed, without prompting, that they met with Weng. Maneniaru made his case for more support for the remaining students in Taiwan. He wasn't to be successful: most of the students' situations did not improve. Some ended up relocating to China; others ended their studies prematurely. Some, like Patricia Luilamo's daughter Georgia, managed to self-finance the remainder of their studies, often thanks to the heroic fundraising efforts of their parents.

Suidani and Talifilu, however, appeared to be more successful in their efforts to solicit pandemic assistance from the Taiwanese. 'If we want support, we have to talk with Taiwan,' Talifilu recalls thinking before the trip. 'But how would this be done? It would be difficult to get anything into Solomons from Taiwan, everything was closed, so the best way to do it is to go and talk and to say, "How are we going to make this thing happen?"'

At the meeting, Weng assured the Malaitans that assistance would be forthcoming. At the time, the meeting went unreported: no Australian or Solomon Islands press got wind of the engagement. Australian officials didn't seem to be aware of the diplomatic episode between Taiwan – a self-ruled island Canberra does not diplomatically recognise – and Malaita – a small island led by anti-China activists with dreams of independence – occurring on Australian soil. The Australian prime minister at the time, Scott Morrison, ruled out discussing the meeting when I spoke with him in early 2023. After the meeting, the Solomon Islanders quietly returned home. Just two weeks later, their country would enforce one of the strictest border closures of the pandemic.

In April, the Solomon Islander community, seeing horrific images from Europe of morgues filling up and entire cities being locked down, increasingly feared what might be coming. In Taiwan, Ministry of Foreign Affairs officials, after their consultation with Weng, readied two shipments bound for Malaita Province. The first would contain 1000 kilograms of rice; the second, personal protective equipment such as surgical masks and testing kits. Taipei had approved the aid, but delivering it to Solomon Islands would prove a logistical challenge. Because relations between Taiwan and Solomon Islands had now ended, the Taiwanese ministry was unable to deliver the aid directly. Instead, it had to arrange delivery through the postal system. It meant that, in addition to securing the equipment, the Taiwanese needed an address to send the shipment to and a freight company that would deliver the consignment despite the border restrictions. The aid was separated into several loads. One was sent to a personal address – that of M4D's Richard Olita, who by now was working in Premier Suidani's office as an advisor. No one, it would appear, had considered the bizarre optics of an individual Malaitan, who had previously been in the spotlight for his involvement in the anti-China movement, receiving a shipping-container's worth of medical equipment from the Taiwanese government. He would eventually receive a knock on the door from the Royal Solomon Islands Police, who had been informed that the shipments were in contravention of the Sogavare government's new China policy.

Another batch of the aid was accidentally addressed to the Sogavare government's Foreign Ministry headquarters. The unknown Taiwanese official who addressed the package clearly hadn't been informed of the sensitive political nature of the operation.

Despite these mishaps, two shipments did manage to get through to Auki, and the delivery was revealed through a series of carefully orchestrated public events. The premier and his team assembled the bags of rice and medical equipment in large piles, which they draped with the Malaitan and Taiwanese flags. A4 posters reading 'We Love Taiwan' were plastered on the walls behind the premier, who knelt in front of the consignments with a large grin upon his face, posing for the local media.

Daniel Suidani

The aid that reached Auki was modest. It did little to alleviate the structural issues facing Malaita's healthcare system, or to address food security for the island. But it served an important strategic purpose for the premier and his team. The response from the Sogavare government was apoplectic: it admonished Suidani and his team, accusing them of bowing to the demands of M4D 'henchmen'. The delivery embarrassed the national government, who were still in a honeymoon phase with the new Chinese personnel in Honiara, who had yet to establish their embassy.

The Chinese were also angry. In a poorly considered statement, China's incoming ambassador to Solomon Islands expressed displeasure at the Taiwan–Malaita partnership, explaining that it 'hurt the feelings of the Chinese people'. To the Malaitans, the Chinese statement looked weak; it only worked to further undermine Beijing's standing in the province and beyond.

For Suidani, the mobilisation of Taiwanese aid had been a triumph. It had four clear benefits for Malaitans opposed to the Switch. First, it agitated the Sogavare government and the Chinese embassy officials. Sogavare's visceral reaction buoyed the Malaitans and gave credibility to Suidani's argument that Honiara was not listening to the people of Malaita. The rebuke from the Chinese embassy, meanwhile, made Suidani look powerful – that he had solicited such a reaction from Beijing demonstrated his influence on the national, and even international, stage.

Second, the active courtship of the Taiwanese by Suidani signalled to both Taipei and the West that the Malaitans had chosen a side. While the policy implications were minimal – no Western donor or partner would upend its existing aid or development strategy to reward Malaita's allegiance – Malaita's overt partnership with Taiwan was visible to, and widely discussed by, a global network of China hawks, who saw in Suidani's determination to push back against China an attractive moral story.

Third, the aid was genuinely needed. Malaita's health system was, and remains, ailing. The procurement of basic protective equipment, such as surgical masks, would have stretched the provincial government's budgetary capacities. And the additional food aid allowed the MPG to distribute large quantities of rice to those who had been most adversely affected economically by the early restrictions imposed by the pandemic.

Fourth, for Suidani, the fierce resistance to China was a political masterstroke within Malaita. His public ceremonies unveiling the Covid-19 aid were calculated; he had leaned into the momentum created by M4D and, understanding the will of his people, identified a strategic way to appease their political and practical desires.

Malaita's interests in the Covid-19 aid saga, then, were clear. But why did Taiwan play along? The sudden repudiation of Taiwan by the Sogavare government wasn't only politically scarring for the Taiwanese; for many, it was also personally devastating. Oliver Weng and his colleagues were forced to pack up shop almost overnight, their visas instantly terminated and their personal and professional lives in tatters. Many of the personal relationships the Taiwanese had cultivated during thirty-six years of grassroots diplomacy evaporated in an instant or were at least rendered meaningless. One could understand if, given the ugliness of the Switch, the Taiwanese had simply moved on. But in Malaita, the Taiwanese saw something different. And the island, known for its resistance to central rule and now for its fierce repudiation of China, would soon emerge as a central character in a new experiment in Taiwanese foreign policy.

*

As Solomon Islands' borders remained shut, in April 2022 I decided to take advantage of Australia's opening up and headed abroad to find out exactly what this new Taiwanese strategy looked like on the ground. In April 2020, six months after the Switch, I had read of a new relationship Taiwan had struck that was being framed as a 'victory' for Taipei's quest for legitimacy. In the unrecognised 'breakaway' nation of Somaliland, in the distant Horn of Africa, Taiwan had announced the establishment of a new embassy. It was the first diplomatic breakthrough Taiwan had had in Africa for a generation. Just like in the Pacific, African countries had, one by one, been switching to China. When Burkina Faso switched its recognition from Taipei to Beijing in 2018, Eswatini, whose king's personal affinity for Taiwan had been reflected by his seventeen visits to the island, was left as the only African country with ties to Taiwan. As in other parts of the world, some Taiwanese representation remained on the African continent. Cultural and economic offices emerged in the handful of countries that would still allow this unofficial Taiwanese presence. One of those offices was in the city of Hargeisa, the capital of Somaliland.

In 1991, Somaliland had split from Somalia. The separation came after years of civil war and genocide, which had killed over 100,000 people in Somaliland. Ever since, Somaliland has maintained de-facto independence, successfully resisting attempts to rule by authorities in Mogadishu, the Somalian capital known for being among the most dangerous cities on earth. In contrast to Somalia, Somaliland is generally safe. It has forged a détente with the Al-Shabaab militants that in much of Somalia serve as a proxy government, and has no internal opposition threatening peace and stability. Today, foreigners and Somalilanders alike can travel relatively unencumbered in the country, without immediate threats to their personal security. This stability has allowed the local economy to grow. When I arrived in Hargeisa, it was undergoing an economic boom thanks to large numbers of returning expatriates. It was even experiencing a housing crunch, as prices soared with the growing demand. Simply, Somaliland presented itself as a success story to the world. For thirty years, governments in Hargeisa had been trying to leverage this story to achieve diplomatic recognition. But even with its strong case, Somaliland remains stranded in diplomatic limbo. No country recognises it, despite it showing all the hallmarks of a legitimate sovereign state. Somalia rejects Somaliland's independence claims and has received support from China to do so. But here, in this fledgling, unrecognised nation, Taiwan saw an opportunity.

To make ends meet during my trip, I'd pitched a story to the ABC about the unusual diplomatic tactics Taiwan's newly established embassy had undertaken since 2020. Although the deserts of the Horn of Africa seemed a universe away from the tropical island of Malaita, a complex relationship with Taiwan bound them. As in Malaita, Taiwan saw the unrecognised country of Somaliland as an avenue for diplomatic relevance in a region where its legitimacy had long waned. It was in Somaliland that Taiwanese foreign minister Joseph Wu, whose resignation had been rejected by his president after Honiara switched to China, saw the best chance to revive Taiwan's international standing.

To execute Taiwan's new diplomatic gambit in Africa, Wu placed his faith in an impeccably dressed, well-coiffed Taiwanese diplomat, Allen C. Lou. Earlier in his career, Lou had been responsible for securing diplomatic ties with the small Caribbean nation of St Kitts and Nevis. He had opened an embassy before. He was single and wedded to his work, and Wu hand-picked him to head to Africa and broker a new partnership with the Republic of Somaliland. If successful, such a partnership would not only deliver Taipei a new ally, but could also serve as a platform for Taiwan to reassert its influence in Africa.

Somaliland represented a major pivot in Taiwan's diplomacy: running short of allies, it was now willing to consider working with unrecognised republics. When I spoke with Lou, he was clear about what his country was trying to do. We met in a small conference room at Taiwan's embassy in Hargeisa – the title 'embassy', rather than 'representative office', a sign of the diplomatic recognition between the two de-facto states. Lou made the case that Taiwan was the 'gateway' to Somaliland's wider recognition. He said the entire Somaliland strategy was 'the baby' of Joseph Wu. The orders had come from the top – a message that was likely to have ricocheted throughout the Taiwanese Foreign Ministry, incentivising aspiring diplomats to hunt for their own unusual opportunities.

As the relationship between Somaliland and Taiwan deepens, Taipei is providing diplomatic credibility and tangible economic support to Somaliland. Perhaps more importantly, it is also facilitating relationships with key diplomatic personnel across the world, especially in the United States. Just before I arrived in Hargeisa – which bore many aesthetic similarities to Honiara – the Somaliland president had concluded a week-long tour of the US, meeting State Department officials and members of Congress, pitching Somaliland's independence. The tour was aided by Taiwan, which leveraged its connections with China hawks in the US Congress to facilitate the visit. Taiwan's desire was clear: it wanted the US to formally recognise Somaliland, and in doing so, expected Somaliland to extend formal recognition to Taipei.

Taiwan's audacious diplomatic efforts in Somaliland were born of necessity: with a dwindling number of allies around the world, it was left with no choice but to try to create new ones.

*

Several months after the drama surrounding the Taiwanese aid consignments had simmered down, Premier Suidani began to experience acute headaches. He was beginning to feel the pressure. He had, by now, become a central player in his country's national politics, his every move and manoeuvre covered extensively by local and international press. But it became clear that the headaches were more severe than those caused by stress or anxiety.

Given the inadequacy of local medical services in Auki, Suidani's advisor, Celsus Talifilu, suggested that the premier travel to Honiara for a diagnosis. In March 2021, Suidani crossed the Indispensable Strait to the capital, where he would undergo examination at the National Referral Hospital.

The NRH, however, was unable to accurately diagnose the premier's condition, and instead recommended he travel to Australia to receive a formal diagnosis for what was now feared to be brain cancer. If confirmed, the NRH further recommended he undertake his treatment in Australia – a treatment plan that would likely see Suidani sidelined from politics for a considerable period. Initially, Suidani and his team, led by Talifilu, tried to keep the health scare private, and, upon the advice of the NRH, started the complex work of securing financial and visa support for the trip to Australia. But almost immediately, they began to hit roadblocks.

Initially, Suidani had requested financial assistance from the Sogavare government. Talifilu, however, alleged that the Sogavare administration immediately used the premier's plight as leverage. In exchange for the government's help, Talifilu alleged, Suidani would have to back down on his vocal stance against China. In August 2021, Talifilu told me that to do so would 'be like shaking hands with China', and that the premier had refused the offer.[1]

They then turned to the Australian government, hoping for more support. By now, the geopolitical significance of Solomon Islands' China relationship, and Malaita's ongoing dalliance with Taiwan, was well understood within the Australian government. There was a reluctance, however, to be seen to interfere in the personal health matters of a politician now at the centre of growing domestic political tensions in Solomon Islands. Australia had a formal policy not to extend unconditional medical support to political leaders in the Pacific and neighbouring countries, a formal policy that irked some in the Australian cabinet.[2] The logic was simple: by providing healthcare to one high-profile Pacific Island politician, a precedent would be set, and soon, dozens of mid-level political operatives from the countless subnational jurisdictions in Solomons, Papua New Guinea and beyond would be knocking on the doors of Canberra's representatives throughout the region. Adhering to this established policy, Australia's high commissioner in Honiara, Dr Lachlan Strahan, rejected Premier Suidani's appeal for health assistance, but arranged to fast-track his and Talifilu's visa to enter Australia.

In Brisbane, Suidani received a diagnosis – later described as a 'brain space-occupying lesion' – and was told that treatment was expected to cost around AU$100,000.[3] The premier – a former schoolteacher, now two years into governing one of the world's poorest jurisdictions – was simply unable to afford it. Although a modest effort was made to fundraise for the premier's treatment through a GoFundMe page, it was clear he would still fall short. He needed help.

By the time Suidani fell ill, his cult status as an anti-China crusader had made him something of a hero to a niche global audience of China hawks. His rebuke of China's advances was routinely covered in most major international newspapers. In any story about the Switch and its aftermath, journalists, myself included, would invariably note Malaita's staunch opposition to China and loyalty to Taiwan – usually omitting the complex range of views that is found across an island as vast as Malaita. In contrast to the murkiness and uncertainty that surrounded the Switch, Suidani's pro-Taiwan position appeared unequivocal. To some Western scholars, it was inspiring. When Suidani had begun voicing his opposition towards Beijing, he knew it would stir up controversy. What he didn't know was that it may well save his life, too.

As Suidani sought financial assistance, Canadian academic Dr Cleo Paskal, who had been closely following Solomon Islands since the Switch, caught wind of his plight. Paskal had been writing a regular column in an Indian online newspaper, the *Sunday Guardian*, routinely praising Suidani's brave stance against China. She also appeared on several Indian TV news channels explaining the intricacies of Malaitan provincial politics, to an audience that enjoyed the David vs Goliath story of individuals taking on the might of India's rival Asian power. Paskal was connected to influential figures in India, including Professor Madhav Das Nalapat, an international relations academic at Manipal University. A well-known scholar, Professor

Nalapat had built his reputation through the publication of numerous books and regular columns covering Indian nationalism and foreign policy, as well as serving as the editor of several Indian newspapers and journals. A democracy advocate, Professor Nalapat is also fervently pro-Taiwan. His official biography claims that it was he who convinced former Indian prime minister P.V. Narasimha Rao to open trade offices in Taipei in 1992, despite India's recognition of the People's Republic of China. Ever since, visiting Taiwanese delegations to India had stopped in to see Nalapat.

By 2020, Nalapat was serving as an editorial director of the *Sunday Guardian*. 'I was contacted in 2020 about the illness of Premier Suidani by a family friend, Cleo Paskal,' he told me. Paskal told Nalapat that the Australian government was refusing to help Suidani. Nalapat saw Australia's inaction as symptomatic of 'the somewhat condescending attitude that Canberra and Auckland [sic] have demonstrated to the smaller eastern Indo-Pacific Island countries … an attitude that must have proven very helpful to Beijing'.

Paskal managed to convince Nalapat of Suidani's virtues, and of his dire health situation. The professor had an idea. Nalapat explained his next steps to me by email:

An era ago, Dr Tsai [Ing-wen, the president of Taiwan] had been the guest of my university on her only visit to India. Since that visit, Dr Tsai has been kind enough to spare a bit of time for a meeting with me whenever my schedule found me in Taipei, a situation that remains intact as a consequence of her innate courtesy …

Cleo [Paskal] put me in telephonic contact with a close associate of [Premier Suidani], who said that it was a matter of life and death. I got in touch with the President of Taiwan and informed her of the medical emergency.

I have never had the honour of meeting the Premier, but in my sole telephone conversation with him, the impression was of a man who stood by what he believed in, and if necessary was prepared to suffer for it. That he could not afford the money to get treated in Australia showed his honesty, although to this day, the dismissive approach of Canberra to a humanitarian emergency is a bit distressing and remains a surprise.[4]

In May 2021, it was revealed in the *Solomon Star* newspaper that Suidani and Talifilu had travelled to Taipei and were now residing there. Although all parties insisted publicly that the visit was purely on humanitarian grounds, it was hard for observers to ignore the political significance of Suidani's appearance in Taiwan, a country he had been so publicly and controversially courting. At the time, the direct involvement of the Taiwanese presidential office and of Professor Nalapat were not known. But as the story broke, Talifilu used his influential Facebook group, 'Malaita Provincial Development Forum', to explain the premier's presence in Taiwan.

'Suidani has been ill for the last five months with a provisional diagnosis pointing to a probable brain space-occupying lesion', Talifilu wrote. 'Medical doctors in Honiara referred Suidani for an urgent head CT/MRI scan diagnosis and treatment overseas. His case was referred to the Overseas Referral Committee of the National Referral Hospital in Solomon Islands on 5 March 2021 for assistance. But since then, there was no response from the Committee.'

Talifilu said that Suidani was 'fighting for his life' and that the premier 'thanks Taiwan for making it possible for him to seek medical treatment in one of the most advanced medical places in the world'.

In a response that appeared to represent the peak of the dispute between Suidani and Sogavare, the national government formally rebuked Suidani for seeking medical treatment in Taiwan. It issued public statements emphasising that the visit was 'unauthorised' and that Suidani's Taiwan engagements did not undermine the Sogavare government's commitment to its One China policy. It criticised Suidani for listening to his 'henchmen', in a clear reference to Talifilu and M4D. The visit also earned a rebuke from the Chinese embassy in Honiara, which told the *Solomon Star* that it firmly opposed any official contacts between Solomon Islanders and the Taiwanese.

For just over a month, Premier Suidani, along with his wife and Talifilu, stayed in Taipei, as the premier underwent treatment at the National Taiwan University Hospital. After several weeks, Talifilu took to the pages of *Solomon Business Magazine* to announce the imminent return of the premier to Malaita.[5] In Taipei, Talifilu wrote, the premier had received an MRI test, which 'cleared him of the suspected condition'. Talifilu quoted Suidani, who heaped praise upon his hosts: 'I and my people of Malaita province will treasure this historical support for many years to come. This is a testimony of our friendship and the friendship of our peoples', Suidani was quoted as saying.

Talifilu, Suidani and Taiwanese authorities deny that, during the premier's time in Taipei, any political activities occurred. When asked if Australia had any knowledge of or involvement in what occurred in Taiwan, former Australian prime minister Scott Morrison declined to comment, refusing categorically to discuss on the record any intelligence he had received during 2020 about the courtship between Taiwan and Malaita, or about Suidani's medical evacuation.

While in Taipei, however, Suidani didn't only rest and receive treatment. From his hotel room, he gave interviews to the global media, including his appearance on Sharri Markson's program on Sky News Australia. He reiterated his refusal to accept Sogavare's offer of medical funding in exchange for relinquishing his criticism of China. The interviews circulated on social media in Malaita, and by the time Suidani began his journey home, he was emboldened. He had emerged as a Malaitan statesman on the world stage, a champion for the autonomous spirit that so many of his constituents held dear.

The journey home for Suidani would be a long one. In mid-2021, Australia's strict Covid quarantine arrangements were still in force. From Taiwan, in mid-July Suidani flew to Brisbane, where he spent two weeks in hotel quarantine and at least two months continuing his recovery and readying for his return home. In preparation for his homecoming, Suidani and Talifilu spent their time finalising a handful of commitments he planned to announce on arrival in Auki – a signal that, while he may have been away, he still wielded authority.

By mid-October, the plans for his return were finalised. Suidani and Talifilu boarded the weekly Solomon Airlines flight from Brisbane to Honiara, where they met a boat that would take them across the Iron Bottom Sounds and Indispensable Strait. As he stepped ashore at Auki Harbour, the premier was greeted by an extraordinary scene. Thousands of Malaitans had gathered for the ceremony, in what is thought to have been the largest political gathering for a provincial politician in the country's history. A floral wreath was draped over his neck, and he was sat upon a throne carried by six shirtless men, a traditional practice conveying Suidani's stature. Through the dense, cheering crowd, as music played, he was carried to a podium. 'Welcome, Father of Malaita', read one sign. Behind his throne stood a flag upon which soared a giant Malaitan eagle, the province's official emblem. When Suidani reached the stand, he began his speech.

'A boat only rocks when the captain is out,' he declared, before going on to detail nine new development projects – including a pineapple factory, fisheries investments, wharfs for outer islands and a pig-meal processing facility supported by USAID – to rapturous applause. He thanked his constituents for sticking with him in his absence. 'If we continue to stand together, my good people, I believe we will receive good things.'

Suidani's homecoming enshrined his place as Solomon Islands' de-facto opposition figurehead. Abroad, he was now seen by many as a bulwark against Beijing. Sogavare was still dominant, and his office was still the most powerful in the country. But whereas Suidani's popular mandate was clear, Sogavare's public appeal was limited. The images of Suidani, the former schoolteacher just three years into his premiership, being carried on the shoulders of his fellow Malaitans, announcing policy triumphs to an adoring crowd, proved that his power came not from his ability to win over fellow parliamentarians, or from his ability to quash political opponents in parliamentary manoeuvrings. Suidani could claim, at least for now, that his power emanated from the people.

12

HONIARA BURNING

AS THE ENMITIES BETWEEN THE Sogavare and Suidani governments escalated, M4D's leadership began to revamp its pitch to Malaitans and to the country. Its early successes had seen M4D become a household name. The initial protests in the wake of the Switch had emboldened the group, and Olita's legally risky decision to involve himself in the Taiwanese aid saga had been noticed by the entire country. But there was uncertainty among its key personnel as to what M4D really was. Was it a movement? Was it an idea? Or was it a formal organisation, akin to a political party? And after its early achievements in pushing the Suidani government to sign the Auki Communique, what was its next move? What was its ask of the Sogavare government? How would it achieve its pledge to place Malaita on a path to statehood?

To grapple with these heady questions, Knoxley Atu and Richard Olita turned to a veteran activist and protestor, Lawrence Makili, for strategic and intellectual advice. Born on Ontong Java – a tiny atoll, administratively part of Malaita Province but located 500 kilometres to Malaita Island's north – Makili, now fifty-seven years old and based in Honiara, was a stalwart of Solomon Islands' activist scene. Dreadlocked and slightly balding, he had cut his teeth in the 1980s and 1990s, travelling widely across the Pacific and even as far as Paris to protest the French government's policy of conducting nuclear tests in the Pacific. He was a fervent supporter of nationalist crusades across Melanesia, such as the Kanaks' ongoing independence struggle in New Caledonia and the West Papuan efforts in Indonesia's far east.

A self-confessed heavy drinker and womaniser, Makili boasts of having twenty-five children to eleven different women across the world, describing them proudly as the inevitable by-product of his intrepid and hedonistic life as a 'professional, well-trained activist'. As he entered middle age, Makili concentrated most of his energies on environmental crusades, taking on formal roles with Greenpeace and the Earth Institute. His impassioned defence of dolphins had made him many enemies in Solomon Islands, where the animals are sometimes still caught, traded and eaten; in 2008, he had been abducted in Honiara, driven to the outskirts of town and beaten to within an inch of his life by eight men enraged by his dolphin advocacy.

While environmental campaigns had become Makili's profession, he was also a zealous campaigner against corruption in Solomon Islands, which he had been agitating against since the Mamaloni era. In 1998 he had led protests that helped to weaken Mamaloni. His hatred of Sogavare was personal; he viewed him as Mamaloni's 'little boy'. For Makili, the return of Sogavare to power in 2019 was a devastating development. He had protested against Sogavare's elevation in 2006 and 2014 and believed the country was in for another period of tumult. He took to the streets when Sogovare prevailed in the April 2019 parliamentary scrum for the prime ministership and pledged to do whatever he could to oust the now four-time prime minister.

For Atu and Olita, an association with Makili added credibility and experience to the M4D cause. Throughout 2021, Makili's counsel began to influence M4D's strategic vision and philosophical foundations, and when the legal heat became too much for Olita and Atu, Makili began taking on a more formal role as a spokesman for the organisation. The experienced protestor made the case that M4D should frame itself not as a political organisation – political parties rise and fall regularly in Solomon Islands without any major consequence – but as a new political ideology, filling a vacuum in Solomon Islands' largely unideological, tribal politics. Concepts of 'right' and 'left' don't apply to the ever-evolving coalitions of MPs in Solomon Islands, who are more motivated by local issues and the maintenance of power than by Western intellectual traditions. Makili's idea was to create an ideological space, grounded in popularly held democratic values, that could comfortably accommodate all the anti-Sogavare forces – a broad church that would be as much about the principles of democracy and equitable development as about simply opposing Sogavare. To Makili, M4D's utility was as a brand, a label which could be taken up by everyday Solomon Islanders alienated by the type of politics Sogavare had brought to the country. 'An organisation can be deregistered; an idea can never die,' he said. But for Knoxley Atu and Richard Olita, M4D's value remained its ability to mobilise people into protest. To them, the best way to spread the M4D brand – to realise Makili's intellectual project – was to show its force on the streets.

After an extended parliamentary recess, much of which had been filled with tit-for-tat politicking between Sogavare and Suidani, the prime minister decided to recall the national parliament in late November 2021. In the looming recall of parliament, Atu and Olita saw an opportunity to demonstrate M4D's power. They consulted with Makili, and a plan was conceived. M4D would mobilise protestors in great numbers on the opening day of parliament and use the power of the crowd to force Sogavare to accept, or at least consider, a list of demands M4D had previously sent via letter to the prime minister's office, which had been ignored for months. The ten demands were bold and in line with the Auki Communique. M4D wanted the Sogavare government to commit to banning Chinese investment in Malaita, prohibit the 'influx of cheap Asian labour into Solomon Islands who are systematically taking away economic opportunities from Solomon Islanders', and work to better implement the 2000 Townsville Peace Agreement, among other requests.[1] Makili had drafted the demands in August 2021, but nothing had eventuated. M4D believed that with enough pressure from the crowd, however, Sogavare would have no choice but to buckle.

It was a highly improbable, risky plan. Sogavare's stubbornness was well known, and he was never going to allow himself to be forced to negotiate with a group he dismissed as thugs and radicals. To do so would undermine his entire political brand. And given the long history of rioting in Honiara, the mass mobilisation of young men to the capital, who were certain to be angered by a Sogavare no-show, was sure to create a tinderbox that risked being ignited by the faintest spark.

As chatter about the M4D plan grew in Honiara and beyond in the early weeks of November, the public, too, seemed unconvinced of the strategy. Many anticipated a violent day. As did Sogavare, who began laying the groundwork to blame any violence on his political opponents. In the weeks leading up to the return of parliament, Sogavare began issuing warnings about the likely unrest and pre-emptively alleged that Matthew Wale, Peter Kenilorea Jnr and Daniel Suidani were plotting a violent coup. On 21 November, he held a briefing with the Royal Solomon Islands Police Force and other security officials to discuss plans for the reopening of parliament on 24 November. After the meeting, he publicly declared that he had information that Wale, Kenilorea Jnr and Suidani were indeed responsible for whatever was coming later in the week, although his police briefing had included no such details. Sogavare had used the official occasion of his security briefing to give his unfounded accusations against three opposition figureheads a veneer of legitimacy. Those who were planning the protest for 24 November hoped it would convince Sogavare to buckle, or even step down. Instead, Sogavare was preparing to use it to his advantage.

For the next three days, just about every passenger vessel that crossed the Indispensable Strait between Auki and Honiara was full. For weeks, Knoxley Atu had been rallying young men from villages across Malaita to travel to the city. Using his mobile phone, Atu would call five close associates in as many villages as he could, asking each to bring five friends, and for those friends to bring five friends, and so on. The message spread like wildfire. Few could afford a boat ticket; instead, large numbers of young men capitalised on the fact that tickets are purchased onboard after the boat departs. Once the trip was underway, most simply refused to pay; some mentioned M4D or Knoxley Atu by name when they were asked to buy tickets, hoping it would get them out of trouble. Meanwhile, back in Honiara, Lawrence Makili had been busy mobilising the urban Malaitan populations, using similar tactics to spread the word.

Early on the morning of 24 November, the crowd began to gather. Boats were still arriving at Point Cruz Terminal, carrying hundreds of Malaitans. Others already in the city also headed to the terminal, which was their meeting point. As the crowd grew, Atu, Olita and Makili entered the local police station and tried to negotiate, through the police, a meeting with the prime minister. As the three men debated with police, the crowd swelled outside. Soon, several thousand young men were in attendance, and they began to slowly walk from Point Cruz Terminal to Parliament House, some 500 metres away.

The police, acting as intermediaries between Sogavare's office and the throng of protestors, first assured the crowd that an audience with the prime minister would be granted. But as the morning proceeded, and the crowd grew larger, the speeches became more aggressive and the likelihood of Sogavare arriving diminished. In fact, as the crowd was being told that Sogavare would address them, the prime minister was being advised to do just the opposite. Sogavare's minders had conceived a way for the prime minister to safely exit the parliamentary complex. Given the parliament's physical location, an inconspicuous exit would prove challenging. The building is set into a steep hillside, with only a single road running from the front of the complex, up the hill to a two-lane road behind it. All vehicles entering and exiting the premises were clearly visible to the protestors.

There were legitimate concerns for the prime minister's safety. These concerns were held not only by Sogavare and his advisors, but also by the Australian government, who were by now following the situation closely. Sogavare's team had to improvise. The prime minister would be ushered out of the back of the building and placed in a private vehicle, not his official car. He would be driven into the hills behind the parliament, where he would be met by another private vehicle. He was briefly forced to travel by foot on the backstreets of Honiara between the two vehicles. Then, he was transferred to the heavily fortified Rové Police Station, where he would remain for most of the next forty-eight hours.

I spoke to David Wairi, a 31-year-old journalist who was in the crowd that day. He said that by mid-morning, rumours began circulating that 'the MPs had already fled', including the prime minister. The crowd had been promised by the M4D leaders that the protests would lead to real change. Now, it grew considerably angrier as news of Sogavare's escape spread.

With Sogavare gone, the crowd of over a thousand rushed the parliamentary grounds. Soon, a palm-leaf hut adjacent to the parliamentary building was set ablaze, and the police responded forcefully, firing tear gas. No one knows who started the fire. Protestors claim that it was the result of police actions, while the Sogavare government argued it was an intentional act by the violent crowd. Whatever the cause of the blaze, it was the spark that ignited a much more dangerous turn of events. As the fire burned and the crowd spilled into the parliamentary grounds, more tear gas was fired. Hundreds of protestors succumbed to its effects. 'We are not dogs, we are men. Why are you using this on us?' one of the protestors shouted, before being ushered into a parliamentary bathroom by some of the remaining MPs to clean his eyes. Other protestors fled to the nearby University of the South Pacific campus, where Maverick Seda, a 21-year-old student, provided water and milk to ease the burning. The crowd flooded onto the streets of Honiara, where authorities quickly conceded that they were unable to control the riot that was beginning. As in past riots in Honiara, there were some genuine political agitators, but they were outnumbered by opportunists taking advantage of the chaos. Facing little resistance from police, the rioters turned their attention on Chinatown. Within hours, dozens of buildings, mainly Chinese-owned retail outlets and apartment complexes, had been set ablaze, and a thick black smog descended over much of the city. To dissuade the protestors, some building owners placed Taiwanese flags on the front of their shops. Most of these buildings were spared by the rioters, whose targets included police stations and even one of Sogavare's personal residences, which was unoccupied at the time.

As the violence escalated, those responsible for organising the protest had quietly slipped out of town. By mid-afternoon, Knoxley Atu was back in Malaita, while Olita and others had gone into hiding in the hills behind Honiara.

Although he was now safely confined to the fortified police barracks, Sogavare remained quiet for most of the day. There was no public announcement, and no word about his whereabouts or safety until later that evening. In the meantime, Sogavare was joined by Australian high commissioner

Lachlan Strahan. Under the security treaty struck between Honiara and
Canberra in 2017, as a condition of the end of RAMSI, the Solomon Islands'
prime minister was entitled to request Australian peacekeepers should
violence ever descend on the country. Through Strahan, Sogavare now conveyed such a request to the Australian government.

*

In Canberra, the Australian prime minister, Scott Morrison, convened with
national security advisors, who were monitoring the riots, to consider how
to execute Sogavare's request.

Australia's minister for international development and the Pacific, Zed
Seselja, had gathered his staff in his ministerial office. In spite of Australia's multi-billion-dollar efforts in Solomon Islands in the years leading up
to the violence, Canberra had few eyes on the ground during the course of
the rioting. There were no intelligence assets in the crowd, no sleeper agents
monitoring the speeches and actions of the M4D-mobilised group assembled in front of parliament. Instead, Seselja relied on his staff's personal
friends and connections in Honiara to monitor the situation in real time.
They turned to Facebook, where locals were uploading extraordinary and
increasingly alarming footage of the escalating chaos.

There was no doubt in Scott Morrison's mind that Australia would
follow through with Sogavare's call for assistance. Morrison was familiar
with Australia's security obligations and understood the political context.
But the rapid deployment of troops to a foreign country presented genuine safety risks to those deployed, as well as political risks to Morrison's
government. Morrison was on the eve of a re-election campaign. Past peacekeeping operations had led to the deaths and injury of Australian troops.
And the deployment of troops to Solomon Islands was especially complicated given the country remained formally closed due to its strict Covid-19
border restrictions. There was a concern in both the Australian government
and the broader community of Pacific commentators, as well as in Solomon
Islands, that the peacekeeping effort could see Covid-19 enter the country

for the first time. Morrison and his senior Pacific advisors also knew that the Australian action would likely be viewed by some Solomon Islanders as shoring up a deeply unpopular Pacific leader. To address this, the government worked to encourage other countries from the region to join in the peacekeeping efforts. Within hours, Fijian and Papua New Guinean leaders had agreed to the request. Before committing Australia to the operation, Morrison says he telephoned the federal opposition leader, Anthony Albanese, who Morrison alleges was unaware of the rioting occurring in Solomon Islands. Morrison claimed, derisively, that Albanese asked if the troop deployment was to alleviate issues relating to Covid-19, highlighting what Morrison seemed to believe was Albanese's inadequate grasp of Pacific affairs.

As the Morrison government readied its deployment, Sogavare made his first formal statement. It wasn't until 8 p.m. that Sogavare took to the airwaves, releasing a video statement that admonished the protestors: 'I honestly thought the darkest days were behind us,' he said, before announcing a strict curfew. He was angry, but he also appeared chastened. Although he may have been prepared to capitalise on any violence, he appeared genuinely affected by the significance of the disaster. His comments filled an unusually quiet airspace. No other major political figure in Solomon Islands – no one from the government, and no leading opposition figure – made any public statement until after Sogavare had. When I asked opposition figures why they hadn't taken to Facebook or other platforms to call for the violence to end, most didn't have a clear answer. There appeared to be a willingness, within the opposition, to see how events played out – to see whether Sogavare could really hold on this time. The opposition's unwillingness to proactively work to quell the unrest gave Sogavare all the proof he needed to soon begin placing blame for the violence at the feet of his political enemies. Within hours, in his first phone interview with media after his televised statement, Sogavare directly blamed external interference for the riots. His comments were widely interpreted as an indictment of Taiwan's meddling in the country's affairs, and of its support for the Suidani government.[2]

Sogavare's calls for a curfew, however, were in vain. By now, local police had proven entirely incapable of stopping the unrest. Into the morning of 25 November, more buildings were razed. Pitched battles between drunken, stone-throwing rioters and tear-gas-firing police broke out across the city, as thousands of families sheltered fearfully in their darkened homes.

In a military base in Townsville, a city in Australia's far northeast, more than seventy Australian Defence Force personnel were readied for departure. Within twenty-four hours of Sogavare's formal request, this initial contingent was on the ground. As Australian soldiers began patrolling the streets, the violence quickly ended. But the damage – the worst unrest Solomons had seen in a generation – had been done. After two decades of meticulous peacemaking, and just two years after the Switch, Solomon Islands was broken once more. The streets resembled a warzone. Buildings, including the Kukum Police Station, had been turned to rubble. Thick black smoke blanketed the sky, as fires were left uncontained by authorities. From the hills above Honiara Senior High School, Res Lynn, a 22-year-old former student, emotionally watch her old school campus wilt and crumple under the flames lit by her compatriots.

Two days after peace had returned to Honiara, security guard Edie Soa, who worked in Chinatown, was patrolling the district. Inside the OK Mart, a small retail outlet, he discovered the remains of three people. They had been huddled together in a storeroom, where cash and precious items were kept. Their bodies, charred and unidentifiable, were surrounded by debris.[3]

*

Eight months later, I returned to Solomon Islands after the border restrictions eased. Immediately, I made my way to the banks of the Mataniko River, along which Chinatown runs. Time had done little to alleviate the sheer scale of destruction. From the taxi, along the main stretch of Mendana Avenue, blackened apartment buildings, their glass windows having been blasted out by flames, came into view. I stepped out of the taxi and started to walk around Chinatown. It felt as if the riots had happened yesterday.

Few structures had escaped unharmed. Burnt-out cars, crumpled and contorted from the flames, had rusted, as had the exposed steel beams in the countless buildings that had been razed. The area was largely abandoned. A handful of young children played in half-destroyed buildings. Others frolicked in the river, surrounded by piles of twisted metal, cars and rubbish.

Of the buildings that remained, none had escaped the anger of the protestors. Nearly every surface had been defiled by racially charged political graffiti. Many were directed at the prime minister: 'Soga Stand Down', 'Sogavare Go'. Some promoted the Malaitan cause: 'Mala Rule', 'Malaita Forever'. Others carried a far more ominous, racialised message: 'Waku Go Home'.

Riot damage in the capital.

PART V
TWISTED IRON

13

SEEKING PROTECTION

TEN MONTHS AFTER THE SMOKE HAD SETTLED in Honiara, martial arts expert Wanghu was putting his class through its paces in Buala village, on the north coast of Santa Isabel Island. Their feet sank into the black volcanic sand on the beach that served as their classroom. Wanghu's students, children aged between six and ten, were being trained in the art of self-defence by their Chinese instructor. In a tight T-shirt, Wanghu's physique was clear. His shaved head, bulging biceps and head-to-toe black outfit created an imposing figure. But he was not there to intimidate, and his giggling students seemed rapt by his presence.

'What we most look forward to every day now is the afternoon kung fu training,' one child told a local journalist covering the event.

Over several days in October 2022, Wanghu led a group of forty young girls and boys from Buala through a kung-fu course, teaching them basic self-defence skills. He was a representative of the China Police Liaison Unit (CPLU), who had been making global headlines since their arrival in Solomon Islands in early 2022. Images of their other students – members of the Royal Solomon Islands Police Force (RSIPF) – undertaking fire-arms training seemed to confirm in many Western eyes the consolidation of Beijing's grip on Solomon Islands. Chinese weapons had been flowing into the country. Chinese police were alleged to be embedded with local forces. And a cadre of RSIPF officers had been flown to China for a crash course in the Chinese style of policing. China's offer to assist the Solomon Islands police had been on the table since the Switch. But not until the two countries signed a controversial security partnership in April 2022 did the pace of their interactions ramp up. The security deal had become a global story, even rocking the Australian federal election, becoming a central issue in a campaign that ushered in a change of government in Canberra. But in Isabel Province, Wanghu, the smiling CPLU attaché, was welcomed with open arms.

'There have been cases of rape and robbery in Isabel Province,' supervising police commander Rodney Hirovaka told the Solomon Islands Broadcasting Corporation covering the event. 'This training taught young women and children how to protect themselves.'

Wanghu was at the vanguard of the Chinese police force's new tactic: winning hearts and minds. And, at least in Buala, it appeared to be paying dividends.

'We feel the charm of kung fu,' one of the students said.[1]

*

The thousands of angry men who had rioted in Honiara that first week of November 2021 may have hoped the chaos would remove Sogavare from office and put an end to his government's blossoming relationship with China. While many of the rioters were opportunists, others clearly wanted Sogavare gone. But if Sogavare wouldn't go, the crowd at least wanted to make its opposition to the China partnership known. They had hoped that, with an intimidating show of violence, the Sogavare government would reconsider its Beijing rapprochement. Instead, the riots would catastrophically backfire, providing further justification for Sogavare to double down on a controversial security relationship with Beijing that many had long feared.

As early as August 2021 – months before the riots – rumours had begun to circulate in Honiara political circles that the Sogavare government was pursuing a security relationship with Beijing. It was a development that those who most fervently opposed the Switch had been concerned about since mid-2020. The rumours were first flagged by Matthew Wale, the opposition leader, who had heard from an undisclosed source that a small team of Sogavare loyalists in parliament had been charged by their leader with a highly secretive task. They were to begin negotiations with Beijing for a security partnership – a deal that would 'diversify' Honiara's security relationship, allowing the government to be less dependent on Australia for the maintenance of law and order. Having heard of these behind-the-scenes negotiations, Wale decided to warn Australia's high commissioner, Lachlan Strahan.

'I told the Australian high commissioner that there were discussions on something that would lead to a security agreement,' he told *The Australian's* foreign affairs defence correspondent, Ben Packham. 'I was informed by somebody who was in those discussions. At that stage, internal discussions between key ministers were happening, and exploratory – that is the way it was put to me – "exploratory discussions" were being held with China.' He believed his informants were concerned about the supposed arrangement.

At their meeting, Wale saw Strahan writing notes. He assumed the issue would be followed up by Canberra. Just a few weeks later, Strahan was headed back to Australia for the first time since the start of his posting. After a fortnight in hotel quarantine in Queensland, he would make his way to Canberra. Within days of arriving, however, he suffered a debilitating back injury, so severe that he would not return to Solomon Islands for another five months. His able team in Honiara would be left to navigate a turbulent six months without their boss on the ground.

Through the remainder of the year, the negotiations Wale had been alerted to intensified. Weeks after the November riots, as these negotiations continued behind the scenes, the Chinese agreed to a formal, stand-alone request by the Sogavare government to provide police officers and equipment to assist the RSIPF to keep the peace. The offer, announced on Christmas Eve 2021, came seven weeks after Australian forces had arrived in Honiara. For the Australians, it suggested a deeper security partnership was probably on the horizon. Over the next four months, the Australian government would work assiduously to stop a formal security partnership between Beijing and Honiara from emerging. The Morrison government sent several delegations of senior officials to Honiara to convince Sogavare to alter course. Soon, these engagements would become public knowledge. And on the eve of Australia's May 2022 federal election, Sogavare confirmed what some had now come to view as inevitable: Beijing and Honiara would sign a formal security pact.

*

For the most part, foreign observers framed Sogavare's determination to establish the security pact with Beijing as part of a grand geopolitical struggle between East and West. There were legitimate security concerns for Australia and other Pacific countries. Some observers even suggested that the security pact's timing, on the eve of the Australian election, was strategic, intended to embarrass the Morrison government and hurt its re-election chances.

But for Sogavare, the geopolitical dimensions of the security pact with China were almost certainly a secondary consideration. As a man who had ascended to power twice after the violent ouster of his predecessor, he knew that he, too, was vulnerable. Sogavare needed protection.

Sogavare has long feared assassination, or at least a violent coup. At times, his concerns have seemed unrealistic; occasionally, the threats have seemed more acute. In 2006, at the height of his stand-off with the Australian government over the Moti affair and Australia's perceived interference in the country's legal system, an Australian expatriate living in Solomon Islands, Bill Johnson, was arrested for conspiring to assassinate Sogavare. The plot was supposedly 'sponsored by Australia'. Johnson's lawyers claimed the threats consisted of an incoherent rant by a drunken Johnson at his favourite watering hole, the Point Cruz Yacht Club. The charges, almost certainly spurious, were dismissed by the Australian director of public prosecutions. The notion of an Australian-backed plot was laughed at by the perplexed Australian prime minister at the time, John Howard. Regardless, Johnson was deported to Australia.

A few months later, a former Solomon Islands MP who had lost his seat in the 2006 national election, Alfred Sasako, published an article in which he claimed that, before the Johnson arrest, Sogavare had suggested that an attempt on his life was imminent. Sasako wrote that after Johnson's arrest, Sogavare consulted a fortune teller, who told the prime minister that a 'light-skinned woman working close to [him]' would soon carry out an assassination attempt. Sogavare denied Sasako's claims, but his opponents believed he had been paranoid about assassination plots ever since the Johnson incident.[2]

By 2019, Sogavare, now in his fourth prime ministerial term, came to office determined to hold on to power. His first three prime ministerships had all ended prematurely after he lost support on the floor of parliament. This time, he worked to consolidate support among his colleagues. He had seen off motions of no confidence and could count on his comfortable majority to maintain his position. But he still remained anxious about the other threat to his power: the streets.

'Paranoid' is a word often used to describe Sogavare's concerns about his wellbeing, but some of the threats against him have been less fanciful than the Johnson plot. When I first travelled to Auki in the weeks after the Switch, I heard about the violent reception Sogavare's allies had received in villages when spruiking the China partnership. Some had been confronted by crowds, incensed at the Switch, who angrily rejected their arguments and pelted them with rocks. I spoke with a number of people who had organised against Sogavare in Auki, and with members of the public on the streets and in the market. 'If Sogavare came to Auki, what would happen?' I asked one local.

'We will kill him,' the man said.

Certainly, only a small minority of Sogavare's opponents use such rhetoric. But their feelings are real and are widely circulated online. In March 2020, an anti-Sogavare Facebook page, 'Corrupt in DCGA',[3] was launched. At the time of writing, it has over 6000 followers and regularly publishes posts. Although some of its posts share allegations of corruption within the Sogavare government, most of its content is far more personal, threatening and, at times, disturbing. The page routinely vilifies Sogavare, referring to him as the country's 'black prime minister', highlighting his Choiseul origins, which place him in an ethnic minority. It also regularly warns of violence directly targeting Sogavare. In 2021, the page began to issue veiled threats to the prime minister. 'Prime Minister Sogavare soon to face his final judgment day', one post said. Over time, these vague warnings evolved into overt death threats. 'Black Manasseh Sogavare, a stupid prime minister … You are evil and your dead is near. Your dead spirits is watching over you,' said another post.

These sentiments were at the extreme end of the rhetoric circulating in Honiara. But such threats, and the ability of those making them to circulate them widely and potentially to plot against the government, undoubtedly informed the Sogavare cabinet's announcement in November 2020 that it would ban access to Facebook. Although this decision was reversed following an outcry from the public and from the business community, it revealed the government's sensitivity to threats and expressions of dissent.

Rumours routinely circulate in Solomon Islands about more organised armed plots against the government. Their legitimacy is often questionable, but the constant chatter adds to an air of instability in the capital. In July 2021, for example, the *Solomon Star* published a report by Alfred Sasako – the former MP who had previously described Sogavare's alleged visit to a fortune teller – claiming that 'an armed group is reportedly plotting to take down the Democratic Coalition Government for Advancement'. Sasako had been a long-time proponent of the Switch. After visiting China in 2006, he had come home spruiking the economic benefits of a partnership with Beijing and had been an advocate of a switch ever since.[4] His July 2021 report included sensational allegations that 'ex-militants' from Malaita, Guadalcanal and even Sogavare's home province of Choiseul were preparing to forcibly remove the prime minister from office.[5] Sasako, whom Malaitan officials say is a close ally of Sogavare, linked the allegedly imminent armed coup to Daniel Suidani's 'anti-Sogavare stance'. Although the truth behind Sasako's claims are questionable – Sogavare's opponents believe it was used as a pretext to enact stricter security measures in the capital, or perhaps to justify the security deal with China – similar rumours also emerged elsewhere.

In the weeks after the Honiara riot, a front-page story in Papua New Guinea's *Post-Courier* newspaper reported similar rumblings. 'Secret Plot Uncovered: PNG Police Receive Reports of Bougainvilleans Involved in Sect to Overthrow Solomon Islands Prime Minister', read the headline. The story, dismissed by leaders in Bougainville and Papua New Guinea, suggested that experienced militants from Bougainville had been smuggling weapons across the porous Shortland Island border crossing between their island and Choiseul and providing training to a group of Malaitan dissidents.

Even if Sogavare wasn't disturbed by these unverifiable rumours, he was chastened by the November 2021 riots, during which his personal safety was genuinely under threat. Although he was able to call on the Australian government for assistance, that help wouldn't arrive for at least twenty-four hours. In the intervening hours, he was reliant on a personal security attachment he had previously attempted to arm and strengthen, unsuccessfully. Sogavare would also have been aware of Australia's potential reluctance to deploy troops to quell the riots. Conscious of being seen as 'neo-colonial', Australian governments of all persuasions have traditionally been averse to such deployments. And while Australia may have been treaty-bound to send troops, they also knew that doing so could be perceived as support for Sogavare personally, undermining Australia's credibility with his opponents and large swathes of the Solomon Islands public.

When the Australian deployment came, supplemented by forces from New Zealand, Fiji and Papua New Guinea, there was pushback. Ironically, much criticism of the intervention echoed the anti-intervention rhetoric that Sogavare had made famous. 'Australia, Fiji, PNG and New Zealand are here to protect Sogavare', one source close to the Malaitan government told me. 'Australia can't bring answers to Solomon Islands. They been here fourteen years using Australian taxpayers' money ... look at what they left behind.' The Malaitans were also concerned about rumours that an Australian navy vessel was 'floating outside Auki Harbour' and that there were 'drones over Auki'. 'Quite risky if the boat will anchor here in Auki', my source warned.

Sogavare was aware of this criticism and of Australia's sensitivity to it. His reliance on Canberra left him feeling vulnerable. By enacting a security partnership with Beijing, he had achieved two strategic objectives. First, he knew that Australia's reluctance to intervene would now be significantly curtailed. Canberra would be loath to see Chinese military personnel patrolling the streets of Honiara if another spate of violence broke out and would therefore be much more likely to deploy security personnel quickly. Sogavare had deftly leveraged Australia's anxiety about China to put the might of the Australian Defence Force at his beck and call. He extracted a commitment by Australia that its troops would remain in place until the 2023 Pacific Games, all but ensuring peace on the streets until the end of the parliamentary term.

Sogavare's security partnership with China had also tempered the likelihood of widespread unrest in the future. The Solomon Islands community may have been sceptical of China, but many also feared its brutality. Solomon Islanders know of the Tiananmen Square massacre. Some know of the atrocities against Uyghurs in Xinjiang. They understand that protest and dissent in Xi Jinping's China are quashed with violence and oppression. When riots break out in Honiara, local police are rarely able to handle the situation: the community do not fear the police. When Australian and other regional troops are deployed to keep the peace, they do so on a strictly non-confrontational basis; their mandate is usually limited to the protection of key public infrastructure, such as airports and parliament, and to providing security for political figures. These foreign forces rarely apprehend rioters and never engage with them. The prospect of confronting Chinese security personnel on the streets of Honiara is another story. The outcome of a Chinese military deployment to quell violence, particularly violence directed towards the ethnic-Chinese community in Honiara, is unpredictable.

Anyone planning a major protest in Solomon Islands could now be certain of coming face-to-face with either Australian troops or well-armed Chinese soldiers. Sogavare had control of the streets, as well as the parliament.

*

As Sogavare's defence of the security pact intensified, his frustration with the media coverage of the deal deepened. His rhetoric focused on sovereign decision making – on the right of any nation, no matter how small, to make its own foreign policy decisions. For the international media observers now hanging on his every word, much of his language appeared coded, designed to subtly criticise the concerns emanating from Canberra. But Sogavare's most passionate and direct critiques were targeted at the international press.

'I think so far, what has been put out in the media has been ... misinformation. There are places to go to get proper information – our office is always open, officials are always there, I'm also available – but we are concerned about media organisations that deliberately put out misinformation after a lot of explanations. We have issues with these kinds of people.'

Upon hearing about Sogavare's new open-door policy, I grew optimistic that my endless requests for an interview might be accommodated. Between September 2019 and June 2022, I had approached the prime minister's press team six times; on each occasion, I was politely rebuffed by the PM's genial, well-respected press secretary, George Herming.

I was not alone. As the world's attention was increasingly focused on Sogavare in the wake of the Switch, he went to considerable lengths to avoid speaking with reporters whom he viewed as hostile to his interests. In November 2019, two months after the Switch, Australian TV program *60 Minutes'* Liam Bartlett – one of the program's longest-serving reporters – travelled to Solomon Islands to investigate Honiara's ties with Beijing. The resulting episode, 'Seeing Red', was deeply problematic. It framed the Switch in predictably narrow terms, going so far as to dub China's new relationship with Solomon Islands as a 'soft invasion'. Perhaps sensing the likely hyperbole, Sogavare refused to speak with Bartlett, resulting in almost comical scenes. In one sequence, Bartlett chased Sogavare, who had just stepped out of a meeting, to his waiting car. Although *60 Minutes'* framing of the story was shallow, the images of Sogavare running away from a high-profile Australian reporter consolidated a caricature in many Australians' minds about him. Agitated by the *60 Minutes* ambush, for the next two years Sogavare's press office appeared to implement a near-universal blockade on interviews with the foreign press. It continued even as some of the world's most respected foreign publications turned their attention to the opaque world of Honiara politics.

By the time Solomon Islands' borders opened in July 2022, many of the once obscure characters of Solomons politics had become fixtures in the global press, some even writing opinion pieces and appearing on TV and YouTube news channels abroad, and thereby amplifying their prestige at home. With the exception of a handful of appearances on Chinese state news broadcasts, however, Sogavare remained conspicuously absent from direct engagement with journalists. He never extended interview opportunities to Western media and rarely took questions from local reporters.

During the Australian federal election campaign of May 2022, Sogavare's China deal became prominent in Australia's national debate and was framed by the Labor opposition, as well as much of the Australian commentariat, as a failure of the Liberal government's Pacific policy. Nevertheless, repeated attempts by Australian journalists to contact Sogavare were rebuffed. 'Prime Minister Sogavare's office was contacted for comment' became a routine coda to countless stories about Solomon Islands in the lead-up to the Australian poll.

Sogavare's refusal to engage with the media was sometimes deeply personal. In July 2022, while drinking cheap SolBrews at Honiara's Coral Sea Hotel, I received a late-night email from Michael Miller, *The Washington Post*'s Sydney correspondent. Miller had been covering the Pacific from Sydney since 2020, and like me had taken advantage of Solomon Islands' newly opened borders to report on China's Pacific Games construction projects and the Malaitan backlash. He was now on the final day of his assignment, and I invited him to join me at the Coral Sea for a debrief. When he arrived, I asked if he'd managed to get an audience with Sogavare. 'He was on my plane,' Miller said.

When Miller's flight to Honiara earlier that week had reached cruising altitude, a flight attendant told him that Sogavare was in seat 1A. Miller audaciously inched his way to the front of the plane and politely introduced himself. Miller was transparent about his intentions, telling Sogavare he was coming to Solomon Islands to report on the country's relationship with China and was hoping Sogavare might find time for an interview to tell his government's side of the story. Sogavare was polite, Miller said, and suggested Miller take up the matter with his nearby staff. Initially hopeful, Miller soon realised he was being rebuffed. After a few days in the capital, Sogavare and his staff refused to speak to him.

At first, I was convinced that Sogavare's reluctance to engage with Western journalists was probably based on poor advice. Perhaps the genial George Herming was telling the prime minister that it wasn't worth the effort. Despite my personal view that politicians' direct and frequent engagement with the media is a pillar of any democratic system, it is also true that no leader is at the beck and call of foreign reporters, no matter how prestigious the journalist's publication. Sogavare's media strategy, however, was becoming increasingly clear. In directly denying Miller's request, it was obvious that Sogavare was driving the media blockade.

Throughout his fourth prime ministership, Sogavare's reticence became further entrenched, and this had consequences. Routinely, he gave up opportunities to explain and argue for the extraordinary policy changes he was driving, and his silence allowed the growing international narrative that Solomon Islands was on the road to autocracy to go largely unchecked. Perhaps the Moti affair, for which Julian Moti himself had partially blamed a feverish Australian press, still weighed on Sogavare. Perhaps the *60 Minutes* ambush had confirmed in his mind that he was unlikely ever to get a fair hearing with foreign, and especially Australian, press. Whatever the reason, his reluctance to play the media game only served to create a vacuum. Sogavare was being caricatured as a quasi-dictator with a Trumpian belief in a grand media conspiracy, cosying up to the tyrants in Beijing. His political opponents were all too willing to fan this narrative flame: routinely, opposition leader Matthew Wale would label Sogavare an autocrat, knowing that the world was watching. Hungry for quotes, the foreign press would incorporate Wale's views into their stories. Sogavare was being defined by those he opposed.

14

RED LINE

IN EARLY 2022, AS SOGAVARE PREPARED to finalise the security pact with China, several thousand kilometres to his south, Australian prime minister Scott Morrison was bracing for a bruising, uphill election battle. Morrison had won a 'miracle' election victory three years earlier, defying opinion polls to narrowly triumph against his Australian Labor Party opponent, Bill Shorten. At the 2019 election, Morrison was still a relative unknown, but he leveraged his approachable persona against Shorten's unpopularity to prevail. By 2022, however, Morrison was a known commodity. He had made significant mistakes that raised questions not only about his polices, but also about his character. The Labor Party was quietly confident that, after nine years in opposition, 2022 would be their year.

News of the security deal between Solomon Islands and China first broke with a Reuters story on 24 March 2022, and it became a major Australian news story after a detailed document, leaked by Celsus Talifilu, was tweeted by New Zealand security academic Anna Powles the same day. Publicly the Morrison government claimed to have been blindsided. Zed Seselja, minister for the Pacific, told media that Australia only found out about the deal when it had leaked online. Australia's foreign minister, Marise Payne, offered a similar line. Some members of the Morrison government and some Australian intelligence personnel had been aware of a potential deal, however, for over a year. They had quietly dispatched several senior public servants to Honiara in the early months of 2022 to argue against any such deal. Seselja and Payne's insistence that the Australian government was unaware of the deal masked the considered diplomacy that had been occurring in the background.

This was all but confirmed on 27 March 2022, when Jim Molan, a back-bench Australian Liberal senator, was interviewed on Sky News Australia. The host just happened to be his daughter, Erin. 'This came as no surprise,' Molan said of the leaked draft security arrangement. 'I've been watching the prime minister and the national security ministers working on this for some time.'

It was soon reported in *The Sydney Morning Herald* that the leak had been orchestrated by Australian intelligence personnel, who had acquired a draft version of the supposed deal earlier in March. It was suggested that Australian intelligence officials, knowing that the deal was likely to proceed, had organised the leak, hoping it would place renewed public pressure on the Sogavare government, and potentially convince him to back away from the agreement.

Around the same time, Talifilu, who had widely distributed the leaked deal on social media, had begun to involve himself directly in the Australian political conversation. On 29 March, in an opinion piece for *The Sydney Morning Herald*, he wrote that Solomon Islands, under Sogavare, risked becoming 'a puppet state'.[1] 'The Sogavare government's proposed security agreement with China ... is bad news for both the Solomon Islands and the South Pacific region', he wrote.

Gone were the heavily capitalised, invective-laden Facebook posts that Talifilu had become known for. Instead, he was writing for a new audience, sounding an alarm and making Malaita's opposition known, but doing so in the language of a statesman – someone demanding to be taken seriously by the Australian establishment and leaning into the anxieties of the Australian public and Australian policymakers about China.

'China is intentionally dragging the Solomon Islands into their geopolitical battle with the United States. The people of the Solomons will suffer the fallout from this contest, just as they did when Japan invaded during World War II. But unlike 1942, China is using our own so-called leaders to accomplish their goals,' Talifilu wrote. He admonished the whole

Solomons political establishment, labelling them 'corrupt' and 'kleptocrats'. 'The nation is now an oligarchy, not a democracy.'

*

In the weeks after the deal was leaked, and just days before the 2022 Australian federal election was called, Scott Morrison recognised that there was a need for the Australian government to press its case to Sogavare publicly. In the government's view, Australia needed to be seen to be explaining directly to the Solomons leader that Australia repudiated Honiara's security deal with China, and that the deal would impact the bilateral relationship. Quiet diplomacy had failed to this point. But there was also a political imperative to take a more visible course of action. The Morrison government's reputation was by now being tarnished by a perception that it had failed to do all it could to stop the security deal proceeding. Although the Australian government recognised that changing Honiara's mind would be challenging, it also knew that, without a concerted, visible effort to do so, perceived inaction would harm its re-election prospects.

Internally, there was a debate as to which Australian minister should be dispatched to try to persuade Sogavare. Morrison himself could not undertake the mission. The election campaign was all but upon him, and the likely rejection of his pleas to Sogavare would have been a political humiliation. It was suggested Marise Payne, Australia's foreign minister, might undertake the task. As foreign minister and in her previous role as defence minister, she was familiar with Solomon Islands and with Sogavare. However, she was reluctant to make the visit, which caused consternation among some members of the Australian government. Finally, in late March, it was decided that Zed Seselja would meet with Sogavare to request, one final time, that the security deal with Beijing be rejected.

As preparations were being made for Seselja's visit, however, he was struck down with Covid-19. Under pandemic restrictions at the time, he was required to isolate for seven days and would not be able to enter Solomon Islands until he had tested negative for the disease. It would take nine days for Seselja's PCR tests to return to negative; by then, the writs had been issued for the Australian federal election, sending the Morrison government into caretaker mode. Conventionally, incumbent governments are not permitted to undertake major political or policy activities during this caretaker period. The national security implications of the looming China security deal, however, prompted the Labor opposition, led by Anthony Albanese, to accept the necessity of Seselja's audacious, last-ditch gambit.

On the morning of 13 April 2022, Seselja and Ewen McDonald, the senior Australian diplomat in charge of the Office of the Pacific, along with their staff, boarded a C17 Royal Australian Airforce transport plane in Canberra, bound for Honiara. Given the lack of commercial aircraft flying during the pandemic, the delegation was forced to rely on this much slower, more austere military transportation; the trip took much of the day and required a refuelling stop in Brisbane. The delegation sat in the cargo hold at the back of the aircraft, where the noise was so loud that it prohibited any preparation for the meeting during the flight.

When they arrived in Honiara late in the afternoon, they were quickly whisked away from the airport to briefings with Australian high commissioner Lachlan Strahan, now back in the country after recovering from his spinal injury, and his staff, ahead of their meeting with Sogavare, which was scheduled for the following morning.

The Australians were not confident that they could convince Sogavare to reverse course completely, but they were not entirely without hope. Intelligence officials had informed the Australian government that the pressure being placed on Sogavare from Australia and internationally may have been starting to shape his thinking. If he wasn't going to completely withdraw from the China security deal, it was thought, he might agree to amend certain provisions, to lessen the chance of a Chinese military base being established in Solomon Islands in the future. Once in Honiara, however, Seselja and McDonald were informed that it would not just be Sogavare and his senior advisors in the meeting. Instead, a large number of pro-China MPs who had vocally supported the Switch would be joining them. The Australians believed that these MPs had muscled their way into the meeting to ensure that Sogavare would not cave to Australian pressure. This would fundamentally change the dynamic of the conversation. Instead of a candid one-on-one between Sogavare and Seselja, the Solomons prime minister would have an audience of his most important parliamentary backers to entertain, and to cater for.

Before the pandemic, the Australian minister for the Pacific would have expected a rigorous travel schedule. One of the portfolio's key responsibilities is managing Australia's relationships with governments and other organisations throughout the vast Pacific Island region. But Covid-19 had made that impossible, and Seselja's last-minute dash to Honiara was his first visit to Solomon Islands.

The Australians' strategy focused on highlighting the Australian government's commitment to Honiara, as demonstrated by the troop deployment it had made, on Sogavare's request, after the November riots. They wanted to press home that Australia remained a reliable partner – that when Sogavare required it, Australian military personnel were dispatched almost immediately, rendering any similar arrangement with the Chinese unnecessary. To stress this point, the delegation met with senior Australian Defence Force and Australian Federal Police personnel on the ground in Honiara the morning of their meeting with Sogavare, thanking them for their contribution to the peacekeeping efforts, before heading down Mendaña Avenue to the Office of Prime Minister and Cabinet.

There, the delegation was ushered into a large meeting room. While there were just four Australians present – Seselja, Ewen McDonald, Lachlan Strahan and Seselja's chief of staff – Solomon Islands were represented by a large number of ministers, MPs and their staff, as the intelligence officials had forewarned Seselja and MacDonald. After a few minutes of pleasantries and introductions, Sogavare entered the room, and the atmosphere quickly changed.

Sogavare was visibly tense. He began by expressing frustration that, despite his repeated assurances that he would not be changing course on the China security deal, he was again being confronted by an Australian delegation asking him to do just that. A few months earlier, a detachment of senior Australian bureaucrats had come to make the same request; Sogavare said he was struggling to see the point in this exercise in futility.

The Australians were taken aback by Sogavare's frustrations, but proceeded with their original strategy. Seselja led the meeting and began by emphasising how quickly the Morrison government had responded to Sogavare's requests for assistance during the November riots; ADF and AFP personnel were on the ground within twenty-four hours of Sogavare's formal ask. This demonstrated not only Australia's commitment to Solomon Islands, Seselja argued, but also its capacity to deliver. A security deal between Honiara and Beijing, by contrast, would not be in the interests of Solomon Islands, Australia or the Pacific region more broadly. Seselja cited the case of Djibouti – a small country in the Horn of Africa – which in 2015 had permitted China to establish a military base on its soil. The Australians argued that, ultimately, this had led to an undermining of Djibouti's sovereignty, and that without appropriate safeguards, Solomon Islands would be next. Australia, in contrast, respected Solomon Islands' sovereignty, and the existing security relationship between Canberra and Honiara had proved effective.

Sogavare seemed surprised at just how forcefully Seselja made these points. But he had heard all these arguments before. After politely listening to Seselja, Sogavare rebutted with an extended, impassioned rejection of Australia's demands. The security deal with China, he said, merely provided Solomon Islands with an alternative option should there ever be a breakdown in the relationship with Australia. He promised Australia remained Honiara's 'partner of choice'. He denied that any military base would be established by China on Solomons soil. Even so, he suggested, Western powers were in no position to criticise China for its aspirations to have military bases around the world, given America's global military footprint, including in Australia.

Sogavare then began an extended diatribe expressing his scepticism about Australia's interests in Solomon Islands. John Howard, he argued, had never wanted to undertake the RAMSI mission; Howard's commitment to Solomon Islands had not been sincere. Without mentioning the

Julian Moti affair or the 2006 AFP raid on his office specifically, Sogavare claimed that during his previous prime ministerships, Australia had intentionally undermined him politically. As for Australia's involvement after the November riots – the Australian peacekeepers, he alleged, had refused to protect the Chinese embassy in Tandai. This persistent rumour was not true; the Australians had protected the embassy, along with countless public buildings and key pieces of infrastructure. Seselja and McDonald stressed this to Sogavare, but Sogavare didn't budge.

Recognising that they would be unable to convince Sogavare to back down from the China deal entirely, they began to lobby him to make amendments to the pact, including a formal confirmation that there would be no Chinese base in Solomon Islands. Seselja also suggested that the bilateral deal be made public, in line with the broader expectations of the region, not just of Australia. Sogavare did not refuse either of these requests, but explained that he could not unilaterally agree to them without first consulting the Chinese.

It was clear to the Australian delegation that Sogavare was using the meeting as an opportunity to perform for the most important bloc of supporters in the parliament: the pro-China MPs who, early in 2019, had threatened to oust him should he not wholeheartedly support the Switch to China. Sogavare may have been perceived, by now, as an all-powerful leader, but he remained vulnerable to any shift in sentiment among his parliamentary backers. Recognising this, he didn't give an inch in the meeting. In the process, he further consolidated the support of the bloc of pro-China MPs who were in the room.

Since returning to the prime ministership in 2019, Sogavare had openly told Australian officials that his chief concern was to remain in power for the rest of the parliamentary term. Despite knowing this, and knowing that Sogavare's political survival depended on the support of the pro-China MPs in his parliamentary coalition, the Australian government proceeded with a meeting that included this bloc of MPs, giving Sogavare a platform from which to consolidate his parliamentary supporter base. Instead of weakening the Solomons–China relationship, this last-ditch gambit by the Morrison government, designed primarily to save face before a bruising Australian election campaign, had only strengthened it. And once again, Sogavare had deftly shaped a potential threat to his personal political advantage.

The Australians had ultimately failed. The security deal with China was signed six days later, on 20 April 2022. Its final details were never made public.

*

By the time Zed Seselja returned to Australia, Scott Morrison had set the election date for 21 May. His government had five weeks to convince the Australian public they deserved another three years in power. Their chances of re-election were low, but almost immediately, a series of clumsy gaffes by the Labor opposition leader, Anthony Albanese, dented Labor's confidence and kept the Morrison government in the fight. On the second day of the campaign, Albanese was asked a simple question: what was the Australian unemployment rate? He faltered, awkwardly stating that he couldn't recall. This small mistake was seized upon by Morrison and damaged morale in Labor's campaign headquarters.

After a difficult first week, the Labor campaign was hoping for a better week two. But then it received even worse news: Albanese had contracted Covid-19 and would have to quarantine in his inner-Sydney home for the next seven days, deputising much of the public campaigning to his front bench. For Labor supporters who had watched a potentially victorious campaign flounder in 2019, it felt like déjà vu. At Labor's austere Surry Hills campaign headquarters, strategists had to get creative.

Typically, foreign policy issues make little impact on Australian elections. Votes are won on hip-pocket issues: the Australian electorate wants to know who is better positioned to make its economic life easier. Occasionally, this has been disrupted by external events. Australia's 2001 election was held just two months after the September 11 attacks on the World Trade Center, allowing the Howard government to leverage its national security credentials and brutal asylum-seeker policies. The 2001 election was an anomaly – but in the months leading up to the 2022 election, the regular media coverage of China's encroachment into the Pacific had once again thrust national security onto the election agenda. Usually, this dynamic would favour a conservative government in Australia, and Morrison was confident this would hold true for the 2022 poll. The Liberal–National Coalition's foreign and security policy is generally more blunt, harsh and nativist than that of the Australian Labor Party, and this hardline rhetoric has often been favoured by the public, while Labor's more nuanced positions have made it vulnerable to accusations of weakness. But the Pacific, and China's growing presence in it, had become a weak spot for the Morrison government.

Many critics accused the government of having been 'asleep at the wheel' in the Pacific. In fact, it had implemented a suite of big-spending initiatives under its 'Pacific Step-up' agenda – one of Morrison's first major policy initiatives after he assumed the party leadership in September 2018. Morrison, a devout evangelical Christian who had travelled widely in the Pacific with his family as a child, was personally popular in much of the region, and despite a few clumsy interventions from his colleagues, the language he used when discussing the region was often well received in the Pacific.

But Morrison and his government had a major weakness when it came to dealing with the region: climate change. The Morrison government's inability to implement meaningful policy to reduce Australia's carbon emissions had become a sticking point. For years, Pacific Island countries had been publicly calling out Morrison and his conservative predecessors for their tepid climate policies. For many Pacific countries, climate change is the pre-eminent challenge, and also a profound opportunity. Although Pacific countries are vulnerable to the effects of climate change, mitigation measures in these countries are creating investment opportunities and allowing the Pacific to play an outsized diplomatic role on the world stage. With its inadequate policy settings on climate, the Morrison government was missing an opportunity to strengthen and broaden the Australia–Pacific relationship, while giving Pacific countries an incentive to find other development partners.

By May 2022, the Pacific's vocal frustration with the Morrison government's climate inaction had become an election issue. For Labor, it presented an opportunity to undermine Morrison's foreign policy credibility and neutralise the government's advantage on national security. In the months leading up to the election, Labor's foreign policy team, led by South Australian senator Penny Wong as shadow foreign minister, and with Pat Conroy as shadow minister for international development and the Pacific, began quietly crafting a comprehensive policy announcement that it would use to create a point of distinction on the Pacific between the two parties.

In planning for the Pacific announcement, Labor's campaign strategists had two aims. First, as Albanese was off the campaign trail, Labor wanted to give its most talented frontbenchers airtime. Penny Wong, among the most formidable and skilful politicians in the Australian parliament, was one of those talents who could command attention while Albanese was recovering from Covid. By proving the party wasn't a one-man show, Labor would be demonstrating to the electorate that it was ready to govern.

Labor strategists were also eager to play on voters' anxiety about China and to demonstrate that only a Labor government could counteract it. Despite Sogavare's assurances that the security deal would not lead to a Chinese military base in the Solomons, that risk was being widely discussed in Australia. Australians were on edge about the perceived threat, and Labor had repeatedly blamed the Morrison government's ineptitude in the Pacific, including it poor track record on climate, for the emergence of these threats.

To capitalise on this anxiety, Labor strategists planned to make the Pacific announcement in Australia's far north. They initially planned for Penny Wong and Pat Conroy to do it in Townsville, in northern Queensland. It was from Townsville that, five months earlier, Australian Defence Force personnel had scrambled to Honiara to quell the unrest. Labor wanted to highlight this proximity, subtly reminding Australians that, if China were to have a naval base in the Solomons, it would only be a two-hour flight from one of Australia's largest military bases.

As Labor readied for the announcement, however, it heard that Morrison would also be in Townsville and decided to move the press conference to Darwin. The largest city in Australia's Northern Territory, Darwin is no stranger to foreign attack: in 1942, it became the only city in Australia to be subjected to Japanese air raids. More recently, the city had become a case study in the Liberal–National government's mismanagement of the relationship with China. In 2016, when Morrison was treasurer under his predecessor as prime minister, Malcolm Turnbull, the Port of Darwin was leased to a Chinese-owned company, Landbridge.[2] The sale came after an open bidding process, with Landbridge offering significantly more than its competitors to secure control of the strategically critical port. It was a controversial decision. President Barack Obama even expressed US concerns about the deal. Morrison government ministers responded to the criticism by accusing Labor of being 'soft on China' – the defence minister even accused his counterpart of being a 'Manchurian candidate' during the campaign – but the Darwin Port saga suggested to some Australian voters that the Liberal government, rather than the Labor opposition, was leaving Australia vulnerable to Chinese expansionism. Labor's Pacific announcement would reinforce that narrative.

In the days leading up to the announcement, Penny Wong began laying the groundwork, deploying increasingly sharp rhetoric criticising Scott Morrison's inability to keep Australians safe. On Wednesday 20 April, Wong told the ABC that the Solomons–China security pact was 'the worst foreign policy blunder in the Pacific that Australia has seen since the end of World War Two ... it is going to make our region less secure and this has all happened on Scott Morrison's watch.' She admonished the government for having sent a 'junior woodchuck' in Pacific minister Zed Seselja to lobby Sogavare to abandon the deal. The pressure was getting to the government, causing unforced errors. When asked about the criticisms, Australia's deputy prime minister, Barnaby Joyce, conceded the seriousness of the threat, arguing that Australia 'didn't want a little Cuba on its doorstep', a reference to Cuba's hosting of Soviet nuclear missiles just 120 kilometres from US soil in the 1960s.

Sensing its strategy was working, Labor continued its attacks. The shadow treasurer, Jim Chalmers, stated that the Morrison government's cuts to foreign-aid spending were to blame for the security deal. 'The fact is the government cut aid. And it is a common view across the national security establishment that this has been detrimental to our interests in the Pacific', he said.

The Morrison government's handling of the security deal had become a useful proxy for the government's broader failures. It spoke to its inadequacies on climate change and Morrison's tendency not to take responsibility for his government's mistakes, and it shone a spotlight on the government's deteriorating relationship with Beijing.

Until this point, Morrison had been reluctant to change his tune. His usual response to questions about the security deal emphasised Solomon Islands' sovereign decision making. He rejected criticism of his decision to send Seselja rather than foreign minister Marise Payne to lobby against the security deal, saying he had acted on departmental advice. But by 24 April, he had changed tack. When pressed about the China threat, Morrison responded forcefully. 'We won't be having a Chinese military base in our region and on our doorstep,' he said, adding that this would be a 'red line' – a line that Australia shared with the United States, New Zealand and other Pacific countries.

Morrison added that Sogavare 'clearly shares our red line', but the comment was nonetheless viewed as a veiled threat to Honiara. Reporters began asking what Australia's reaction would be should that 'red line' be crossed. Was Morrison suggesting military intervention? Was he suggesting trade sanctions? Would he consider some of the wilder forms of retribution suggested by some commentators, such as barring Sogavare and his allies from accessing Australian visas, or ending the flow of migrant workers from Solomon Islands? The meaning of Morrison's 'red line' comment was unclear. But it demonstrated that he had lost control of the narrative and in some respects the campaign.

Two weeks later, Sogavare took to the floor of parliament in Honiara, accusing Morrison of treating Solomon Islanders like 'kindergarten students'. Morrison's comments, Sogavare said, could be understood as a 'warning of military intervention'.[3]

The morning after Morrison made his 'red line' comments, Wong and Conroy flew to Darwin to announce Labor's detailed Pacific policy package. It was a sweeping program, covering seven policy areas including clean energy and security, Australia's soft-power projection, an expansion of traditional aid investment and an increase in senior political visits to the region. The policy was significant, but equally important was how it was delivered. 'The vacuum Scott Morrison has created is being filled by others who do not share our interests and values,' Wong said in Darwin, suggesting that only under a Labor government could Australia's relationship with Sogavare be repaired.

The politicisation of the Solomon Islands' security deal with Beijing was not the only issue which helped the ALP win the 2022 election. But Labor insiders believe it was essential in turning their campaign around after a turbulent first week. The ability of Wong, Conroy, Chalmers and Albanese to leverage the security deal to Labor's political advantage shifted the momentum of the campaign back towards the Labor Party. Labor's success in capitalising on the security deal also reinvigorated the party's morale. For the rest of the campaign, the focus returned to traditional 'bread-and-butter' economic issues: jobs, wages, interest rates, housing affordability. But the Solomon Islands issue continued to re-emerge every couple of days. Sogavare's face was on Australian TV screens regularly, and the media were hungry for any information about the extent of China's involvement in the region. Australians were scared, and they were scared about an issue they now believed the Morrison government had no capacity to influence.

On 21 May, Australian electors overwhelmingly rejected the Morrison government. Anthony Albanese would be Australia's new prime minister, and the first Labor leader to win a majority in Canberra in fifteen years.

The Sogavare relationship was now his to fix.

15

ARC OF ANXIETY

BEYOND SOLOMON ISLANDS, THE SECURITY PACT crystallised the fears of international observers for whom documenting China's 'capture' of Honiara had become a preoccupation. Throughout the rest of 2022, a cavalcade of commentators weighed in on Sogavare's security deal, often stoking dire warnings in the Australian and international press about the country's imminent descent into dictatorship.

In August 2022 in *The Australian*, Cleo Paskal and Anthony Bergin co-authored an article detailing the 'coup' Sogavare was attempting to mount in Honiara. The catalyst for the article was Sogavare's absence from a World War Two commemoration. August 2022 marked eighty years since the commencement of the Battle of Guadalcanal, the six-month-long campaign by Allied forces that had successfully recaptured the Solomon Archipelago from Japan between August 1942 and January 1943. The campaign is widely considered a turning point in the Pacific War. It also carries particular symbolism for the United States: future president John F. Kennedy, aged twenty-six, has been justifiably feted for his actions during the campaign, after the patrol boat he commanded was struck by a Japanese warship. After Kennedy's boat sank, he embarked on an extraordinary physical feat, swimming back and forth between the shipwreck and an island several kilometres away, each time rescuing a fellow sailor. Stranded on the island for days, Kennedy relied on locals to sneak communications past the Japanese patrols nearby. A coconut inscribed with a plea for help was carried by local islanders Biuku Gasa and Eroni Kumana to Allied forces, who were then able to rescue Kennedy and his crew. The coconut sat on the Resolute Desk in the White House during Kennedy's short presidency; he experienced crippling back pain related to the events for the remaining years of his life.

So important was the eighty-year anniversary to the United States that Washington dispatched the new US ambassador to Australia, Caroline Kennedy – the daughter of John F. Kennedy – to Honiara for the event. The symbolism was clear. A dawn service was held at Bloody Ridge, the site of a decisive Allied victory early in the battle, with senior American and Australian representatives in attendance.

Prime Minister Sogavare, however, 'didn't bother turning up to the commemoration', as Paskal and Bergin wrote in *The Australian*. He was 'busy putting forward a bill to postpone the scheduled 2023 elections', they speculated.

Sogavare's intention to delay the 2023 elections was by now causing genuine concerns, locally and internationally. His argument that the country didn't have enough money to host both the games and an election in the same calendar year was hardly credible and invited legitimate criticism. But Paskal and Bergin's commentary went further, invoking a contemporary version of the Cold War 'domino theory': if Solomon Islands were to descend into autocracy, they argued, the contagion would spread:

> Sogavare's move is an attempted coup against the people of Solomon Islands. He is trying to turn his country into a clone of China, by taking control of media, signing secret security deals, using bribery to change the constitution, and preparing to instigate and then crush dissent ... It's a coup with Chinese characteristics, and if it's not stopped in the Solomons, it will spread.[1]

Paskal and Bergin's arguments were alarming. But they merged genuine concerns about Sogavare's disregard for democratic principles with less convincing grievances. The absence of Sogavare from the World War Two commemoration wasn't necessarily intended as a slap in the face to the West. The Sogavare government was represented at the commemorations by a minister, and no other head of government had travelled to Solomons for the ceremony. Instead of being seen as the triviality it was, however, the episode became caricatured as evidence of Sogavare's unrelenting opposition to the West.

From a Western perspective, the significance of the ceremony may have been unambiguous. The Allied victory in Guadalcanal set in train the events that saw America prevail over Japan. But within Solomon Islands, the legacy of that battle is more complex. Some still feel a deep pride about the role Solomon Islanders played in assisting Allied forces, but the conflict doesn't carry the same 'coming-of-age' significance as it does in the US and Australia. After the ceremony, US deputy secretary of state Wendy Sherman told Australian TV's Sarah Ferguson that the Battle of Guadalcanal was crucial in enabling a 'free Solomon Islands, a democracy, an independent country',[2] but it wasn't until 1978, thirty-six years later, that Solomon Islands emerged from the colonial yoke as a nation of its own.

For many Solomon Islanders, the consequences of the Battle of Guadalcanal aren't a distant memory; they still impact daily life, even in the capital. In the year leading up to the August 2022 ceremony, four people were killed in Honiara by unexploded American-made World War Two bombs, thousands of which remain shallowly buried under Guadalcanal's topsoil. At a Mother's Day party in May 2021, fifty-year-old Honiara resident Maeverlyn Pitanoe was cooking over an open-pit barbecue at the house of her friend Rusilla Posala. Without warning, a tremendous explosion engulfed Pitanoe and the thirty other guests. After she regained consciousness, Pitanoe noticed her 'arms, legs and torso were shredded', and saw 'two fingers hanging, one ... already gone'.[3] After fifty-three days in hospital, she returned home. Two people were killed in the explosion: Charles Noda and Raziv Hilly, young men who had 'led exemplary lives and were on the way up in their professional careers'.[4] Noda died several days after the blast, succumbing to catastrophic injuries at the poorly equipped and understaffed National Referral Hospital. Hilly – Posala's nephew – died instantly. Speaking to media in the wake of the blast, a shocked Posala noted the irony that her uncle, Biaku Gasa, had been one of the islanders who helped rescue John F. Kennedy during the war; decades later, 'the war has now claimed [Gasa's] great nephew'.[5] In the *Solomon Times*, Honiara resident Andrew Koronihona lamented: 'WW2 was someone else's conflict thrust onto our shores without our consent, permission or even collaboration. The co-conspirators have moved on and yet 79 years on, [Solomon Islands] is still counting the high cost. Two local elite young men, in the prime of their lives with a bright future, had to be tragically cut short by the ongoing post-war fallout.'

In framing minor episodes such as the World War Two memorial as part of a battle between the West and Beijing, analyses such as Paskal and Bergin's may be problematic, but they are not all hyperbole. They are right to express concerns about the state of Solomon Islands' democracy, and Sogavare's actions demand intense scrutiny. I share their concerns about democratic backsliding in Solomon Islands. Solomon Islanders I know cherish their democracy and are often fearful of China's growing presence – both real and perceived – in their daily lives. Some don't believe Sogavare has the capacity to withstand Chinese coercion. Concerns about Sogavare's approach are shared by a diverse set of internal critics, many of whom have been able to gain considerable influence within Solomon Islands by presenting themselves as fierce opponents of the prime minister.

With such intense scrutiny on Sogavare, however, trivial events such as the World War Two commemoration ceremony have been taken out of context and analysed through an altogether foreign lens. Often, this has been encouraged by Sogavare's political opponents, whose description of him as an 'autocrat' are invariably reported by international media, and who, with considerable savvy, have been able to shape a deeply unflattering caricature of the prime minister, improving their own political fortunes in the process.

The longer I analysed the emerging public commentary on Sogavare, the louder the chorus of voices expressing opinions about his psychology seemed to grow. It appeared many international analysts aspired to become authorities on this exotic soon-to-be dictator, irrespective of their experience in Solomon Islands or their familiarity with its history.

Two weeks after Paskal and Bergin's article, Dave Sharma, a former Australian ambassador to Israel and recently deposed member of Australia's federal parliament, warned in *The Australian* that Sogavare's Solomon Islands posed a threat to Australia. Citing a number of genuinely concerning developments – the security deal, Sogavare's decision to delay the election, Huawei's investment in the country's telecommunications infrastructure and a reduction of state funding of the national broadcaster – Sharma declared that Sogavare was 'redolent of an autocratic leader in the time of the Cold War'. Critical of the new Albanese government, Sharma argued that Canberra must focus not only on supporting 'development and infrastructure' when dealing with Solomon Islands, but also on 'institutions and governance', omitting to mention that the primary focus of Australian development assistance over two decades in Solomon Islands had been on exactly that – and that this approach had accrued power and control in Honiara, frustrating Solomon Islanders and making the country particularly amenable to foreign influence. 'The prospective establishment of a client-state autocracy in our neighbourhood – a Cuba in the Pacific – demands urgent action,' Sharma warned, without specifying what type of action.[6] This unhelpful caricature – *A Cuba in the Pacific* – would stick, with *The Australian* using the term to describe Solomon Islands in future editorials, including one published the morning of a visit by Sogavare to Canberra.[7]

Sogavare was also growing in notoriety beyond Australia. One Canadian academic took to the pages of conservative US magazine *The National Interest* to make the case that Australia should abandon its policy of 'non-intervention' in Solomons, citing among other reasons Sogavare's 'Western antipathy', as demonstrated by his 'absence from the August 2022 Second World War Memorial'. Again invoking an antiquated Cold War, 'slippery-slope' framing, the author continued: 'If the threat of a deterrent intervention is foreclosed against the Solomon Islands, neighbouring island nations will see the benefits of playing China against the coalition of liberal democracies, creating a ring of hostile bases as the Japanese did during World War II. There are plenty of other socio-economic dislocations in Micronesia and Melanesia for China to exploit.'[8]

It is tempting to dismiss such analysis, but it doesn't occur within a vacuum, and it isn't only consumed by foreign audiences. Within Solomon Islands, international commentary is closely followed and widely distributed. Each time I have written an article for an international newspaper or provided a comment to another journalist on anything to do with Solomon Islands, it isn't long before I see my words spreading across the many active Facebook groups dedicated to Solomons affairs. The same is true of most commentary about the country, especially any related to its relationship with China. Even obscure articles from distant countries and YouTube videos by bedroom analysts became part of the daily content feeds of Solomon Islanders. Paskal's *Sunday Guardian* commentary – which often praises Sogavare's opponents such as Peter Kenilorea Jnr and Daniel Suidani while denigrating the prime minister – is routinely shared in influential Facebook groups such as 'Malaita Provincial Development Forum', in which Celsus Talifilu posts daily. Increasingly, Facebook has become Solomon Islanders' primary public square.

In October 2022, the Australian Strategic Policy Institute (ASPI) released an investigative report, *Suppressing the Truth and Spreading Lies: How the CCP Is Influencing Solomon Islands' Information Environment*.[9] Over the preceding years, ASPI had produced compelling research into China's influence campaigns and into human rights violations in Xinjiang. The organisation had become so influential in calling out China's abuses that it had stoked the ire of Beijing. In November 2020, a list of fourteen 'grievances' that China had with Australia was leaked to Australian journalist Jonathan Kearsley, one of which was a direct criticism of ASPI. China was incensed that the Australian government 'provided funding to [an] anti-China think tank for spreading untrue reports, peddling lies around Xinjiang and so-called China infiltration aimed at manipulating public opinion against China'.[10]

Beijing's diatribe was clearly directed at ASPI, which had only recently released an extraordinarily in-depth examination of the establishment of detention centres in western China. I was glad to see the research and its impact. In April 2018, I had taken the long bus ride from Ürümqi, the capital of Xinjiang, to Khorgas, a border town straddling the Kazakhstan–China frontier. For thirteen hours I sat next to a young ethnic Kazakh doctor, who, despite spending her whole life in China, was hoping to flee over the border. Her husband, also a doctor and ethnic Kazakh Muslim, had been 'disappeared' in Xinjiang several years earlier. When I disembarked in Khorgas, I was confronted with a dystopian scene: armoured vehicles and heavily armed police on every corner. ASPI's exposé on China's activities in Xinjiang was thorough and damning and inspired international condemnation. That the influential ASPI had now turned its attention to China's focus on Solomon Islands reflected just how central to Australia's own security conversation the Beijing–Honiara relationship had become.

The ASPI investigation into China's influence in the Solomons focused on traditional and social media and attempted to examine the efficacy of China's influence activities in the wake of the November riots. It found that China's most consequential efforts came in the traditional media space. 'CCP official-led articles published in local media – including opinion pieces, press releases and other quote-based articles – are the most effective method of propagating CCP narratives in Solomon Islands' online information environment,' the researchers found. But in the online realm, China's efforts were found to be largely ineffective. ASPI researchers painstakingly scoured thousands of comments in public Facebook groups from the days after the November 2021 riots. It found that China's state-run media outlets 'had little impact on and penetration into the Solomon Islands' online information environment'. China-produced media reports were 'rarely shared in public Facebook groups and, when they were shared, received mostly anti-China comments in response'. In its sentiment analysis – a research technique examining key words and phrases to ascertain the views of commenters – ASPI found only marginal success by China's influence machine in shifting public views in Solomons.

ASPI's research also noted the establishment of a Facebook group in the aftermath of the November 2021 riots called 'Solomon Islands for china [sic]'. The group had just over 1000 members and shared a plethora of content, ranging from explanations of an upcoming Chinese holiday to YouTube videos documenting China's planned 2033 Mars mission. Most posts in the channel registered no user activity: although there were more than ten posts a day, there were no reactions or comments on the vast majority. This was in contrast to the large and very active Facebook groups that had a much greater influence on the day-to-day discourse in the country.

Ultimately, the ASPI investigation made clear that, while there may be some desire by Chinese authorities to influence social and traditional media in Solomon Islands, their efforts thus far had amounted to little. China remained deeply unpopular with digital audiences in the country, who appeared resistant to whatever attempt to control the narrative Beijing was making. When ASPI released this measured research, however, media coverage of the report suggested the opposite – that China was undertaking a deeply sophisticated and even *successful* influence campaign, focused on undermining Australia's brand in the country. Such an interpretation was furthered by ASPI's executive director, Justin Bassi. A former senior advisor to Australian foreign minister Marise Payne, in an interview about the research Bassi suggested that Australia's brand in the country had been undermined by a coordinated effort to blame the November riots on Australia and the United States.[11] This interpretation appeared to contradict the detailed findings in the report, which in many respects demonstrated Solomon Islands' resilience, rather than its vulnerability, to rather poorly coordinated Chinese propaganda campaigns. The ASPI report further suggested that there be more training for Solomon Islands' journalists, so that they would be able to be resilient in thwarting Chinese propaganda. This recommendation seemed to mirror an already established entity: the Pacific Media Assistance Scheme, a program that sees the Australian Broadcasting Corporation send journalists to Honiara to run training annually.

Whatever the merits of the ASPI report, its very existence demonstrated just how central Solomon Islands had become to Australia's national security debate. But the interpretation of the report was also illustrative of a deeply diminutive view many observers had of Solomon Islanders, even if subconsciously. The report did document a desire by Beijing to shape public opinion in Solomon Islands. This reflects a broader international propaganda mission by Beijing and is a legitimate concern. But the research also demonstrated that despite these efforts, most Solomon Islanders remained unconvinced, and unmalleable to foreign viewpoints that directly contradict their own. Solomon Islanders remained generally critical of China's approach in their country and publicly said so. Despite Sogavare's relationship with China, a clear majority of everyday Solomon Islanders remained deeply sceptical. China's influence campaign appeared to have had more of an effect on Australian public opinion, which tended to exaggerate the scale of the threat, rather than on opinions in the country it was supposedly victimising.

By mid-2022, Solomon Islands had become a 'big deal',[12] having metastasised into an issue on which many of Australia's most powerful voices were discussing. But despite this coverage, an overwhelming gap remained: the voice of everyday Solomon Islanders. Just as Sogavare's brand had started to be defined by those outside the country, Solomon Islands itself was becoming caricatured – emerging as a vector for Australian and international anxiety about China, and as a totem of the foreign policy mistakes of the broader West.

PART VI
WHERE THE NORTH ROAD ENDS

16

HENDERSON CONCESSION

ON 28 JUNE 2022, PRIME MINISTER SOGAVARE took to the podium in his office. In just three days' time, he announced, Solomon Islands' border would be normalised. From 1 July, two and a half years of strict border enforcement would come to an end. With the easing of restrictions, I quickly booked a flight back to the country, returning on the fourth Solomon Airlines flight into Honiara. For the first time, I had brought my girlfriend Emily with me, determined to show her the country I'd been regaling her with tales about since my last visit. Typically, the plane contained few tourists. Most of those heading to Honiara were Solomon Islanders coming home, or Australian and Chinese officials entering on business. In the row in front of us sat three Australian army personnel, coming to Honiara to negotiate the final details of Canberra's promise to deliver marine patrol boats to Solomon Islands.

As I arrived back in the country, it felt as if nothing had changed. The austere immigration and customs infrastructure was still in place, despite the various new processes necessitated by Covid-19. The dilapidated, pot-holed road linking Henderson Airport to the capital remained unimproved. The ramshackle market stalls selling betel nut and coconut were still there. The distinct smell of the humid air, mixed with burning rubbish and tropical life, struck the same as ever.

*

It had been two and a half years since I had last seen Richard Olita, when we had sat by Lake Ozi, drinking SolBrews, overlooking the lapping waves, talking about his grand plans for Malaita for Democracy. I'd worked diligently to maintain our relationship, and it would prove a fruitful one. Although Olita has his own agenda and could be provocative, if not untruthful, in telling certain stories, he nevertheless remained a central character in the story of Malaita's push against the Sogavare government. He wasn't only a useful source, providing colourful commentary on the endless oscillations of Solomon Islands' politics – he was a gateway to others. As the investigation into the November riots drew on, much of the focus descended on three men who allegedly 'masterminded' the plot: Olita, Lawrence Makili, and the hitherto behind-the-scenes leader of M4D, Knoxley Atu.

On our first night in Solomon Islands, Emily and I waited at the front of the King Solomon Hotel as darkness fell. We were there to meet Olita and his M4D colleague, Knoxley Atu. At this hour, Honiara becomes a little more tolerable. The sun casts an orange hue down the west–east oriented streetscapes; the afternoon breeze takes the sting out of the heat; and the chaotic scrum of daily life in the capital cedes to a quiet rhythm more aligned to the island life of my imagination. As we waited, we speculated about which approaching car might be Olita's. I'd imagined a beaten-up mid-1990s Toyota Corolla, hundreds of dilapidated examples of which can be found on Honiara's many potholed roads. I was wrong.

Blaring down the road came a large, showroom-quality GM pick-up truck. Chrome blue with alloy wheels and a tray detailed with military armour–style trimmings, the vehicle had tinted windows so dark we couldn't see inside from just metres away. It pulled up hurriedly, stirring up dust in the twilight. Out stepped Olita.

Olita, now thirty-eight, appeared much the same as when we had last met in Auki. His beard and his waist were thicker, but his handshake remained firm and his outwardly serious demeanour could still be penetrated with a well-timed, self-deprecating joke about my Australian intolerance of the equatorial heat. Olita presents himself as a strong man, but in person, he is easy to disarm. His betel-nut-stained smile is large when he first greets you, and his laughter is bellowing, befitting of his stature.

I had promised Emily, an overworked and underpaid schoolteacher, an island holiday – an escape from the frigid midwinter of Adelaide to chase the warmth of the South Pacific. Instead, we were heading out for an intimate evening with a man on trial for arson, rioting and treason, on the unlit fringes of outer-suburban Honiara.

In the driver's seat of the ute sat Olita's cousin, Hayden. In his early twenties and standing more than six feet tall, Hayden had recently inherited a considerable fortune. His father, an MP and successful Malaitan business-man, had passed away in 2020, providing Hayden with enough money to buy what would appear to be one of the most expensive cars in Solomon Islands. Emily and I took our seats (leather and unnecessarily equipped with a heating function), and we began driving through the backroads of the capital. As we inched up behind Kukum, where a police station had been burned during the November riots, Olita, from the front passenger seat, went out of his way to explain the significance of the area.

'Just at this corner,' Olita said, 'was where the RAMSI officer was shot.'

On 22 December 2004, Andrew Dunning, a 26-year-old Australian Federal Police officer, received two fatal gunshot wounds from a high-powered rifle while on patrol in this district. It was an orchestrated assassination – the only attack of its kind during the fourteen-year peacekeeping operation.

As we continued to snake our way up the mountain roads, the relative modernity of downtown Honiara was replaced by dark slums.

'Look at all the fires,' Emily commented, noting the thick smoke that was hanging low in the deep valleys of the hills district.

'Dinner time,' said Olita.

Populated largely by Malaitan émigrés, the communities on Honiara's urban fringe house the most acutely disadvantaged people in the city. Eking out an existence here has always been a challenge. Most young men – by some estimates more than 60 per cent – are unemployed. Unlike in the rural villages, there is no opportunity to cultivate crops and survive off the land. For decades, the economic disenfranchisement evident in these improvised, quasi-legal squatter settlements has provided fertile ground for political instability. Now, it had also become a temporary home for those awaiting the legal repercussions of their alleged involvement in the November 2021 Honiara riots.

Olita had led us to this dark corner of Honiara to collect a man who, until now, had been an enigma to me. I'd spent considerable time in Malaita, speaking to agitators and members of Malaita for Democracy. But Knoxley Atu, the supposed founder of M4D, had so far remained elusive. He had finally agreed to meet, but given he had been charged with eight crimes associated with the riots, it was only possible if we did so in private, and without informing any authorities. In the months after Honiara burned, Atu had been on the run.

Forty-eight years old and with a grey beard, receding hairline and small, recessed eyes, Atu had achieved national infamy. Having first gained notoriety as the enigmatic, behind-the-scenes leader of M4D, his stature had risen considerably since the riots. It was Atu, as well as Olita and a handful of other, unspecified dissidents, who had planned what they described as a 'peaceful sit-in' on that November morning. But no matter how adamant the organisers were that their intentions had been peaceful, they were now indelibly associated with the devastating outcome. The government, desperate to pin the blame on someone, had rounded on the head of M4D.

Perpetually dressed in khaki – his trademark outfit includes a floppy beige hat, a sleeveless beige fishing jacket and tattered jeans – Atu appeared almost a caricature of a revolutionary dissident. I'd seen his face, sunken under his hat's sagging brim, regularly in the *Solomon Star*, which had reported with relish his now infamous escape from the RSIPF earlier in 2022. Atu's involvement in the riots had always been known by authorities. But by the time his arrest warrant was ordered, he had relocated to his remote home village in northern Malaita. In fact, just moments after the riots began, Atu, sensing the day was spiralling out of control, had fled back to Malaita in a banana boat. Three months later, in February 2022, the police decided to raid his village but were met with fierce resistance by Atu's friends and neighbours. The police, who fired tear gas on the angry crowd, were soon forced to retreat. Meanwhile, Atu had escaped, seeking refuge in a makeshift jungle encampment where he would live largely in solitude for almost three months.

Atu had been persuaded by his older brother to turn himself in; they had hoped he would soon be found innocent. When Atu returned to the capital, however, the gravity of the charges he was facing became clear. He was charged with eight different counts, including the inciting of riots and arson, as well as several misdemeanours associated with his unwillingness to surrender to authorities. He was now on bail. His court case was just days away, but he was eager to meet. He wanted to tell his story.

After a few minutes driving through the backstreets of Honiara, Hayden pulled over to collect an unmistakeable Atu. He and Olita jumped into the tray of the pick-up truck, lit a cigarette and, like jockeys, slapped the side of the car to get it moving. As we wound our way east of downtown Honiara, Hayden began divulging details about his life. He was soon to marry a young Australian girl, whose dad had moved to Solomon Islands a decade ago. For much of the drive, Hayden lamented how he and his brother's newfound wealth, courtesy of their inheritance, had destroyed their relationship. I wondered how much of that wealth had been spent on luxury items such as the GM pick-up truck.

It was 9 p.m. when the car turned off the Kukum Highway, down a dark alley and towards a clearing near Henderson's runway. The house was Hayden's, another result of his inheritance. It had become a late-night meeting place for Atu – a place where he knew he couldn't be overheard. The car pulled up, and Emily and I stepped out onto the grass. Hayden, as if he were Atu's personal secretary, fetched several chairs, a table and bottles of water. We were sitting in the middle of an expansive, overgrown lawn. Behind a distant fence hummed the heavy machinery of a small manufacturing plant; on the other side of the lawn, a row of thick, tall shrubs enclosed the opening. Hayden turned on a powerful floodlight and pointed it towards where we were sitting. I began recording.

I started by asking Atu about the circumstances that had led to his surrender. His suspicions about the authorities, he told me, were validated by the alleged alteration of one of the statements he had given. After he turned himself in, Atu said, he gave two statements: one to the Fijians and one to the Solomons police. 'But then later, we heard that the statements were separate, they were mismatched.'

Olita interrupted. 'There were two separate statements in two separate interviews.'

Both Atu and Olita believed that Atu's statement had been tampered with by the police. The statement he gave to the Fijian peacekeepers, he said, was the legitimate one, whereas there had been details added to the second statement he had supposedly given to the RSIPF.

'I think the RSIPF, they're working on split groups ... [and] getting directives from the prime minister's office,' Olita said.

Both men believed that Atu's surrender, and his statements, were being gamed by Sogavare's office to enhance the likelihood of a prosecution. I was unable to independently verify this claim. But whatever the legitimacy of Atu's allegation, the reality was he was now facing serious criminal charges and risked spending decades behind bars. Prosecutors had charged Atu with crimes related to the deaths of the three people in Chinatown. He was frightened and believed he was being set up.

'They said they have evidence of us holding talks and meetings ... planning burning down buildings,' Atu said. He and Olita denied such plans ever took place. Instead, they insisted, their intentions were purely peaceful.

'On the morning of the riot, we were at Point Cruz, speaking with police, trying to have a dialogue. We were meeting with the police commissioner and the deputy police commissioner.'

I ask what their intentions had been for the thousands of young men who assembled that morning near the parliament.

'The message at the time was, "There is going to be a peaceful sit-in protest at the parliament grounds",' said Olita.

Their plan, they claimed, had been to sit down with the prime minister and put to him 'the demands of the people', and that the crowd only grew angry once it became clear that Sogavare had no intention of meeting with them.

I put to Atu the obvious point that such intimidation tactics were never going to work: Sogavare, of all prime ministers, would be the last person to kowtow to the demands of an angry mob. Surely, I argued, Atu and Olita understood the volatility and the danger of the situation they'd crafted. They had created an expectation among their followers that their strongarming would work. Had they, I asked, not laid the foundation for the violence that was to come?

Atu and Olita claimed that as the crowd grew angry, they tried to settle it down. 'We asked the police commissioner to not give the orders to fire the tear gas. But then all of a sudden, the tear gas went off,' said Atu.

By then, it was too late. Even if the tear gas hadn't been fired, the crowd had become incensed by the rumours that Sogavare had fled parliament. The tear gas certainly escalated the situation, but there are competing claims as to who triggered the initial violence – whether a protestor was the first to rush the parliamentary grounds, or whether a single officer lost his cool and let his trigger finger slip. Atu maintains that as the crowd grew violent, he tried to calm down what had quickly become an unruly mob. Whatever attempts he made were unsuccessful. He quickly departed for Malaita and into hiding.

Throughout our conversation, Olita had been relatively subdued. He showed a clear deference to his older colleague. But when I asked what the pair thought of Australia's intervention after the riots, Olita lit up. He was a sceptic of Australia's military involvement, both historically and in the wake of the protests. He believed the latest intervention was designed merely to support Sogavare personally, and that Australia's previous interventions had been a failure.

'We had RAMSI for fourteen years … look what Australia has done. There are flashy prisons … but the economic infrastructure is not there. Most of the RAMSI money spent is on policing … on security. But after all these fourteen years, look at the capability of the RSIPF. Does it match the time [Australia] spent in the country?' he put to me. 'The question is when will we, Solomon Islanders, see *our* interest pursued?'

Seeking an answer to these questions, Atu suggested, was why M4D was founded. 'Malaita for Democracy is not a group … it is a voice, something like a voice. A movement. Something like that. As a traditional leader, I take their voice, and read to the Malaita Province executive, that these people do not want communism to come into this island. M4D is not a group, it is a voice.'

'You're using that voice very loudly,' I said, prompting Atu and Olita to erupt into laughter.

As our conversation drew on, Olita and Atu both began to express their discontent with Premier Suidani, their once staunch ally, more openly.

From 2019 through to 2021, M4D and the Suidani administration were in lockstep when it came to their uncompromising position towards the Sogavare government. There was no evident appetite in M4D to sit down with Sogavare immediately after the Switch. On my first visit to Auki, Olita had boldly claimed that if Sogavare were to come to Malaita, he would likely be killed – not by Olita or his acolytes, but by angry Malaitans whose visceral hatred of the prime minister M4D was benefiting from.

But the looming threat of jail time had tempered the two provocateurs' enthusiasm for acrimony. Atu and Olita had changed tack and begun pushing Suidani to enter a formal negotiation with Sogavare.

'We have weak leadership,' Atu said, in reference to Suidani and his unwillingness to enter into 'dialogue' with Sogavare.

M4D's desire to resolve the issues facing their province through formal dialogue between the Sogavare government and the Malaitan provincial government was a significant change in approach. And it was clear that this abrupt change was a direct result of the legal threats the two men now faced.

As we sat in the overgrown garden, Atu acknowledged the severity of the charges he faced. When I asked if he was scared of going to jail, his response was surprisingly honest: 'Yes.'

'The conditions are very bad' in Solomon Islands' prisons, interrupted Olita. Atu, whose deep stare was shaded by the brim of his fatigue-green floppy hat, remained silent, puffing on his cigarette.

I asked him about his political ambitions. If M4D was truly the voice of the Malaitan people, as Atu had described it, why wouldn't its bombastic and charismatic leadership take the next step and run for elected office? From a parliamentary perch, Atu would no longer need to scramble just to get his voice heard, and he would be able to confront, face to face, the political adversaries whom he claimed were ruining his country. Atu didn't commit to any political future, but he didn't rule it out. He said he believed that, if he were to stand for office, he would be successful. Both Atu and Olita were eager to claim that the real source of power in Malaita wasn't the premier's office; it was them and M4D. They said that they and their followers had enabled Suidani to ascend to the premiership, and that Suidani's popularity would dissolve if M4D were to withdraw its support. Atu even suggested that he had protected the premier during successive no-confidence motions, pressuring wavering MPs to oppose Suidani's ouster and organising M4D protests in the premier's support.

Knoxley Atu, July 2022.

Atu and Olita's claims about their influence were often exaggerated, but they were not altogether imagined. They had demonstrated a capacity to tap into the deep-seated sense of historical anger and everyday injustice felt by Malaitans, both those living on their impoverished island and those struggling to survive in the hill slums of Honiara. Their rhetoric was skilful and their message powerfully invoked Malaitans' century-old aspirations to independence. Within their own communities, Atu and Olita inspired loyalty, and their ability to mobilise masses of disenfranchised young men was powerful.

Their strategic deployment of this power, however, was questionable. The lack of a considered strategy – and indeed, the occasional disiplay of strategic ineptitude – made me question whether their intention was truly to advance the cause of an independent Malaita, or whether it was to advance their own personal authority within a tumultuous, unpredictable and sometimes violent political culture.

This lack of strategic nous was best demonstrated by their haphazard approach to the question of Malaitan independence. When I asked Atu if the ultimate goal of M4D was a Malaitan state, he said unequivocally that it was. But their strategy for achieving this audacious goal was limited to soliciting the support of their fellow Malaitans through a poorly organised ballot on independence in late 2021 – a tactic that was ultimately dismissed even by Premier Suidani, who had said previously that he supported Malaitan independence. The ballot had no legal or political legitimacy.

To truly achieve independence, emerging nations must embark on a complicated diplomatic, legal and public relations push to legitimise their struggle in the eyes of other countries. Every year, there are many referendums globally attempting to advance the autonomy of one jurisdiction or another. Some of these, such as those in Catalonia in 2017 and Scotland in 2014, bear legitimacy – they're the culmination of decades of struggle and public awareness raising. There have been independence pushes in the Pacific region that were the result of carefully crafted strategies. Timor Leste's struggle against Indonesian occupation at home was accompanied by a dedicated international diplomatic effort. This was crucial in legitimising the notion of an independent Timor Leste. It is easy to look back at successful independence struggles and assume that success was inevitable. But this is rarely the case.

Even when jurisdictions hold legitimate referendums endorsing their independence from a recognised nation state, the extension of diplomatic recognition by other states is not guaranteed. Fundamentally, states are disincentivised from extending diplomatic recognition to separatist movements. Within most countries – even the most stable, economically advanced democracies – there are disenfranchised communities who believe they would be better off alone. Modern states know this, and rarely extend recognition to upstarts. If any jurisdiction could achieve independence simply by voting in favour of it, the stability in global affairs brought about by the evolution of the modern nation state would be compromised; the world would shift from a relatively static bloc of almost 200 recognised states to an ever-evolving landscape of fledgling and weak nations. The rapid proliferation of nation states in the second half of the twentieth century was an inevitable result of the dismantling of global colonialism, but since the collapse of the Soviet Union, only six new nation states have been globally recognised. The last jurisdiction to achieve independence in the Pacific Islands region was Palau, in 1994.

Elsewhere in the region, even successful independence movements have failed to deliver new states. The closest comparable case to Malaita's is in the far west of the Solomon Archipelago, where Papua New Guinea's Autonomous Region of Bougainville successfully voted for independence in 2019. That vote was conditional on a 1998 peace agreement struck between Bougainville's rebels and the Papua New Guinean government, bringing to an end the deadliest conflict in the Pacific since World War Two. The vote, which was deemed legitimate by international observers, saw 98 per cent of Bougainville's voters endorse independence. The referendum commenced a period of negotiations between Bougainville and Papua New Guinea aimed at creating a timetable for independence. But even with the endorsement of Port Moresby, the emergence of an independent Bougainville is not at all certain. To achieve genuine independence, that independence must be recognised by a sizeable majority of global states – and few, if any, states in the region, let alone distant states with no relationship with Bougainville, have an incentive to extend this recognition. Australia remains mum on the issue, seemingly reluctant to hasten the creation of yet another fragile state on its doorstep that could be vulnerable to international influence. Public opinion in Bougainville in favour of independence is clear, and the Papua New Guinean government has, so far, acted in good faith to enable the 2019 referendum result to be realised. But on the international front, a resource-limited Bougainville has been unable to mobilise broad support.

As our conversation entered its second hour, I began to explain the complexities of achieving statehood. Olita seemed unaware of the challenges facing the Malaitan independence movement; he believed firmly that, if Malaitans did vote for independence, America, Taiwan, Japan and maybe even Australia would support them. When I suggested it may be more complicated than that, Olita seemed intrigued, but Atu remained quiet.

'So, are we done here?' he eventually asked, sternly but with a wry smile.

Fearing I was overstaying my welcome, I shook Atu's hand and thanked him for his time. We stepped back into Hayden's plush car and headed back to the heart of the city.

17

EAST TO FATALEKA

AUKI, LATE ON A SUNDAY AFTERNOON, was languid, dirty and vacant. Few shops were open; the handful of locals on the streets were the ones who never leave. A heavy downpour filled potholes with muddy, oily water, and the rusted tin roofs heaved with the weight of pooling rain. Walking around town from hotel to hotel, I found their receptions empty. The doors were open – in one hotel, I walked into the kitchen and made myself a cup of tea while I waited for someone to show – but no one was home. Continuing my search, I headed, somewhat regretfully, to what was alleged to be Auki's finest motel: the Auki Lodge. Its basic concrete building sits atop a hill in the middle of town, overlooking the port, next door to the Malaitan provincial government offices. The doors were barricaded, so I entered through a side gate to see if I could rustle the attention of a staff member. Sweating profusely under the burden of my backpack and the humid air, I saw a man sitting in front of the small reception building, which was locked.

'I didn't know this hotel offered personal check-ins from the premier,' I joked.

Coincidentally, Premier Suidani had just arrived to meet a friend for dinner. Unhappy that I'd had such a hard time finding a room, he called the owner of the lodge at home, who promptly came to check me in. I shouldn't have been surprised to find the premier at Auki Lodge. It is here, on the rickety deck overlooking the centre of town, that Suidani decamps each evening, and where a roster of local men speak to him over countless Sol-Brews, often late into the night.

I hadn't seen the premier since 2019, at our meeting at the Heritage Park Hotel. He looked healthy but markedly thinner than when I had seen him last, and he appeared tired. For the past three years, he had been a man on a mission, and it was taking a toll.

'We're doing okay,' he said. 'My health is okay. But we're worried that the DCGA [Sogavare's national government] will end us in June next year.' He was referring to rumours that Sogavare was planning on forcing provincial governments into caretaker mode ten months ahead of the 2024 election. The move would render Suidani's government unable to legislate or to make any policy decisions, effectively neutering his capacity to govern.

Sensing the premier was growing uneasy at the propsect of an improvised interview with a journalist late on a Sunday afternoon, I quickly asked him about growing rumours of looming Chinese investments in his province. Suidani had become famous for his pledge to prevent Chinese investment in Malaita. But that promise was becoming harder to keep, as an influx of Chinese proposals began to appear across the island. One of these was by a well-known, scandal-plagued company, WinWin Investments, whose overtures in Malaita had been making headlines. A Chinese corporate conglomerate with interests in timber and mines, it had been the subject of corruption allegations associated with Gold Ridge on Guadalcanal. The premier conceded that what he believed to be a subsidiary of WinWin, the New Asia Mining Company, had a delegation of staff currently in Auki. New Asia had their eyes on a titanium deposit in the island's east. Suidani expressed fears that, despite his promises to keep out Chinese investors, he didn't have the authority to prohibit New Asia from entering Malaita after all. 'We can grant the business licences,' he said. 'But we don't have control over the tribal lands. If the [Sogavare] government approves the mine, we cannot stop it.'

Provincial governments across Solomon Islands sit awkwardly in between the powerful national government and highly autonomous and sovereign tribal communities. Often, community elders, in collaboration with the national government, have the ultimate decision-making powers regarding extractive projects in their communities. Although premiers can protest, their legal avenues to contest projects are often significantly constrained. The premier, despite making big promises that China would never enter Malaita, could be bypassed. He knew it, and New Asia knew it. Earlier in 2022, the company had dispatched one of their representatives, an ethnic-Chinese resident of Malaita married to a local, to begin lobbying the East Foufoumela community about a proposed mining site. The site was selected due to its expected quantities of titanium deposits. In truth, no one really knows what lies under the ground in Malaita. The British never conducted geological surveys of any serious nature. This has left the Malaitan market open to the most adventurous speculators. Rumours abound that the proposed catchment area of the mine also houses rich deposits of gemstones.

New Asia was aware that the Foufoumela community had an appetite for extractive projects. For decades, communities across East Fataleka, the Malaitan ward in which Foufoumela sits, had been home to a small-scale logging operation. Although the community didn't benefit significantly – it remains languishing in subsistence – certain tribal leaders did financially benefit from granting commercial operators permission to undertake the logging. New Asia had dispatched its representative to Foufoumela, recognising that it was a community that would be receptive to external economic stimulus.

On 1 December 2022, Premier Suidani received a visit from a collective of tribal leaders from across Fataleka. They were pushing him to support the New Asia project. It put him in a challenging, high-pressure situation. Were he to endorse the initiative, he would be moving away from the fervent anti-China position that had made him famous. But if he rejected the tribal leaders' request, in all likelihood, the project would proceed regardless, making the premier look weak and emboldening his critics – both those on the Sogavare side of the argument and his former allies in M4D, who, as Knoxley Atu and Richard Olita had told me, had now begun publicly criticising the premier for 'weak' leadership.

As I arrived in Auki, the New Asia deal was attracting attention. A number of ethnic-Chinese businessmen had arrived in Auki on the same boat as I had, accompanied by bodyguards. A draft version of the proposed mining project had been leaked, and it was an appalling example of the bad behaviour unscrupulous foreign companies sometimes attempt to get away with in Solomon Islands. New Asia would provide the Foufoumela community monthly royalties of just SBD$700, around US$80, and pay SBD$100 (US$15) for each hole it drilled during its prospecting. The deal substantiated the fears of those who had been pushing back against the extractive industries in Malaita for decades. But for the community, even this modest income stream appeared better than nothing.

Foufoumela is a small village in the highlands of a region known as Fataleka, a place I had been determined to explore since beginning to investigate the fallout of the Switch. Fataleka is a remote area largely isolated from neighbouring regions due to a lack of accessible roads, and it is where Suidani had his political start. Fataleka was also where Knoxley Atu was now residing, after his months of legal troubles in Honiara had begun to subside. I wondered, as I spoke with Suidani, how the community that had spawned the two key actors in Malaita's now globally renowned opposition to Chinese expansionism had come to be the first community in Malaita to buckle under the allure of big Chinese mining money.

*

I didn't know how to reach Fataleka, but I had a vague plan to head along a track known as the North Road, leaving the gritty confines of Auki and travelling a circuitous route around the northern headlands of Big Malaita, before returning to Auki via a mountain road that begins on the eastern side of the island, at the southern end of the Fataleka region. I would travel any way I could.

Rural Malaita is a vast tapestry of villages. They sprawl across every available piece of land, emerge out of dense forests, straddle sandy beaches, and seem to grow and change at a rapid pace. The island is thriving with humanity. Because of this, almost all maps of Malaita are outdated, rendering detailed planning impossible. I decided to make things simple by breaking my mission into bite-sized pieces. First, I was to get to Gounatolo, where the North Road ends. Once at the terminus, I'd haggle and improvise my way on foot and boat down the east coast, to the small village of Atori, where I hoped to reconnect with the dirt track west and find a ride back to the capital.

In Auki, I began knocking on the windows of parked trucks, eventually waking up a man who introduced himself as Robert Roboranvanu.

'Are you heading to Malu'u?' I asked him. Malu'u was the biggest town on the way to Gounatolo. He nodded and let me sit up front as he collected dozens of passengers in his tray.

Robert was in his early fifties and had two children – a boy, fourteen, and a girl, twelve – both of whom lived in Honiara with his wife. He had moved back to his home community of Malu'u during the pandemic, leaving his family behind. 'I lost my job in the city, so I came back home to drive trucks for my uncle,' he explained.

As we left Auki, the North Road quickly turned from a potholed strip of tarmac into a dirt track in varying states of disrepair. Occasionally, the gravel was even and refreshingly smooth. Often, the track was marred by potholes several feet deep and filled with water. At times, it hewed close to the shore, where the potent combination of coastal erosion, made worse by rising sea levels and the over-harvesting of mangroves for firewood, could see entire sections of the road under water at high tide.

In the weeks before I arrived in Auki, Prime Minister Sogavare had made a visit to Malu'u. It was his first to the island since the standoff with Suidani had begun. I asked Robert what he thought of Sogavare's arrival.

'The community was excited to receive him,' he said, arguing that all the trouble around China was just 'naughty boys' trying to 'take advantage' of the situation arising from the Switch. His community liked the prime minister, he said. They were proud that he had chosen Malu'u as the location to begin his rapprochement with the Malaitans.

More practically, Robert argued that, since the Switch, Malaita had seen no economic benefits as a result of Suidani's anti-China stance. Robert had no skin in the game. His views weren't informed by any ideological argument or philosophical stance, and he had nothing against Daniel Suidani.

He simply couldn't see any material benefits from Suidani's campaign. Meanwhile, his life had been getting much harder. 'Diesel is now SBD$17.50 per litre. It costs over $1000 to fill up the truck,' he said. In addition to rising fuel prices, inflation had been skyrocketing, even in the black-market economy.

The North Road passes over numerous streams that have yet to be bridged. Where there are bridges, they are often in an incomplete state of construction, supposedly half-finished by a New Zealand contractor. Where the road has been destroyed by the creeks, communities take it upon themselves to fix it, at a price. As we rounded a corner, a large bamboo boom-gate blocked the path ahead. A shirtless man walked over to the driver and demanded a toll. Behind him stood a small boy, maybe seven or eight, who had war paint on his face. We made eye contact. Robert, who had told me the tolls were getting much more expensive, negotiated the price down from $100 to $30, but said he wouldn't dare refuse to pay altogether.

'Sometimes, if they get drunk, there could be trouble,' he said.

After five hours in the truck, Robert dropped me at a small motel on the edge of Malu'u, the 511. 'The prime minster stayed here a few weeks ago,' Robert told me, as he introduced the owner, Job Kabui, a sixty-year-old former CEO of Solomons Ports.

Semi-retired, Job now spends his days tending to his modest six-room motel and indulging his guests in lengthy conversations about politics and Malaitan history. The Kabui name is well known in Solomon Islands: Job's brother, Frank, served as governor-general between 2009 and 2019, and his nephew, Albert, still worked as an advisor to Prime Minister Sogavare. Despite his proximity to the centre of power, Job remained a cynic. 'We have many problems. It is because of the politicians,' he said.

Nevertheless, he had seized the opportunity to host Sogavare and his team. 'The prime minister wanted a room with a balcony, so we put him in Room 1,' Job said. Sogavare had been travelling with twenty-five armed security guards, who slept on the floor of the old shop Job used to run on the ground floor of the guest house. 'The prime minister was scared to come here. My nephew, Albert Bagui, is the prime minister's personal secretary.

He rang me and asked, "Uncle, is it safe?", and I promised him the prime minister would have no problems here.'

For Job, the troubles whipped up by M4D, and Premier Suidani's politicking, didn't represent his community of Malu'u. M4D, he said, was 'only for Auki', and had achieved no tangible benefits for people elsewhere on Malaita, other than undermining the province's reputation.

I asked Job if he thought there was any truth in the argument that Sogavare's administration had been withholding support from Malaita as punishment for its stance on China.

'The government isn't giving any money to the province ... because the provincial government isn't doing its job,' Job said.

Rather than being a conspiracy by the Sogavare government to withdraw funds from the Malaitans, Job believed that the removal of grants through the CDF program was due to legitimate administrative errors by Suidani's government, not payback for its adversarialism. 'The projects ... nothing happened, because we were disqualified. We were disqualified because, one, we had no provincial secretary ... he was removed several years ago.' Second, he said, 'The [provincial] budget was not approved, because the Public Advice Committee did not examine it.'

This key bureaucratic check on public spending in the province was effectively ignored, Job claimed, which meant some of the spending of the provincial government was technically not allowed under national law. Suidani's provincial government, Job argued, 'didn't do their job properly'. And the impact in Malu'u was real. A planned administration block for the Malu'u region never happened. A building to house nurses, approved by local leaders in Malaita, was also unable to proceed as a result, Job contended, of maladministration by the provincial government, not because of a strategic intervention by the national government. 'You got to have the conditions there [to receive the grants], but then they started to blame the Sogavare government,' Job said. 'The provincial members feel bad about it, too. Because they wanted projects in their wards, too.'

Job also believed that, fundamentally, Suidani was determined not to help Malaita, but to seize power for himself in Honiara. Earlier in 2022,

Suidani had created a new political party, Umi 4 Change, or U4C, which he promised would field candidates across the country in the 2024 national elections. Whether Suidani himself would be one of those candidates was unclear. 'The premier is trying to run away from his position ... he is pushing the U4C party, he is trying to go national,' Job said. 'There will definitely be a change [of government in Malaita]. When there's a change, I don't know what the fate of the Auki Communique will be. It could be wiped out. It's nothing binding.'

In Job's view, Suidani was 'pushing his U4C party', with the help of Celsus Talifilu. 'Do you think there could be a relationship with Taiwan?' I asked.

'Definitely, definitely,' Job said. 'I have heard stories ... When there was the Switch, Taiwan sent some money.' Job said that the secret deal between Malaita and Taiwan in 2020, and the resulting delivery of Taiwanese aid during the early months of the pandemic, had amounted to nothing in Malu'u. 'They promised us some bags of rice ... not even a single ten-kilo came through here. Nothing came,' he said. He understood why Taiwan had courted Malaitan support: 'Taiwan wanted Malaita to vote for them ... when it becomes a country. But we can't survive [as an independent state].'

For Job, the idea of an independent Malaita wasn't just fanciful. It was fundamentally wrong. He believed the only way to achieve independence would be through violence. 'If bad comes to worse,' he said, 'we will have to fight. But what are we fighting for? It's nothing. You have to have something out the back, you cannot fight for nothing. Malaita has to work with the government, to work together.'

Despite his opposition to the actions of the provincial government, Job insisted he was a proud Malaitan. And he had the record to prove it. 'When I started this project,' he said, referring to his 511 Motel, 'people said, "Hey Job, go and build this in Honiara." But I am from Malaita. I have to build Malaita. Who else is going to build Malaita? So this is my little contribution.'

*

In northern Malaita, cars are rare. After a day waiting, hoping to find a ride, not a single vehicle had passed me. I spent my time exploring central Malu'u, walking back and forth along the sleepy road. Since I was unavoidably conspicuous, I leant into the experience. Small children ran from their homes to follow me as I strolled along the seaside at a leisurely pace. Men chewing betel nut and discussing the ways of the world in beachside huts would step away from their group and shake my hand, offering me a smile and a 'Good afternoon' before going back to their business. Young women giggled and hid behind bushes or shelters as I walked past.

Some of the less shy locals came out to join me. One was Ramos, a seventeen-year-old aspiring engineer who was studying as a boarder at Aligegeo High School in Auki. Ramos' dream of becoming an engineer was born of the woeful state of infrastructure he saw on his regular commute, on the back of a truck, between Malu'u and Auki. The drive, around sixty kilometres, takes over five hours, thanks to the dilapidated condition of the road. Dozens of creeks and streams that cut through the road are yet to be bridged, and many small crossings remain half finished, their iron scaffolding and stabilising beams rusting in the humid, salty air.

'Life can be very tough here,' Ramos said, as we walked past a soccer game being fiercely contested by two groups of friends. His parents made ends meet by growing vegetables, mainly a variety of broad bean, which they sold at a weekly market in Malu'u. It was a lifestyle that Ramos' family had been living for generations. To outsiders, it might appear idyllic. But for Ramos, the work was hard, the reward was low, and the desire to build something better for his family was overwhelming.

'Are you watching the World Cup?' I asked.

That morning, Portugal had beaten Switzerland 6–1. Most Solomon Islanders were backing Brazil, whose team colours matched the Solomons' national team stripes. In other towns, where 4G internet had recently arrived, locals were captivated by the cup. As I travelled the islands, kids would shout 'Neymar!' and 'Messi!' in support of their favourite superstars. Shops in Honiara and Auki were selling the flags of every country that made it to the finals, and these flags could be seen flying high behind pick-up trucks, and draped over the shoulders of young men on the streets. In the city, the usually chaotic morning traffic had noticeably quietened, as taxi drivers and workers slept in after staying up all night watching game after game.

Ramos, however, hadn't been following along. 'There is not good enough service here in Malu'u to watch. The tower is usually not working, or it is very slow.'

He pointed to the summit of a nearby mountain. If I squinted, I could faintly make out a distant metal structure. It must have been 500 metres above sea level, up a steep, jungle-covered mountain that looked impenetrable to the casual observer.

'That is the 3G tower for Malu'u. Often it isn't on because it runs out of power. It is run on diesel. The boys have to carry the diesel on their back, up the mountain, so that the tower can work. It takes three days for them to turn the tower back on, so often it doesn't work.'

One piece of infrastructure, however, was changing the lives of people in Malu'u: the new wharf, which Ramos showed me now. On first glance, the structure looked modest, even insignificant. The small concrete pier only stretched fifteen metres into the water and was perhaps four metres wide. It was incomplete: fences protecting people from falling into the water were yet to be erected, and materials to broaden the wharf were lying in wait nearby. But the wharf, however simple, had changed everything for the people of Malu'u. Until it was built, the quickest way to travel to Honiara was to find space on the back of a truck, endure the bumpy five-hour drive to Auki, and then take the three-hour fast boat to Honiara. For many people, however, the fast boat, at around US$30 a crossing, remained prohibitively expensive. Their only option was to catch one of two large, creaking ferries – the *Fair Glory* and the *Taimereho* – which take seven to eight hours to cross the strait. With over 500 passengers on board, many of them seated on an open deck, the ferries are considerably more dangerous. In April 2020, the *Taimereho* set sail from Honiara for Auki, despite warnings that the emerging Cyclone Harold had whipped up dangerous seas. Twenty-seven passengers lost their lives when they were swept overboard by a large wave.

The new wharf at Malu'u meant the two fast boats in service could now dock in the village, removing the need to travel by road to Auki. The cost remained the same, but for those who could afford it, the weekly service to Honiara dramatically upended their isolation. The wharf also provided a means for traders to expand their markets: instead of selling their fruits, vegetables and fish only at markets in Malu'u and neighbouring villages, traders could now sell into Honiara, with goods being ferried from the wharf every Saturday and arriving at the capital three hours later. The wharf was a simple intervention, but it was the right one. And it was funded not by the Malaitan provincial government, or by any foreign donor. It had been a gift from the national government – and Sogavare was eager to claim credit.

In October 2022, Sogavare, along with a large entourage of security personnel and government ministers, arrived at the Malu'u wharf and was greeted by a crowd of over 1000 cheering Malaitans. Initially, Sogavare's team had expected to meet Suidani at the port. When I spoke with Job Bagui, he claimed to have overheard a phone call between his nephew and the Malaitan premier, however, in which Suidani made last-minute excuses to avoid turning up. 'He said he had a family member that was ill, so he wouldn't come, but it was all excuses. He was being told what to do by his advisors,' Job said. 'We were disappointed ... we were all disappointed.'

Instead, Suidani dispatched his deputy premier, Glen Waneta, who was also the local member of the Malaitan provincial assembly for Malu'u. It would prove to be a strategic mistake. As Sogavare stepped ashore onto Malaita for the first time since assuming the prime ministership in 2019, wearing a beige safari suit and a beaming smile, the reception both from the locals and from Waneta was overwhelming. The crowd was rapturous, smiling as Sogavare worked a rope line and shook people's hands. When Waneta took to the stage, his comments reflected the growing division within the MARA government over its anti-Sogavare posturing.

'I speak from my heart. Even if you do not say anything today to the people gathered here to witness the occasion, it is okay with us, as we are very happy with your leadership as prime minister,' Waneta said. 'Actions speak louder than words. You are one of us. You are a son of Malaita.'[1]

Waneta's comments spoke to the growing resentment towards what some viewed as the futility of Suidani's stance against Honiara. While there were many Malaitans who were still with the premier and felt angry about Sogavare's presence on their island, others were, by now, tired of the fruitlessness of the MARA government's position. It had led to few development outcomes, it had harmed, in some eyes, Malaita's reputation, and it had alienated everyday Malaitans – those who don't pay attention to political and ideological debates but who must navigate the complexities and hardship of island life – from the rest of their countrymen. Waneta's comments spoke to this segment of the Malaitan constituency – the 'peace loving' Malaitans, as he and the prime minister called them.

Sogavare seized the moment, delivering a speech that took credit for the port and took a swipe at the divisive tactics employed by Suidani and his team.

'This is an example of how much can be achieved if we work together for the advancement of our people. I will continue to drive home this point that we can only achieve such development projects if we work together. Working together is the only way forward. There is no other way. If we do not work together, our people will suffer'.

The prime minister then turned to the crowd, and with a deft political eye, used the moment to look beyond the politicians and speak directly to the people, making a bold claim about their support for his administration.

'Your attendance this morning,' he said, 'demonstrates your continuous cooperation to the DCGA government in fulfilling its national priority to strengthen and allow people in rural Solomon Islands communities to participate in socio-economic development – and to maintain peace, in the *entire* country'.

*

From Malu'u I continued north, flagging the only car I could find to take me the thirty-five kilometres to Gounatolo. The road wound through the dense jungle, at times inching so close to the sea that it was at risk of being inundated by even the most modest swell. After two hours, the Lau Lagoon, Malaita's largest, stretching thirty kilometres from the island's north-east, down the coast towards its centre, appeared in front of me. The lagoon represented the end of the North Road and was the gateway to Fataleka. Disconnected from any roads, north-eastern Malaita is home to some of the most unique cultures of the Solomon Archipelago. As I made my way down the coast for the next few days, moving village to village, I hoped to try to understand how everyday Malaitans, far from the ruptures in Auki and Honiara, felt about their future.

Among those undisturbed communities were the Saltwalter People of the island of Sulufou, a man-made clump of land that sits in the turquoise waters of Lau Lagoon. Situated just a few hundred metres from the end of the North Road, Sulufou is the largest of these artificial islands. A century ago, in the mid-1920s, as tribal conflict ravaged northern Malaita, a handful of dissidents came up with a bold idea to escape the island's violence: they'd build their own land, removing themselves once and for all from the territorial disputes that had plagued the mountainous north Malaitan headland. Over several years, these once coastal communities literally moved into the sea, through an extraordinary feat of engineering and manpower. The first Sulufouans stitched together large rafts using coconut palms, placing upon them enormous stones, which they then pushed 300 metres out to sea at low tide. One by one, they placed the stones on top of each other, until a new island rose from the lagoon floor. The exiles called their new home Sulufou, roughly translated as *stones on top of stones*, and they began to build a new life, away from the troubles on their former island home.

Sulufou thrived. Its population grew rapidly. The island housed over 1500 people by 1958, when it first came to the attention of authorities after a horrific fire tore through every building in the tightly packed community, killing at least one child. But the Saltwater People didn't leave; they had rebuilt by 1963. Soon, their unique way of life provided a model for dozens of other exile communities, who established their own man-made islands nearby. Even today, frustrated locals still leave the land: the lagoon is littered with small man-made islands in various stages of construction. Sometimes, their diameter is no more than ten metres, their population just a single family.

A flurry of activity followed my exit from the car by the wharf of Gounatolo. As I had come to expect in rural communities, the older men stepped forward first to greet me. Most spoke impeccable English, acquired from their schooling in pre-independence days or through their association with their local church. One man, Clay, asked why I had come.

'I want to go to Sulufou, to the man-made island. I want to meet the Saltwater People.'

Clay left, and returned a few minutes later in the company of an angry-looking young man. Bearded, the young man wore a tattered baseball cap, faded blue jeans rolled up to the knees and a sun-bleached T-shirt reading *The Mighty Maroons: All Fired Up.*

'This man will be your captain,' said Clay. 'He can take you to Sulufou.'

The angry man never spoke to me. Instead, he quietly went about refuelling the outboard motor on the back of his banana boat. I waded through the warm, clear water and stepped into the boat for the short trip across the lagoon. As we skipped across the flat water, we passed several man-made islands. Each was much smaller than Sulufou, which dominated the horizon. Some were used as homes, others as farms growing taro, cassava, coconut and pawpaw. Many Saltwater People no longer had access to arable farmland, having sacrificed their land claims by moving onto the water.

Sulufou, a circular island 100 metres wide, was heaving with people. That much was clear as we approached the rotting staircase, made of tree branches, that serves as its dock. At the edge of the island, dozens of shanty homes straddled the artificial land and the water itself, with half the homes propped up by stilts in the water, which is around two metres deep. More than 500 residents are squeezed onto the tiny island. When we docked, I stepped up the rickety wooden ladder. My gruff skipper, still barely acknowledging my presence, stepped ashore to explain to the islanders what was going on, and to find the man I was hoping to talk to: Chief Sam Owka.

Owka, tall with betel-nut-stained teeth and immaculate English, welcomed me to his island with a smile. He offered to give me a tour, starting with the small graveyard that housed every chief of Sulufou dating back to the 1940s. As we walked the circumference of the small island, the chief walked me through the various challenges the islanders were facing.

'We don't have enough clean water, no sanitation. We need more canoes so we can paddle to shore,' Owka told me.

As the population on the tiny island has swelled, so have its difficulties. Like almost everywhere in rural Solomons, there are no government-delivered services. Instead, the Sulufouans eke out what they can extract from the ocean around them. Because of their lack of land, the people of Sulufou are unable to engage in many traditional activities. No mainland community has a lack of canoes: if they need one, they can simply cut down a tree and create one. But on Sulufou, there is only a handful of trees, certainly not enough to sacrifice for canoes. Instead, the islanders must buy canoes from communities on land, at a price few can afford. The lack of trees has also seen the Sulufou islanders decimate the mangroves that once surrounded their island. To cook, most rural Solomon Islanders still rely on wood-burning fires. On Sulufou, the only nearby wood was the mangroves. After generations of harvesting the mangroves for firewood, the trees have now all but disappeared, forcing the Sulufouans to return to shore to either barter for cooking fuel or steal wood from the land they thought they could leave behind.

As the chief walked me through his village, we discussed Atu and Olita's campaign. It didn't sit comfortably with Owka.

'We don't want to be involved in the politics', he said. 'Whether Taiwan, whether China. Everyone is welcome here.'

The very reason for Sulufou's existence, Owka said, was to avoid the complexities of tribal island politics. His ancestors may have been exiles, but their descendants were proud of the motivations of those who had founded their community. It wasn't Sulufou's place, Owka suggested, to get involved in what he saw as the asinine, never-ending grievance cycle that fuelled political infighting and instability elsewhere in the country.

All Owka wanted was more drinking water and a handful more canoes, so he and his community could get on with living a peaceful, if arduous, life in one of the world's most picturesque settings.

Although Owka was largely apolitical, there was one cause he fervently opposed, and that was independence.

'We are Solomon Islanders,' be proclaimed, forcefully rejecting the notion that Malaita might one day become a nation of its own.

*

I stepped back into the banana boat and asked my captain to head south as far as he could take me with the US$100 I had given him for fuel. South we headed, via the vast, turquoise lagoon that hugs the northeast corner of Malaita. Here, where the North Road transforms into an ocean pathway, Auki and its turmoils felt like another country.

For an hour, we navigated past artificial islands and dodged fishermen and women in long dugout canoes, before turning inland up a shallow inlet. My angry captain, who was yet to speak a word to me, now wedged his fibreglass boat into the beach and told me we'd arrived. This would be the end of my journey via boat: to keep heading south, I'd have to continue by foot.

I'd disembarked by the large village of Forau. As I put my shoes on, a large crowd gathered, some laughing, some pointing at me and shouting in the local Fataleka dialect. I composed myself and approached an elderly woman, who, amid the chaos, remained sedate and measured; she appeared undisturbed by my arrival.

'I'm searching for Bethel,' I said. 'Do you know the way?'

The old woman pointed towards a thin clearing between the village huts. So through the huts I went, a cluster of five young boys following closely behind. They were to become my guides, the Forau Five. For the next two hours, we walked south, past surprised villagers and along thin paths that hugged the white-sand shores and crocodile-filled mangroves. They insisted on carrying my bottles of water, but I resisted them carrying my heavy pack.

Sometimes one of them would dart ahead with a machete and return with a fresh coconut he'd retrieved from one of the palms that shaded the walk. Eventually, the Five reached their terminus, and I was left alone.

The winding beachside path had given way to an overgrown jungle road. I kept trekking south, before stumbling upon a construction site, with five men shovelling piles of gravel into wheelbarrows to lay a foundation. I asked where I was, and one man, who introduced himself as Martin, laid down his tools, took off his orange hard hat and invited me into the semi-constructed shelter that he and his crew were using as a lunch room.

'This is Songarai village,' Martin told me. 'I'm the foreman of this building. I'm also the chief of Songarai.'

'I was told the North Road reconnects here – that there is a car down to Bethel village,' I said. 'I'm looking for Knoxley Atu.'

The men heartily laughed. There was no car today – perhaps, they told me, there wouldn't be another for a week.

'Tomorrow, our truck will go south,' Martin said, before inviting me to stay in his guest house in Songarai for the night, which I readily accepted.

Martin's village typified those elsewhere in this remote corner of Malaita. It brimmed with youthful energy – children gathered any time I stopped walking – and it was meticulously maintained. The chief ushered me towards a newly constructed guest house, which sat handsomely at the edge of the village, shadowed by a mango tree that soared twenty metres into the air. He showed me to a small, empty room, in which his wife had put out a thin floor mat for me, and then he took me on a tour of Songarai. The village of forty households had a central dirt road, sandwiched between stilted thatched houses and a handful of concrete community structures. At the end of the road, which ran about 100 metres, sat an enormous church, the Church of St Peter, painted in bright yellows, reds and greens. This was the heart of Songarai. Twice a day – at dawn and at dusk – the church bells ring, summoning 300 men, women and children from their homes to pray.

Next to the church sat an unusual structure. Raised on stilts, the building resembled a futuristic sailing boat. Its walls were slightly rounded and its roof peaked sharply. Towards its front extended a generous octagonal

Songarai village.

deck, laced with ornate decorative woodwork. Martin told me this was the village's stage. It was here that the chief would lead his community's weekly meetings, and where guests would come and deliver sermons or lectures.

'Knoxley Atu has been here to speak to us about the China Switch,' Martin said. 'He would travel here to Songarai and talk to us about communism and about politics.'

I pictured the man I'd met on the outskirts of Honiara perched centre stage, his bellowing voice projecting heated rhetoric over an otherwise tranquil community composed mostly of children. The bombast seemed a surprising juxtaposition, but Martin said they supported Atu and his mission here in Songarai. 'Knoxley is our brother,' he said.

Martin was clearly proud of Songarai. He took great satisfaction in its physical beauty: in the church and the guest house and the stage; in the warmth and friendliness of its people. But he was most content with the system of governance he had helped install. When he had become chief some ten years ago, Martin had wanted to rebuild his village, catering for a swelling local population and creating a community they could be proud of. He wanted to build the guest house, refurbish the church and tidy the village gardens. To do so, he had needed money. Although Songarai was a subsistence community, the villagers had agreed to pool the produce they grew and sell it, with a portion of the money raised remaining with the village. Martin had successfully implemented a flat tax, which would create a centrally governed pool of money; he and an elected council of elders, including a treasurer, oversaw its spending on community projects. The funds would support weddings and funerals and subsidise villagers' transport on the East Fataleka Constituency Truck – the only form of public transport in the region.

That night, I slept restlessly on the hard-wood floor, before rising early to wait for the truck south. It was driven by an eloquent English-speaker named Bradley, a former soccer star who'd played for Solomon Islands' national team in his early twenties. I climbed aboard the truck's tray and was joined by dozens of other locals travelling to a funeral in a neighbouring village. We drove through the thickly overgrown jungle paths, south towards Bethel.

18

MUSTAFA RISING

AFTER MOST OF ITS PASSENGERS had alighted, Bradley's truck continued south before slowing down next to an unassuming cluster of houses.

'This is where Knoxley's brother lives. He will help you from here.'

I stepped out of the truck and looked up at a small building on a nearby embankment. Standing there waiting was Nixon Atu.

'I can tell you're Knox's brother. You look just like him,' I said, trying to punctuate the awkwardness and make him laugh.

Instead, Nixon firmly shook my hand, and, without even a smirk – his thin, greying moustache didn't move a millimetre – looked me in the eye. I could tell he was suspicious.

'What are you doing here? Why do you want to see Knoxley? We have had a lot of problems here this year.'

I stressed that I had already met his younger brother in Honiara, and that he and Richard Olita had promised to welcome me to his community if I ever made it. But I hadn't been in contact with Knoxley for six months. Now, I was worried he wouldn't even remember me, and that I'd be forbidden entry.

'I've come all the way from Auki, along the North Road, to see your brother. From Malu'u to Gounatolo and Forau, last night in Songarai, and now here to Bethel. I want to understand what happened here in February.'

I explained my project, my reporting on the Switch, and my concern for the wellbeing of the community after the police raid earlier in the year.

Nixon's scepticism waned, and he introduced me to a small boy named Alex.

'This is Knoxley's son, Alex. He will show you the way,' Nixon said.

I could also see Knoxley's face in his son's. Alex didn't say a word, but began walking down a path just off the road. It was so thin that I wouldn't have seen it from a car. The path rose briefly, then began to descend. Overhanging the path were enormous trees – coconut and mango, predominately – creating an avenue leading to what felt like a private jungle kingdom. After several hundred metres, a large clearing appeared, with a smattering of beautifully kept huts and gardens. This was Bethel village, Knoxley Atu's home. High in the trees, children clung to branches, staring at me as I walked past, like sentries keeping watch.

Bethel was like no other village I had seen in East Fataleka, or elsewhere in the Solomons. Whereas many communities are relatively open and accessible – some have roads running through them, beach access, or are exposed to neighbouring villages – Bethel was characterised by its privacy. It seemed a secret world, tucked away from all the troubles beyond the canopy. The clearing on which the village was situated was sprawling and open, perhaps the size of two soccer pitches, and surrounded on every side by thick jungle. The trees served as a natural barrier between the village and the ferocious open Pacific Ocean, blocking the breeze and the sound of pounding waves, creating an eerie quiet. At the heart of the village sat a green Anglican church, surrounded by about forty traditional huts and communal areas.

As Alex led me towards one end of the village, my entourage expanded. Soon, a dozen children and young men were walking behind me. In the distance, I could see a welcoming party: a large gathering of men under a modest shelter, taking their places alongside the man I'd travelled half an island to see.

'Welcome, my brother,' uttered Atu as I stepped into the shelter and shook his hand.

Atu was topless and covered in sweat, droplets of which sat on his thin moustache. Decorative blue and white bunting pinned to the pane-less window frames fluttered in the breeze, flapping above Atu's bald head as he told me what had happened since our last meeting.

'I just returned only on Wednesday from Honiara. The court order keeping me in Honiara was lifted, because they couldn't get anyone to testify against me.'

Atu's return to Bethel village was a long time coming. He'd been forced to stay in the capital for at least six months, as the RSIPF and prosecutors worked hard to gather evidence against him.

But Atu already looked settled at home. He had re-entered the daily rhythm of life in Bethel village. His days started at dawn when his wife, Dorothy, would prepare him a simple meal, usually of rice and fruit. He'd wash it down with sweet cups of three-in-one Nescafé instant coffee, which he called tea, and then tend to the daily business of village life, much of which revolves around talking politics with the village men. Never far from Atu were his six children. One of them, his youngest daughter Alice, was adopted.

It struck me that the police mustn't have been looking particularly hard for the evidence to prosecute Atu. As soon as I entered the community, his acolytes proudly told me about his role in orchestrating the riots. And when I asked Atu about the protest, he told me directly how it had come together; how he had worked the phone to enlist young men from every major village in north and east Malaita. He also had detailed knowledge of the protestors' targets, such as one of the prime minister's private residences, which was razed on 24 November. Atu denies, however, that he had intended for such destruction to occur. He orchestrated the protests, but he said violence had not been part of the plan.

He boasted that he was protected by the loyalty of those who supported the M4D cause. 'They asked sixty people to testify, and no one would testify against me,' Atu said.

The veracity of Atu's boast was uncertain. But what was clear was that the case against him had gone awry. By the end of 2022, the Magistrate's Court had even begun selling pieces of evidence held for Atu's case as mementoes – fragments of signs, broken bottles and improvised weapons – that were supposedly key to convicting Atu and his M4D allies. As it seemed less certain that Atu would in fact be convicted, the cash-strapped court thought selling these items was more productive than preserving them for a doomed trial.

By the time I arrived in Bethel, it had been almost nine months since the police raid on the village. In the early months of 2022, as stability returned in the wake of the riots, the police had yet to apprehend anyone responsible for the violence. As time went on they were placed under considerable pressure to bring those responsible to justice. The police were aware of Atu's involvement, however, and by March 2022 had decided to pursue the M4D leader and bring him – and perhaps his movement – to heel.

On 16 March, the RSIPF dispatched a special response team of twenty officers to Malaita. Their mission was simple: capture Knoxley Atu. To this day, the Bethel villagers believe the RSIPF's orders came directly from the prime minister.

At 4 a.m. on 17 March, members of the police team exited their patrol boats a few kilometres to Bethel's south. It was low tide, and they walked quietly up the beach and snuck into the heart of the village. Nixon Atu, who by now had joined his brother and me in Bethel for tea, recalled the raid.

'We have a community policy here … if anything happens at late hours, you have to give a signal to alert the community what is happening. That is a normal rule,' he said.

A young man who happened to be awake heard a suspicious noise and quickly reacted. He raced to the church, where he hit an old gas cannister with a metal pole to wake up the rest of the village, the same way the local priest did at 6 a.m. each day to rouse the village for prayers. At first, some of the villagers didn't believe the young man, who had a severe intellectual disability. After a few moments, however, his warning proved true.

'There were about fifteen [police in the village] … Five of them were in the boat, and the other fifteen were here in the village,' says Nixon Atu.

As the villagers emerged from their houses, the police panicked. They raced as a group to the communal kitchen, the space we were sitting in now. This space is a dead end: the bush behind the building is so thick that it would be hard to penetrate. The only way out was back the way they had come in.

247

According to Nixon Atu's account, the police, unable to find their suspect, and having roused the entire village of 200, began fighting their way out.

'They were armed with the type of guns with the smoke … and the other guns … they used the rubber bullets,' Nixon said. 'They sat behind the kitchen and they just shot out with the rubber bullets and the tear gas. These guys' – he pointed to the group of young men surrounding us – 'retaliated. Because the police showed they didn't have mercy … they kept shooting with rubber bullets and tear gas, so the community retaliated with stones.'

Nixon said the men of the village ordered the women and children to stay inside their huts as the tear gas began to spread through Bethel. Initially, the men had run out of their houses unarmed – 'if you could expect there is an enemy you might bring bow and arrows, but they were shocked, so they came empty handed' – but soon they were fighting fiercely. Some threw stones while others raced back to their huts to retrieve slingshots and bows and arrows. The stand-off behind the kitchen went on for a considerable time – perhaps as long as an hour – before the police managed to find their way back to the beach. From there, the men of the village chased them through the dawn light for more than six kilometres, to the mouth of a small inlet where their boat was waiting.

Only in the full daylight did Nixon Atu realise the extent of what had just occurred. He gathered the community together to check if anyone had been hurt.

'We are so lucky … even though they get a lot of shots, none of us got injured. It must be God's blessing for us. All the buildings were filled with smoke, but no single child, no single woman [was] affected by the smoke.'

Once he had ensured everyone was okay, Nixon and a few other men began gathering the evidence that had been left behind. They traced the steps the police had taken and collected a number of dispensed tear-gas cannisters and rubber bullets, which the community now holds as proof of their account of events, and which I was shown while in Bethel.

Having gathered the evidence, Nixon Atu took photos and sent them to a friend – Celsus Talifilu.

'I said, "Celsus, can you please help us, just upload what has happened to us here in this early morning hour?"' By 6 a.m., just two hours after the raid, images of its aftermath were circulating on Facebook.

On 18 March, the RSIPF confirmed they had been to Bethel village, but their account differed from Nixon Atu's. The police claimed that the villagers had attacked first, and that the police use of tear gas was merely defensive:

> The Police Respond Team (PRT) were at that location cordoning the house of the suspect when the villagers were alarmed and came out in numbers and attacked the PRT team, with dangerous weapons such as spears, stones, slings, bows and arrows, etc. The PRT team deployed less lethal munitions (smoke) to protect themselves and tactically withdraw. Despite that, the villagers with men, women and children continued to attack the PRT operators until they boarded their transport.[1]

All parties could agree, however, that the raid had failed. Knoxley Atu, although he had been in the village at the time, was not apprehended. As the police descended on Bethel, he had managed to sneak into the jungle.

The villagers had been significantly affected by the raid. For the next two months, Nixon told me, 'Every day, we are living in fear. Especially the children and the women, every time they hear an engine, they suffer, they live in fear.' Nixon said that two months after the incident, he had asked a doctor and a lawyer to visit the village to collect formal statements and assess the health of the community. Although there was no evidence of physical ailments associated with the use of tear gas, the doctor, Nixon said, told the villagers, 'You are so badly affected, most of you are almost traumatised because of this event.'

Some of the villagers believe there had been direct health consequences from the raid. One older man had died two weeks after it occurred; another elder told me angrily that the tear gas had certainly ended his friend's life, although this is unverifiable. What was verifiable was the extent of trauma in the community. Young Alex, Knoxley Atu's ten-year-old son who had welcomed me into the village, hadn't spoken a word the whole time, an affliction his father claims only started after the raid. While I was in Bethel, many people, including both Atu brothers, became apprehensive after nightfall. They had invested in high-powered handheld floodlights. At any minor disturbance – a distant rustling of leaves, a louder-than-usual barking of a stray dog – they would race to grab their torches and shine them in the direction of the disturbance. When we went to bed, Knoxley insisted he sleep within a few metres of me, promising to protect me from whatever threat may come in the night.

The raid was 'the craziest day in our village's history', Nixon said.

Knoxley, ever assured of the righteousness of his cause, had not been dissuaded by the heavy-handed police tactics. Instead, the incident seemed to embolden him to agitate even harder against the Sogavare government. But Nixon had been chastened.

'After that experience, that is why sometimes I have to talk to Knox. I want to discourage him from associating with any other political parties. I don't want such things to happen in the future.'

Nixon was convinced that his younger brother was being used as a pawn by the country's biggest political players. He believed Knoxley had become a useful scapegoat for the Sogavare government, representing many of its grievances: to capture Knoxley Atu would be to decapitate the anti-China and anti-Sogavare movement. Knoxley's most loyal followers in Bethel were convinced that the raid was ordered directly by the prime minister, intended to display Sogavare's reach and his capacity to impose law and order in every part of the archipelago.

In the days and weeks after the raid, Nixon said, no one heard anything from the government. They had hoped they would receive an apology. Instead, they were met with silence. Two months later, however, the MP for Fataleka, Rex Ramofafia – a minister in the Sogavare government who was feeling considerable political pressure from his constituency about the raid – paid Bethel a visit. He was there to achieve reconciliation. On behalf of Sogavare's government, he gave Bethel village SBD$10,000 in compensation. It wasn't an apology, but it was an olive branch, and for Nixon, it was enough.

'We just wanted things to be normal,' he said.

But for Knoxley, the two months following the raid were anything but normal. Once I had settled into Bethel village, he asked if I wanted to go for a walk. He had something to show me. He put on his trademark aviator sunglasses and a singlet with a picture of an African tribal figure on it and started walking towards the beach. I followed him along a path through the thick jungle. Some other village men, and what looked like half the village's children, joined us. It was high tide; the water lapped at our feet as we walked south along the coastline. We navigated the beating waves for fifteen minutes, before Knoxley stopped. He took off his shirt, had a brief swim and then came back ashore, directing one of the young boys to climb a tall palm to fetch two coconuts for us. Then, he ushered me into the thick jungle.

'This is where I lived after the raid,' he said, as we stepped into a cavernous jungle clearing. Protected by thick mangroves on the beach side and impenetrably thick jungle on the other, Atu had created a secret hideaway less than one kilometre from Bethel. He had constructed a small bed out of tree branches and palm leaves, with which he would cover himself when the rain dripped through the canopy above. For three months after the raid, he hid here, fearing the authorities could return to apprehend him at any moment. Village children would bring him food, and several times he returned to Bethel during the day to visit his wife. But otherwise, he remained alone in the jungle, waiting for his legal troubles to blow over.

When the boy arrived with two coconuts, Knoxley prepared them and we sat on the frame of his handmade bed, drinking coconut milk. As our conversation slowed, Knoxley's adopted daughter climbed onto his lap. He drank his coconut, sitting in reflection, as the waves crashed behind us.

*

Throughout northern Malaita, the presence of the New Asia Mining Company, and their visits with Premier Suidani and his team, were well known. The company hadn't arrived overnight. Instead, they had been cultivating a relationship with key elders and tribal leaders across the Fataleka region since early in 2022. These engagements had led to the signing of an agreement between the Chinese-owned firm and a handful of tribal leaders just a week before I arrived in Bethel, in early December 2022.

Nixon had been at the signing ceremony. While Knoxley had spent much of the past year evading authorities in his jungle hideout, Nixon's life was much more conventional. He spent most of his days in an air-conditioned office in Atori, the regional centre, working as a low-level administrative officer for the provincial government. In this capacity, he had been invited to the signing ceremony as a witness.

'New Asia had arrived with bags of cash,' he told me. 'They would give SBD$1000 in cash to every tribal leader who signed the paper.' This was not done with any secrecy, he explained, but in full view of the public. Twenty tribal representatives had signed on to the deal, representing various villages in East Fataleka.

Beyond these payments to individual tribal leaders, the draft New Asia deal offered little else to the community, as was clear from the deal that had leaked, which had appeared remarkably advantageous to the Hong Kong-registered company. Few locals seemed to benefit, apart from the elders who had received the sign-on bonus.

For three years, Atu and his allies had been pushing the Malaita provincial government to prohibit Chinese investment. They had mobilised thousands of angry young men to make that point on the streets of Honiara. But now, a handful of savvy Chinese businesspeople had managed to secure a lucrative opportunity, with almost no resistance from the community, only kilometres from where Atu had fended off the police raid. The deal was controversial, but it demonstrated that Atu's anti-China campaign was not universally supported, or particularly well understood, in much of Malaita. Many Malaitans remain apathetic or uninformed about the advantages and disadvantages of dealing with China. In Fataleka, there was no evidence of any benefits from aid or investment relationships with traditional Western donors: the region remained mired in subsistence living and acute poverty. Most of the villagers had no income and no access to essential medical care or basic medicines. In Songarai, a few days before I arrived in Bethel, I found myself offloading Panadol and Nurofen to elders who kept asking me if I had anything to relieve their various ailments. Given the economic disenfranchisement of the area, it is understandable that the temptation to sign up to a resources deal, no matter what country it originated from, was too great to resist.

But from Knoxley Atu's perspective, New Asia's encroachment into Fataleka was not proof that he was wrong, nor did it convince him to listen to his brother and back down. Instead, it increased his ideological fervour. To Knoxley, the New Asia proposal was evidence of 'weak' leadership. It proved to Knoxley that Suidani was incapable, as he had suggested to me at our first meeting in Henderson. It proved that Sogavare was willing to facilitate a Chinese takeover of his province and of the country, just as Knoxley had warned. After a year of legal woes, controversy, violence and a life on the run, it would have been understandable if Knoxley had decided to back down. But he was determined to do the opposite. Now released from legal scrutiny and no longer worried about being imprisoned, Knoxley Atu was free to plot his next move.

*

After my first night in Bethel, sleeping on the floor of Knoxley's half-built two-storey home in the heart of the village, he offered to accompany me all the way back to Atori, the small village from where I'd be able to find a ride back to Auki. The journey, by banana boat, would take the better part of a day.

I'd slept restlessly. Atu, having positioned himself two metres away from me to provide me with security, snored his way through the night. Two of his six children had decided to place their sleeping mats between me and their father. I'd woken in the night to Atu admonishing one of them for shifting too close to my mat in his sleep.

At first light we woke, had our sweet tea and a biscuit, and then headed south. Atu had invited his wife, Dorothy, and his son Alex along – it was an opportunity to visit relatives too far away to reach on foot. Dorothy was dressed elegantly, draped in a flowing white dress with her hair tidily bunched. Atu, too, had dressed up for the journey, covering his usually bare chest with a sleeveless shirt. Alex remained in the same clothes I'd first seen him in. As we walked south, streams of Bethel villagers were returning in the other direction. They had spent the night watching the World Cup semi-finals in another village some eight kilometres away, which had the only TV in the area. Most were disappointed: loyal Brazil fans, they were dismayed when the South American giants were eliminated by a plucky underdog, Croatia.

To reach Atori, we'd need to walk ten kilometres south and then travel by boat from the village of Faunikari, Atu's birthplace. The two-hour walk gave me time to learn more about him and his campaign. When I asked him why he was so opposed to Chinese communism, particularly considering Solomon Islands' close relationship with Cuba, another communist state, he didn't have an answer.

'Perhaps you could provide me with some literature on communism,' he laughed.

'Sogavare is a communist,' Atu would often declare when discussing politics. But to Atu, communism didn't have the same connotations as it might to those outside Malaita. Atu's economic aspirations for his community revolved around state intervention; he had an innate scepticism of private capital and unchecked market forces. Nor did he associate communism with irreligiosity; he was unaware, for example, of the Chinese Communist Party's crackdown on religious minorities. Instead, 'communism' had become a useful shorthand for any political force he was opposed to and for now, that meant Sogavare.

As I tried to unpick his political philosophy, we paused in a village at the halfway point of our walk. Forty-seven years old and overweight, Atu was struggling with the long trek and had chided me several times for walking too fast. As we rested in the shade of a tree, he pointed out that this village was one of the few Islamic communities in Malaita. I'd heard of the slow penetration of Islam into the island. A handful of communities had been converted over the past twenty years, sometimes to the concern of their neighbours. Most of these communities were located on the main thoroughfare between Auki and Atori; the road allowed ideas and people to travel.

But I was surprised that here, in a remote corner of East Fataleka, one tiny cluster of households had abandoned more than a century of Christianity.

'How did they become Muslims?' I asked Atu.

'I converted them,' he said, to my surprise. 'After the Tensions, I converted to Islam in Honiara. I changed my name to Mustafa Atu and pledged to come to my home island and convert as many people as I could.'

Atu lived up to his pledge. He honed his rhetorical skills, travelling village to village, spruiking the Quran. His proselytising was a success: he had converted a dozen or so communities across the Kwaio and Fataleka regions.

'They were easy to convert,' he said. 'But after some time, I realised I was wrong. I was born a Christian, and I decided I had to become a Christian again.'

After five years as an Islamic firebrand, preaching and converting, Atu returned to his Christian roots. He resettled in Bethel and continued to expand his family. Instead of politics or religion, he spent his time making buildings. As we walked to Faunikari, Atu proudly pointed out structures he had constructed – a school here, a clinic there. Having spent his twenties and thirties as an agitator, first as a member of the Malaita Eagle Force during the Tensions, then as an Islamic preacher, Atu, it seemed, had settled into village life. It wasn't until Sogavare's re-election in 2019 that he had decided to re-enter the fray.

We resumed our walk, following the road as it snaked through several more colourful villages, before arriving at the riverside village of Faunikari. In the 1970s, as Faunikari's population swelled, a handful of families had headed north to create Bethel, which was built on land owned by families who still lived in Faunikari. The two villages, despite their distance, remain intimately connected. Atu, his wife and son were warmly embraced as we entered Faunikari. Soon after we arrived, heavy rain began to fall. I was ushered into a small shelter, where six women gossiped and laughed and asked me questions in pidgin about my life in Australia, and how I knew their bombastic relative Knoxley. Meanwhile, he was holding court with a group of men in an adjacent hut, discussing his political vision with characteristic flare and aggression.

After the rain subsided, our banana boat to Atori was readied. Having bidden farewell to his family and friends, Atu ushered me along a small path. We would meet the boat downstream, near the river's entry into the grey, brooding Pacific.

'I just announced that I will be running for parliament in East Fataleka Ward,' Atu said. 'And I told them that you are my political advisor.'

I laughed awkwardly, assuming Atu's comments were in jest. But he appeared serious. As we walked towards the boat, I recalled other remarks by the villagers in Bethel that did, in fact, suggest Atu had been telling people I had travelled to Fataleka to give him political advice, not to report on his crusade. A day earlier, Nixon had quietly thanked me for advising his brother, whose political activities worried him and his family. I had dismissed the comment, saying it wasn't my place to provide advice. But it was becoming clearer that, for Atu, my presence was advantageous. The fact that a foreign journalist had travelled such a vast distance to visit him amplified his prestige. He was spinning my visit, using it for his own political benefit. I had become a useful prop in his nascent campaign.

We stepped into the small boat and puttered our way out into the lagoon, before pitching south towards Atori. The skies ahead were deep grey, and light rain was falling. The ocean on the northeast of Malaita was dark, and waves pounded the lagoon's edge. Atu asked the captain to head out further to sea, so he could drop a line in and try to catch his dinner as we headed south. Over the roar of the engines, there was little conversation. Atu did, however, point towards one section of the coastline, just a few kilometres south of his home village.

'This is where the mine is being built,' he yelled.

The rain fell harder. The captain slowed, circled back and chased distant birds, hoping to appease Atu's desire to catch a tuna. But there would be no catch today. For an hour, Atu's bait and hook drifted aimlessly behind the boat, all the way to Atori.

Atori is one of few gateways between northeast Malaita and the provincial capital, Auki. From Atori, a muddy and damaged road passes through the highlands towards the large west-coast village of Dala, connecting it back up to the North Road. But despite its importance as a link between east and west Malaita, Atori is a desolate and uninviting place. We disembarked, and entered a place as grimy and seedy as any other port town, albeit with a population of less than one hundred. Its broken pier jutted out across a lagoon, which at low tide transformed from a tepid, shallow entry point for boats into a mudfield. On top of the mud sat several houses and shops on stilts, with families of up to ten people in each small dwelling.

Atu told me he would find me a room, and I could wait here for the next two days for a ride back to Auki. As he stepped off the boat in search of Atori's chief, several men gathered, eager to speak with him and to hear about his tribulations since the riot. He soon returned with the chief, a genteel, quiet man named Arnon Kekei, who gathered plastic chairs for us.

'This is the big man responsible for the riots,' one of the assembled men told me, pointing towards Atu with a large smile.

With an audience, Atu switched into campaign mode. He commenced a lengthy speech, listing Malaita's historical grievances, its unique power and his determination to oust the Sogavare government.

In pidgin – the audience didn't speak Atu's native Fataleka language – he outlined a century of injustice. He cited the 1927 Malaita massacre, the British crackdown on Maasina Ruru, and how the governments of Solomon Mamaloni had worked to divide Malaitans against one another. He lambasted Sogavare, whom he decried as a corrupt and malign leader with an innately anti-Malaitan agenda, and soon descended into racially charged criticism of those in Honiara.

'When we Malaitans go anywhere, we run the place. We are sick of being run by small people,' he yelled, before denouncing the New Asia mine as another example of the mistreatment of the Malaitan people.

I noticed, in his diatribe, that Atu was incorporating information from our conversation over the previous days. The evening before, we had discussed the Pacific Games. I'd mentioned how Sogavare had personally travelled to Vanuatu to lobby for the games, and that the Pacific Games Council had voted for Honiara with just a one-vote margin. I had mused whether the fuss over the games was due to Sogavare's determination to 'cut the ribbon' at the event and enshrine his legacy. Now, Atu seamlessly incorporated my words into his stump speech, mocking the prime minister for having personally begged for votes in Vanuatu because he was only interested in 'cutting the ribbon' on the games, rather than looking after the interests of the Malaitan people.

Atu also spruiked a populist, almost certainly unachievable economic message. 'We want the lifestyle they have in Honiara to be here in Atori, here in Malaita,' he pronounced.

At the end of his speech, he declared his intention to run for parliament. But there wasn't rapturous applause. Instead, the assembled men seemed uninspired, perhaps used to the endless unfulfilled promises of politicians.

'You're going to have to buy a suit,' I said, and Atu and his audience laughed.

As the men started chatting, Atu explained some of his more specific motivations for running for parliament. He said he wanted to become the minister of police, so that he could investigate the raid on Bethel. Perhaps, I thought, a desire for revenge was fuelling his plan to enter national politics. In any case, he was already making promises that would be very challenging to keep.

Arnon, the village chief, agreed. After decades in Atori, he had seen no change, despite many pledges of assistance.

'When the British were here, we had no water, no sanitation, no roads, no wharf. We thought when independence came, we would have all those things. But we still have no water, no roads, no sanitation, no wharf,' he said.

Many villages in Malaita proudly display signs declaring them 'No Open Defecation' villages. Atori isn't one of them. Instead, villagers living in crowded, stilted shanties above the mangroves relieve themselves in the open water, which at low tide recedes entirely to expose human waste and rubbish for several hours, until the water rises again. There is no electricity and no running or clean water. There is very little economic activity, save for one small shop, which sells rice, canned fish and mie goreng noodles.

As Atu left to head back to Faunikari, he shook hands with the assembled men and then with me. I thanked him for helping me reach Atori.

Arnon set up a small bed for me in his home by the wharf, and I settled in to wait for a car to the other side of the island. For two days, I waited. I lay on a mattress on the floor as cockroaches raced across my makeshift bed. I quickly realised that any attempt to kill the critters only made things worse. The second I squished one, thousands of red ants would appear, hoovering down the dead bug. So I made a détente with the roaches, who seemed the lesser of two evils, while I read my paperback and felt time slow to a crawl.

Atori is particularly miserable at low tide, as the muddy mangroves are exposed and the mosquitoes come out of hiding. But at high tide, it also has its problems, with the lapping water covering much of the wharf. Arnon's village, already exposed to the brutality of abject poverty, is on the frontline of an environmental crisis that threatens the only life the villagers have ever known.

I was thankful when a car came, bound for Auki. For six hours, it bumped along the broken road back to the capital, back to where the North Road began.

On the road in Malaita.

19

MAKING A MARTYR

MY JOURNEY AROUND MALAITA IN LATE 2022 was my last after a year of intense travel. After I made it back to Auki, I quickly caught the Pelican Express to Honiara, where I tidied up some business before travelling home to Adelaide, excited for an Australian Christmas. For a few weeks, I put the islands to the back of my mind and reconnected with family, basking in the summer heat and preparing for the year ahead.

Meanwhile, back in Solomon Islands, Daniel Suidani and Celsus Talifilu were starting to feel the political sands shift beneath their feet.

It was becoming clear that Suidani's strong anti-China stance – the mission that had made him internationally famous – wasn't universally accepted at home, with even some of its staunchest supporters starting to question whether their champion could deliver on his rhetoric. Many Malaitans did appear genuinely ambivalent about Chinese companies operating in their communities. But this view wasn't universal, and it was rejected by many who needed immediate assistance. As I had travelled the North Road, apathy towards Suidani's anti-China crusade was the most common sentiment I encountered. Others expressed outright opposition to Suidani's posturing. All along the North Road, there was a desperate lack of basic infrastructure investment. The World Bank–funded Fiu Bridge project, which Suidani had scuttled after a Chinese company won a competitive tender to construct it, was just one of dozens of bridges that had fallen into disrepair. If the Fiu Bridge project wasn't going to proceed, what chance was there for the rest of the road to receive the investment it needed? For those living in the remote Lau Lagoon area, at the terminus of this broken road, calls for assistance to address a lack of drinking water and overpopulation were falling on deaf ears in Auki. Some community leaders felt that Suidani's government was more focused on proving its anti-China credentials than delivering materially on the ground. Others simply saw little utility in the ongoing skirmishes between the Sogavare and Suidani governments. Although few Malaitans revered the prime minister, many along the North Road seemed less perturbed by his actions than the M4D activists and Suidani's team might suggest. What they did see in the ongoing division between the Malaitan and national governments was development inertia, and a threat to the revenue streams that paid for the few basic services that existed in Malaita. Some, too, were deeply suspicious of Celsus Talifilu. Rumours were circulating widely that Suidani was effectively being controlled by Talifilu, whose lengthy political career contrasted with the relative inexperience of the premier and whose position, as an American-style political advisor with a public profile, was unique in Malaitan politics. Malaita, largely as a result of its sudden global relevance, had come to be viewed as a monolith: a place where Suidani's views and vision were unanimously supported. But this was a caricature fanned by external commentators, often for their own ends. Suidani's support, once indisputably iron-clad, was by the end of 2022 indisputably weakening.

These sentiments had been brewing throughout Suidani's term as premier. But they began to be much more openly discussed in the wake of the 2021 riots, which angered many in Malaita who disagreed with the volatile tactics of M4D. For generations, Malaita had been warding off an ugly reputation as a hostile, backwards place. Prior to travelling the North Road, I'd be warned by those in Honiara and elsewhere that the journey was far too dangerous – that I'd be robbed or attacked, and that Malaitan people were innately suspicious of foreigners. Malaitans had long been unfairly maligned and stereotyped, and the 24 November riots reinforced these shallow stereotypes, tarnishing the province's reputation. For a growing number of Malaitans, the blame for this fell squarely with their premier. Suidani certainly hadn't conceived of or supported the riots. But he had conspired with

M4D in the past, was slow to condemn M4D's actions, and was viewed as an architect of the policy division between the national and Malaitan governments that had set the stage for the worst violence since the Tensions. Patience was wearing thin.

As opposition to Suidani gathered steam, he was also facing pushback from his long-time M4D allies. By mid-2022, Knoxley Atu and Richard Olita had begun openly expressing their dissatisfaction. Some of this division had emerged the previous year, when Olita was dismissed from Suidani's team of advisors. Olita and Talifilu have different stories of this dismissal. Olita claims he voluntarily stepped aside because of his increasing public profile, whereas Talifilu told me that Olita was sacked for refusing to receive a Covid-19 vaccine. Wherever the truth lay, the cosy relationship between M4D and the Suidani team had begun to wane as early as 2021, and by 2022 the rift was clear. When I first met Atu at Henderson in July of 2022, he was quick to belittle Suidani. Atu was angry that Suidani had not publicly endorsed M4D's November protest strategy and frustrated that Suidani's high-profile pledge to hold a Malaitan independence poll had never materialised.

By late 2022, the promise at the heart of the Auki Communique – to resist Chinese investment in Malaita – was also beginning to come unstuck. As Suidani had conceded to me at the Auki Lodge, his government had little power to prohibit Chinese investment in the province. Early in 2022, Manasseh Maelanga, a Malaitan MP closely allied to Sogavare, had been the first to circumvent Suidani's Chinese-investment firewall, receiving backing from the Chinese embassy for a project in his constituency: the resurfacing of the Atori wharf, the desolate outpost on north Malaita where I had waited for my ride back to Auki. Maelanga even held a ceremony with Chinese and Solomon Islands flags flying next to each other as Chinese-funded supplies arrived at the small village. Suidani's government was powerless to stop such events, but pictures of Chinese flags flying proudly a few kilometres from Knoxley Atu's East Fataleka homeland incensed the M4D leadership.

Having seen just how hard delivering on the Auki Communique would be, Suidani and Talifilu began equivocating on the true meaning of the document. I spoke with Talifilu in the gardens at the front of Auki Lodge, Premier Suidani's favourite drinking hole, in December 2022. With Chinese businesspeople now travelling back and forth to Malaita, Talifilu told me that the Auki Communique wasn't really intended to prohibit all Chinese investment in the province, but merely to ensure that any such investment would benefit Malaitans. It was a reasonable argument that reflected the legal reality of the situation. But to the anti-China hardliners, this nuanced approach conflicted with their purist interpretation of the Auki Communique. Suidani's welcome of the New Asia Mining Company to Malaita Province – or at the very least, the inability of Suidani's government to prohibit the company from prospecting in East Fataleka – looked like a softening of Suidani's commitment to the Auki Communique. For M4D, it was the last straw.

Meanwhile, Suidani and Talifilu's Umi 4 Change party was gathering momentum. The party was designed to bring together pro-Suidani MPs, and to run candidates in national elections, using Suidani's popular appeal to extend his power to Honiara. Atu, Olita and their advisor, Makili, were deeply dismissive of Umi 4 Change, which they saw as evidence that Suidani craved more power. Atu even promised to run against any U4C candidate in the 2024 national elections, were they to nominate one in his constituency.

As Christmas 2022 approached, it was clear that Suidani's once firm grip on power had become fragile, less than eighteen months after his return from Taiwan as a hero. He had been hailed as the Father of Malaita, the island's champion, and a 'symbol of Pacific resistance to China'.[1] Now, his opponents had united against him, previously apathetic Malaitan voters had been awakened by the riots, and M4D had soured on his leadership. His profile, however, remained high. And his supporters outside of Solomon Islands remained as dedicated as ever to the Suidani story.

In early March 2023, the Malaitan provincial government was readying to reassemble after its Christmas break. Sensing the political tide was turning, Martin Fini, a Suidani critic and the de-facto opposition leader in Malaita, saw his opportunity to strike. He planned to table a motion of no confidence in the Malaitan assembly the day it resumed and worked aggressively to shore up his numbers as the day approached. Suidani and Talifilu were not as confident as they had been when facing a previous motion of no confidence. On that occasion, in October 2021, the motion had not been put to a vote, as major protests in Auki prevented parliament from opening.[2] Atu and M4D had taken credit for Suidani's protection that day, although that claim is disputed. Then, they were backing a winner. By March 2023, Suidani's position was much more tenuous.

To fend off the motion, Suidani and Talifilu began to aggressively link Fini's actions to Sogavare and to Chinese money. They alleged that the Chinese were buying assemblymen's votes and that Sogavare was pulling the strings. It is certainly plausible that Chinese business interests, particularly the New Asia Mining Company, had communicated with Fini and his allies. Similarly, Sogavare's desire to remove Suidani was well known. But there is no evidence that any 'Chinese money', certainly not money directly distributed by the Chinese state, had flowed to Fini and his supporters. Nor was there evidence the motion had been orchestrated by the prime minister's office. Rather, Fini's timing was astute. Although he knew he could count on the backing of the Sogavare government, Fini's intervention was typical of the opportunistic nature of provincial politics in Solomon Islands, where governments can rise and fall on a whim depending on the capacity of individuals to mobilise votes in support of a motion of no confidence.

As the day of the vote drew near, Suidani and Talifilu recognised they would lose. To delegitimise Fini's motion, Suidani instructed his supporters to boycott it. Fearing the vote would lead to major protests like those in support of Suidani in October 2021, the police sent riot squads to Auki. The town braced for violence. On the day of the reopening of the provincial assembly, however, the streets were quiet. Fini and his supporters entered the small assembly hall, while Suidani and his supporters remained defiantly at home. The first order of business was the motion, and it passed unanimously.

After three volatile years, Suidani's premiership was over. The reaction to his ouster within Solomon Islands was muted. It was certainly a major news event, stoking fierce debate online, but there were no public protests.

Given how fractious the political debate had become, the quiet came as a surprise. But it reflected the distance that had grown between Suidani and the Malaitan hardliners who, in previous years, had been willing to mobilise their people in his support. This time, M4D sat on the sidelines.

For a few days, it seemed as if the Suidani story could have quickly faded into the background, and that the three-year stand-off between Sogavare and the Malaitan government had reached its end. But Suidani's opponents in Honiara were not satisfied simply by his removal as premier. They wanted to ensure his career was over for good, and that his U4C party would pose no threat to their power.

In the days after he was removed from office, Suidani's name was kept in the public eye through a series of extraordinary articles by Alfred Sasako, the *Solomon Star*'s controversial reporter. The first claimed that Suidani had been offered asylum in the United States, which was denied by US officials and by Suidani, while a second, much more salacious piece alleged that Suidani had been involved in trying to orchestrate an assassination plot against Sogavare. Given Sogavare's paranoia regarding his personal safety, the claims likely resonated within his DCGA government, if they weren't orchestrated by it. It was clear that Sasako's unverified, poorly sourced and certainly inaccurate reporting was part of a strategy to muddy Suidani's popular reputation, and to pave the way for further punitive actions against the former premier.

On 20 March 2023, Suidani received a letter from Sogavare's minister of provincial government and institutional strengthening, Rollen Seleso, a close ally of the prime minister. Suidani wasn't a stranger to Seleso's correspondence. In October 2021, Seleso had successfully nullified the appointment of five of Suidani's ministers, arguing that only with Seleso's direct consent were these ministers entitled to take up their posts.[3] Now, the minister saw an opportunity to leverage his legal powers to end the Suidani affair once and for all. The 20 March 2023 letter referenced Section 15(1) of the *Provincial Government Act of 1997* and declared Suidani in breach of the act. The evidence, Seleso's letter outlined, was focused almost exclusively on Suidani's highly public support for Taiwan.

'I have perused statements by yourself made in the various daily news-papers, in international newspapers including on international television and have formed the view that you … have shown allegiance and adherence to a foreign power, being Chinese Taipei in defiance of the decision of the sovereign government of Solomon Islands,' Seleso's letter said.

The letter noted Suidani's refusal to 'uphold the decision of the Government in switching diplomatic recognition to People's Republic of China', and charged the now former premier with 'repeatedly making statements inciting disharmony and dissatisfaction against the National Government with regards to the decision to recognise People's Republic of China'.

The punishment would be severe.

'In view of the above, I hereby give you seven days to showcase why you should not be disqualified from being a member of the Malaita Provincial Assembly,' Seleso's letter said.

Although Suidani, closely advised by Talifilu, wrote in strong protest against the decision, Seleso's warning soon came to fruition. The former premier's rebuttal was rejected, and on 5 April, Suidani was disqualified.[4] Ward 5 of East Fataleka constituency now stood empty.

As Suidani and Talifilu navigated the fallout, they did so not from Auki, but from Suva, Fiji's bustling capital. In the aftermath of Suidani's removal as premier, Talifilu had leveraged the former premier's martyr-status into an invitation to conduct a speaking tour in the United States. He had been invited by nonprofit Nia Tero, which amplifies indigenous campaigns on environmental guardianship. The premier was scheduled to speak in Hawaii, New York City and Washington, D.C. But after applying for visas in Suva, Fiji's capital, Daniel Suidani and Celsus Talifilu had been rejected. News of the rejection ricocheted through Suidani's supporter base. Leveraging this support network, Suidani and Talifilu managed to contest the rejection with the support of three United States congresspeople, who had been informed of Suidani's visa limbo, and his story. Representative Neal Dunn, a Republican from Florida's Second Congressional District, who has made his anti-CCP credentials central to his political brand, was the most effusive in his support for Suidani's visit, and the most sceptical of the initial refusal.

'The denial of Daniel Suidani's visa application is suspicious and unusual. Mr Suidani displayed tremendous courage in barring CCP-linked companies from his province while serving as premier. He should be welcomed to the US with open arms, not with more hurdles. I support his decision to reapply, and I look forward to assisting him through this process,' said Representative Dunn.[5] His public advocacy for Suidani's plight was matched by that of academic Cleo Paskal, who, in Suidani's bureaucratic tangle, had seen a story of international significance. 'Why so much attention on a visa case for a former provincial premier from a country of less than a million people?' asked Paskal in a LinkedIn post. 'It's because rarely does a single person come to embody the future of a region, of the battle between systems, as much as Suidani has.'

Suidani and Talifilu's visas were granted after a successful appeal. For a month, the two travelled the United States, sharing their story with a receptive international audience. Talifilu's social media feed trickled out a stream of tourist snaps in front of the UN General Assembly, on New York City streets, in the pristine gardens of Hawaii's Manoa University. The two were invited to the UN Permanent Forum on Indigenous Issues, where they would discuss key indigenous guardianship policies which the Suidani administration had tried to implement while in office, all the while making time for interviews with the international media about Suidani's sensational downfall.

As Suidani and Talifilu travelled to Washington, D.C., the streams of social media posts began to show some familiar faces: those based in America who had been central to the global amplification of Suidani's story. On 26 April, Talifilu shared with his influential Malaita Provincial Development Forum group a picture of himself and Suidani alongside Chris Chappell, a YouTube personality whose channel, *China Uncensored*, had routinely covered the Suidani story. The men were standing in front of the US Capitol. For Chappell, the Suidani story offered an alluring narrative through which he could accrue viewers and reinforce his page's agenda. And by affixing himself to the story, Chappell had also thrust himself, a fringe YouTube commentator, out of the recesses of the internet, all the way to the halls of American power. Chappell's channel is associated with *The Epoch Times* media company.[6] Once 'a small, low-budget newspaper with an anti-China slant that was handed out free on New York street corners', *The Epoch Times* has since 'become a leading purveyor of right-wing misinformation'.[7] The company, linked to the Falun Gong movement, was conceived to provide a counterweight to Chinese government propaganda, but over time, has emerged as a distributor of misinformation itself, even winning praise from noted far-right conspiracist and former Donald Trump advisor Steve Bannon. Its partnership with Chappell's YouTube channel was illustrative of its attraction to beguiling stories that undermine Beijing's credibility, irrespective of the degree of truth and the quality of reporting behind them. Many facets of the Suidani story fit that bill, and Chappell was willing to tell his subscribers that every machination of Malaitan politics was the result of intervention by strategists in Beijing, rather than the outcome of internal political activities occurring on an island he was covering but had no evidence of ever travelling to.

In Talifilu's post, Suidani had revealed that Chappell leveraged his audience of 1.7 million people to provide financial support for Suidani and Talifilu's travels.

Nine days earlier, Chappell had posted a video titled 'YOU Can Strike A Blow to the CCP!'[8] 'Today, you have a rare opportunity to stand up to the CCP and strike a win for freedom,' he told his audience in the video. Chappell then continued to tell his version of Suidani's story, arguing his ouster was solely the result of the Chinese government's direct intervention, and that 'Solomon Islands is being turned into Hong Kong,' referring to Beijing's brutal crackdown on Hong Kong's democracy in preceding years.

'Right now, Suidani is visiting the US. And when he returns home, he will almost certainly be arrested, because Solomon Islands has now been almost completely infiltrated by the CCP. And that's where you come in'.

Chappell then asked his audience to contribute to a hastily conceived GoFundMe page, which within twenty-four hours had raised US$27,000. Using the funds, Chappell, Suidani and Talifilu had made it to the US Capitol. There, they briefed Senate staff and met with sitting officeholders.

They also provided official testimony to the Congressional Executive Commission on China, an important institution within the US Congress that gathers evidence on Chinese human rights abuses and political activities. The bipartisan committee, composed of nine senators and nine members of the House of Representatives, provides an annual report directly to the US president. As they provided their testimony, the two Solomon Islanders were sitting next to Chappell and Cleo Paskal.

Back home in Solomon Islands, Suidani's tour was not going unnoticed. Talifilu's sophisticated use of social media had turned it into a widely followed event. In a post on the 'Yumi TokTok Forum' – one of the larger Facebook groups in Solomon Islands – praise for Suidani was common. One user, Andrew Muaki, wrote in awe of the former premier's achievements.

> The soft-spoken and humble man from Fataleka has a [busier] schedule in a land of over 300 million people than any Solomon Islands prime minister or minister in living memory. But unlike our leaders who visit the US at the expense of taxpayers, Hon Suidani manages to do so with the help of those who believe in what he stands for.

IFUTALO'S EDEN

THE SWITCH WAS A SEISMIC MOMENT in Solomon Islands.

With its recognition of China, Solomon Islands came to be caricatured as the next domino to fall in China's grand quest for global domination. It catapulted obscure, inexperienced island politicians into positions of global import. It attracted a global community of China hawks to cast their attention towards islands they'd never set foot on, many of whom saw in the struggle between Suidani and Sogavare a proxy conflict between China and the World; between Good and Evil. It was typical of a foreign, largely Western, tendency to see small, developing nations as chess pieces in *their* geopolitical and ideological struggles, instead of truly seeking to understand the dynamics that were at play on the ground, and the culture and history that shaped them.

The Switch influenced the behaviour of some of the most powerful actors in global politics. Senior officials in the US government reacted promptly to Chinese overtures in Honiara by establishing an embassy of their own and sending some of their most senior diplomats to the country. US president Joe Biden, in late 2022, stood shoulder-to-shoulder with the Solomon Islands prime minister at the White House. Australia, too, radically altered its behaviour in response to the Switch, loosening its purse and throwing more money at Sogavare and his personal initiatives in fear of 'losing' Solomons to a strategic rival. The Switch came to be symbolic of the imminent threat Chinese expansionism posed to Australia, a threat which has been leveraged to reshape Australia's foreign and security policy, now dominated by a multi-decade nuclear-submarine partnership between Canberra, London and Washington known as AUKUS.

The Switch also delivered power to a handful of Solomon Islanders who previously had none, or whose grip on it was tenuous. Suidani's rapid political ascendency had long coat tails, on which rode Celsus Talifilu. His sage advice, constant companionship and political savvy transformed Talifilu from an anonymous bureaucratic functionary to one of Solomon Islands' most influential men. It took Talifilu all the way to the United Nations and to the US capital. Suidani's career in politics may now be over, but his importance hasn't diminished. In 2019, he was running a small construction business. Now, he enjoys a cult-hero status, and is viewed as symbolic of an epochal struggle between autocracy and democracy, between tyranny and freedom. Many foreigners also saw Suidani as a hero – someone whose remarkable story could be used to boost their own prestige, and their own political and philosophical crusades. Domestically, the Switch provided fertile ground for dissidents and activists to prove themselves and build their powerbases. M4D didn't exist in any significant way until the Switch. Now, it serves as an ideological umbrella that aims to reimagine Solomon Islands politics and pursue a volatile, even dangerous dream of an independent Malaitan state.

These seismic shifts transformed lives, transformed regional politics and transformed Solomon Islands. They also transformed the political fortunes of Mannaseh Sogavare, for whom the Switch became a vehicle with which to accrue extraordinary political power. The prime minister, burned by his three previous periods in the top job, has skilfully played the politics of the Switch to his advantage, consolidating his parliamentary base to emerge as the most dominant politician in Solomon Islands since his mentor Mamaloni. The Switch gave Sogavare a unique opportunity. He used it to inject new capital into Honiara and to boost his legacy projects. He used it to strengthen the support of his pro-China parliamentary colleagues. He extracted major concessions from the US and Australian governments. As the dividends of this strategy became clear, Sogavare continued to double down on what he viewed as a lucrative ploy. In July 2023, he controversially led a thirty-person delegation, comprised largely of loyal pro-China MPs, to China, where he declared he was 'home' upon arrival. He used the trip to admonish the conditionality of Australian and Western aid, while praising China's contrasting approach, stirring his political enemies into a frenzy and sending new waves of anxiety through the Western security establishment. Sogavare also used the controversy to sow division in Malaita. Had Suidani successfully unified Malaita behind his cause, Sogavare's career would have been over. Instead, divisions in Malaita have deepened and Suidani has been ousted, leaving Sogavare firmly in control of parliament and of the country.

For all these transformations, however, the status quo on the ground for everyday Solomon Islanders remains the same. The country is still one of the most impoverished places in the world. Any chance of reform has been, during the Switch years, largely sidelined. The net result is a poorer, harsher Solomon Islands. It remains a place where ordinary people are maimed by unexploded ordinance; a place so bereft of medicine that a scratch can lead to a deadly infection; a place so burdened by energy poverty that rural children can't study after dark; a place where the causes of unrest, instability and hardship are still stubbornly, tragically unaddressed.

*

For external partners of Solomon Islands, especially Australia, the Switch and the entrenchment of what is perceived as a 'pro-China' leader in Manasseh Sogavare are often considered failures of foreign and development policy. The perceived cosiness between Beijing and Honiara is viewed by some as having been the direct result of Australia's policy failings in the country, and in the Pacific more broadly. There are often calls for Australia to 'do more' in the Pacific, implying that this would weaken the resolve of Sogavare or those like him to pursue a relationship with Beijing so vigorously. But there is often little specificity in the calls to 'do more', and there is an unwillingness to concede that past interventions, no matter how well intentioned, have resulted in both positive and negative outcomes, many of which were never intended.

In Chapter 3, I detailed the disastrous long-term consequences of an otherwise economically rational British economic intervention. In establishing the Tasimboko palm-oil plantations, the British successfully created an export commodity but, in doing so, fundamentally distorted the cultural status quo, planting the seeds for future conflict. More recent well-intended interventions have created their own challenges, despite outwardly achieving many of their aims.

Consider the RAMSI intervention: the program was an unequivocal military and strategic success. It brought peace to Solomon Islands quickly and created the structures to sustain it. RAMSI successfully removed weapons from the streets. Many thousands of Solomon Islanders remain thankful for the intervention and express a palpable loyalty to Australia.

But alongside its successes, the RAMSI intervention also has a more questionable legacy. Its undermining of Solomon Islands' sovereignty, through what Clive Moore has described as 'the indignity of an imported administrative and police apparatus',[1] animated nationalists such as Sogavare, fuelling an irreparable suspicion of Australia. Sogavare's ongoing scepticism about Australia today is not because of its inadequate climate or development policies. It is because past Australian governments, under the guise of RAMSI, usurped Sogavare's power and offended his nationalist beliefs. Given it was conceived in haste by an Australian foreign minister who admitted there was no exit plan, the RAMSI operation evolved beyond its original purpose, shifting from peace-building to state-building. After peace was restored in 2003, Australian officials remained in key posts of government, and billions were spent on improving the quality of governance. The focus on capacity-building in these key institutions did improve capacity. It also concentrated an extraordinary amount of wealth in the national capital, further exaggerating the economic divide between the small urban elite in Honiara and the rural majority, who still rely on subsistence for survival.

The scale of RAMSI's investment – AU$2.7 billion – also had a perverse political outcome. Some in Australia appear to believe it entitles Canberra to exert unique levels of influence in Honiara today. But despite the investment, Solomon Islands is still rife with grievance, poverty, corruption, greed and an extraordinary lack of access to the most basic of services, such as electricity, healthcare, sanitation, clean water and education, in remote and rural communities as well as in Honiara. RAMSI was vital and, in many critical ways, highly successful. But it did not put food on the table for young families in Malaita, stock clinics in Choiseul with antibiotics, improve literacy in Makira or build sewerage systems on the Nggela Islands.

Even major infrastructure pledges have created perverse outcomes, while appearing outwardly successful. One of the most promising interventions by the international community has been the development of the Tina River Hydropower Plant. The power plant, a 15-megawatt renewable energy project that promises to supply the Honiara grid with 65 per cent of its energy, is the largest public works initiative in Solomon Islands' history. The project, situated in the hills southeast of the capital, was first suggested by the World Bank in February 2006 and aims to revolutionise the country's energy system, lowering energy prices in Honiara and helping the Solomon Islands government to meet its renewable energy targets. Beset by delays and with an estimated cost of US$240 million, the project has received finance from the World Bank, the Green Climate Fund, the Asian Development Bank, the Australian government, the Abu Dhabi Fund for Development and South Korea's development agency.

The focus of donor partners and the Solomon Islands government on Tina River, however, has had unintended consequences. In the sixteen years since the project was announced, only a handful of other meaningful projects on climate and energy have occurred, beyond a few ad-hoc projects. With all the hopes for decarbonising the Honiara grid being placed on Tina River, there has been little effort to reform the antiquated electricity regulations that have hampered the uptake of renewable energy in the city. Solomon Islands' energy market is governed by an electricity act written in 1964 and barely amended since. It grants a unique degree of power to the Solomon Islands Electricity Authority to set the price of power and to serve as its sole generator, institutionalising a conflict of interest. Any private generator of energy who creates over 50kw of power must pay the same tariff as their neighbours stuck on the Honiara grid. This means that if a private energy consumer – perhaps a business or a school – wants to install solar panels on their roof, they will not receive a lower energy bill than if they had remained on the diesel-fired grid, and they would not be able to connect their own energy supply to the Honiara grid. In mature energy regulatory regimes, households and businesses can generate power on their roofs and sell this power back to the grid. These 'feed-in tariffs' incentivise private energy consumers – businesses and households – to invest in cheaper, cleaner energy, hoping that they can both lower their power bills and generate income. They also lower the emissions profile of the grid as a whole. But as of 2023, this is still illegal in Solomon Islands. This has driven up prices, further entrenched the grid's dependency on diesel-generation, and left many householders in Honiara simply unable to turn on the lights.

All the attention focused on the Tina River project has also constrained the capacity of authorities and donors to look beyond Honiara to invest in project development that leads to the provision of basic services. Eighty per cent of Solomon Islanders live outside of Honiara, and 80 per cent of these islanders have no access to electricity. They do not have refrigeration for food or medicine, or sufficient lighting to allow them to study at night. They usually cannot connect to the internet. These individuals will never be connected to any power grid and will never benefit from the investment in the Honiara-focused mega-project.

The Tina River Hydropower Plant will lead to real positive outcomes. But the focus on this single initiative has had a clear opportunity cost. It has disincentivised regulatory reform and distracted from development initiatives in rural communities. And it has further demonstrated to many in Solomon Islands that the priorities of the government and of its donor partners are firmly on Honiara, compounding the divisions and enmities that have continued to spill into violence and unrest for a quarter of a century.

The Seasonal Worker Program is another example. The scheme has real benefits for those who are accepted. But it favours the well educated and comparably well off. It creates a distorting effect on the local labour market, syphoning many of Solomon Islands' best and brightest – individuals with degrees in law, finance, engineering or government – to pick fruit on Australian farms or slaughter animals in New Zealand abattoirs. Meanwhile, local businesses in Solomon Islands struggle to find skilled local labour and must hire foreign consultants to meet critical skills shortages.

These examples illustrate the unique degree of complexity surrounding economic and development interventions in Solomon Islands. Calls to simply 'do more' ignore this complexity. They also ignore the inherent structural flaws in the West's development apparatus and how it is applied to a state like Solomon Islands. The lack of economic progress in the country must stimulate debate about the focus of bilateral and multilateral donors and how aid is delivered. As Solomon Islands' largest development partner, Australia's approach, in particular, warrants scrutiny. It is clear that when such scrutiny is applied, major gaps appear.

When, in 2013, Australia elected a conservative government led by prime minister Tony Abbott, his administration set about reforming how overseas development assistance was implemented. The government formally merged AusAID, Australia's development agency, with its foreign affairs department. The merger was intended to drive operational efficiencies – managerial code for reducing staff numbers – and to better align aid with Australia's foreign policy strategy. In practice, it increased the outsourcing of foreign aid programs to a handful of major private sector contractors. Today, around 30 per cent of Australian aid spending is tendered to private contractors, much of which is consolidated among four major players in the space – ABT Associates, DT Global, Palladium and Tetra Tech (formerly Coffey) – who collectively earn billions each year in Australian government contracts.[2]

Outsourcing projects to specialist contractors is not new. Sometimes it is essential, especially as technical expertise departs Australia's public sector for global conglomerates. But the reliance on for-profit corporations to administer Australia's strategic aid spend creates structural barriers to innovation and change. All aid spending is carefully monitored and evaluated. Each aid dollar spent is typically subject to rigorous analysis during and after the program, in order to identify whether or not the program provided value for money and was ultimately effective. This makes intuitive sense: donors don't want to see aid money wasted, so they have established rigorous protocols to ensure this doesn't occur. But it leads to tried and tested programs being replicated and expanded, while new, riskier and more innovative initiatives aren't considered, and certainly aren't pushed by the private companies delivering on the ground. Major corporate aid contractors do not want to be involved with projects that have a higher chance of failure, even if the potential development dividends for these initiatives could be worth the risk. With billions of dollars at stake, innovation is sidelined, while repetition is rewarded.

In a country like Solomon Islands, where a vast majority live in rural, disaggregated villages, small-scale initiatives are often where the most consequential and direct development outcomes can occur. Take the ailing village of Atori, where I spent my time squishing ants and cockroaches waiting for a ride, as an example. In this community of 200, there is one driver of economic activity: a small wharf. The wharf is administered by the local chief, Arnon, who collects a modest fee from those loading and unloading cargo. Arnon is a passionate Malaitan. And he has a vision for his community's advancement. Each day, he has fishermen come and dock, hoping to sell their catch to local merchants. Because there is no refrigeration, the fishermen cannot transport their catch to communities more than a few kilometres from the wharf. Arnon, recognising this challenge, has longed for a simple fix: an ice machine. He told me of his hopes to have a small ice machine installed at the wharf, powered by solar panels. He would be able to pay for the machine's upkeep with the modest wharf-docking fee, and would sell the ice for a modest price to the fishermen. It would be a win-win for the fishermen, and for Atori. The anglers would be able to preserve their fish for more than a few hours, granting them access to more markets. And it would bring a little more income into the Atori community. Arnon dreams of this intervention. He cannot afford it himself and hopes, one day, donors will be able to assist in turning his vision into reality.

There are innumerable examples of micro-interventions that would stimulate local economic activity, albeit modestly, across rural Solomon

Islands – initiatives that would add to traditional ways of living, rather than displacing them. Despite being low-cost, and likely high-impact, they rarely occur. This is because of the managerial overheads associated with implementing dozens or hundreds of micro-initiatives and the fact that the aid ecosystem is unwilling to embark on these more risky initiatives. In an interview for this book with former Australian prime minister Scott Morrison, who genuinely prides himself on his knowledge and experience of Pacific Island affairs, I asked why these highly effective small-scale initiatives aren't favoured. His answer was brutally honest: 'It's very hard.' Donors and aid contractors instead search for large-scale projects – projects that have healthy margins for the implementing partner, despite their lukewarm development impacts for the recipient country. The focus leaves people like Arnon frustrated: he sees tens of millions of dollars flowing into administrative reform in the capital but has no way of receiving a few thousand dollars to get his ice-machine project off the ground. It is a dynamic that fuels resentment, keeping the kindling that can lead to instability perpetually dry, ready for charismatic agitators to set alight.

These macro trends in the delivery of foreign aid and assistance demand reform. But perhaps more alarming than the inadequacies of international aid policy is the willingness of development partners to use aid and assistance as tools to curry political favour with Solomon Islands' elite. Since the Switch, Australia has funded the pet projects of the Sogavare government, at the expense of more impactful development initiatives. Chief among these has been the Pacific Games. In August 2022, the newly elected Albanese Labor government, which had made the Australian–Solomons relationship a political weapon during the 2022 election campaign, agreed to provide AU$17 million to support Sogavare's initiative.[3] The development benefits of the games are minimal. The support for the games, as noted by esteemed Pacific aid scholar Professor Stephen Howes of the Australian National University, constituted 'over 10 per cent of Australia's total aid to Solomon Islands' during 2022–23.[4] The allocation also contravenes OECD guidelines on aid spending, chipping away at Australia's already shaky credibility as an aid donor. The support for the games demonstrates Australia's prioritisation of the political relationship with Sogavare, a deeply unpopular 67-year-old leader who will certainly cede power at some point, over reinvigorating an aid program that currently achieves little for the country's most disadvantaged. Australian policymakers have reckoned that it is as important to meet Sogavare's political needs, under the questionable logic that doing so would prevent the prime minister going further with the Beijing relationship, as it is to meet Solomon Islanders' complex development needs. This prioritisation is felt in Solomon Islands, especially in Malaita. It is short-termist, politically driven aid delivery. It is an approach that will undermine Australia's longer-term credibility in a region critical to its national security and global relevance.

For the last several years, the chief criticism of Australia's approach to the region has been that its approach to climate change had been insufficient, angering Pacific governments who see global warming and rising sea levels as an existential threat. Former prime minister Morrison argued that the issue rarely came up when he spoke directly with Pacific leaders. But during the 2022 Australian election, the deficient climate policies of the Morrison government were routinely cited by his opponents as a chief reason why the Pacific was cosying up to Beijing.

Critics of this narrative ask why, if Australia's climate policies have undermined the Pacific–Australia relationship, would the region shift towards China, the world's largest emitter? But this question misses the point. Pacific nations understand China's emissions profile: they do not seek out a relationship with China because of its climate credentials. But climate isn't the only issue that Pacific leaders care about. And in lieu of Australian leadership on the issue, Pacific nations have sought alternative sources of financial and diplomatic support, both to practically benefit their economies and to impose a strategic cost on Canberra for Australia's perceived inaction on climate.

The breadth of the climate challenge, and the diverse suite of activities associated with mitigating its worst effects, however, does provide an opportunity for Australia to consolidate its relationships in the region in a way that is mutually beneficial. Being serious about climate at home isn't all that matters, but it is Australia's ticket to working deeply with Pacific countries on the issue that is most central to the region's long-term prosperity. In this sense, Australia's policy of pushing back against Chinese interference in the region – a policy known as 'strategic denial' – can best be achieved if Australia first becomes a climate leader. This is a precondition to working intimately with the Pacific region.

Analyses that place the blame for Solomon Islands' myriad economic and governmental failures squarely at the feet of its international donor partners, however, are not fair. Much of the responsibility does lie, too, with Solomon Islands' decision makers. Successive governments in Honiara have been unable to provide the leadership needed to improve the country's anaemic economy. Corruption is endemic. Few bills pass the national parliament, where many politicians prioritise the micromanagement of their constituencies and self-enrichment over the pursuit of national revitalisation.

Perhaps more pernicious than the poor policy making and the incapacity to stamp out corruption is the Solomon Islands government's inability to craft a narrative and a national mission that inspires the public. Travelling around the islands, I have often asked locals about the aspirations of their communities – whether the children and young adults have hopes, dreams or plans for the future. I am conscious that my perspective – that of a Western-educated, 32-year-old man who lives in a developed city with a population larger than the entire Solomon Islands – will always differ from those across the archipelago. But the answers were still often saddening. Some young people hope to get an education and to pursue a career, or to build a more stable life for their families. Others simply don't see the point, recognising that nothing has really changed in their communities, in terms of economic or development outcomes, for generations. There are, of course, many communities where a simple, subsistence life is idyllic and sufficient to satisfy. But in others, people just do not believe that progress is possible. So much Western thought over the past century has been premised on the idea, however flawed, of linear progress: *if I work hard, I will get ahead and build a better life, and leave the next generation better off.* In much of rural Solomon Islands, there is no expectation that this kind of progress will eventuate. I often thought, when trying to fall asleep on the floor of a village guest house, about a world in 2050: a world where countries like mine would see extraordinary progress and technological advancement, while the village in which I was sleeping would remain exactly the same, if not even more challenged, as its people bared the brunt of an increasingly hostile environment, fuelled by the apathy and greed of those thousands of kilometres away.

*

Alongside debate about what the international community, including Australia, should do in Solomon Islands is the question of what it should *not* do. After the Switch, countless foreign actors – governments, for-profit international development firms, academics, YouTube quacks, politicians, businesspeople, journalists and authors, including myself – saw an opportunity. For me, the Switch became a vehicle through which I achieved many of my journalistic ambitions, some of which had sat with me, unfulfilled, since childhood. In this remarkable story and its aftermath, I was presented with a rare platform and a chance to tell a story that wasn't my own. I was conscious of this dynamic, and often guilty about it. Was I displacing local storytellers? Was this book the right thing to do?

But as I grappled with this moral dilemma, I witnessed others leverage the Switch and its colourful characters to achieve their own ends, often with far less introspection. Academics and commentators jumped on the story, seeing a chance to legitimise their opinions about China's rise. Australian politicians used the Switch to improve their political fortunes, and Australia's national security complex used it to justify military expansionism. Shady Chinese-linked businesses saw a chance to enter a market that was poorly regulated to make a quick buck. In short, outsiders saw in the Switch not a risk to Solomon Islanders, but a chance to pursue their interests. It struck me as not too dissimilar to the motivations of the gold-hungry Spaniards, or the British labour traders, or the warring parties in the Second World War, who used this archipelago for their own ends, scarring it in the process for generations to come. For centuries, outsiders had used Solomon Islands as a vehicle for their own ambitions. The Switch was no exception. And the outcome was this: an island chain richly endowed with cultural and physical attributes sits languishing, among the least developed nations on earth.

Ultimately, all international actors – be they Solomon Islands' traditional donor partners, multilateral institutions, new partners such as China, or outsiders looking in like me – need to be humble enough to recognise that our expectations of what progress looks like might not always align with what is desired on the ground; that our proven path to prosperity might not appeal; that our way of living is fundamentally different, but not better or worse, than that of everyday Solomon Islanders, who will have their own visions of what progress means, for themselves and for their kin.

*

As a cool breeze whipped through the shared dining room in 511 Motel, in the small fishing village of Malu'u in North Malaita, I sat next to a man named Roger Ifutalo. He was waiting for his dinner, which was being prepared by another man in the kitchen. As I prepared my instant noodles, we started to talk.

'It is his turn to cook', he said, pointing to his colleague slicing chillies by the stove.

Ifutalo was shirtless, hairy-chested, and fifty-six years old. He and his colleague worked as technicians for Solomon Power, the state electricity utility, and their jobs involved regular travel to every inch of the archipelago.

'Wherever there is a problem, we will go. I've been across Malaita, to Western, to Isabel, even as far away as Taro in Choiseul,' said Ifutalo.

The electrician had spent the past twenty-six years working a respectable, well-paid job for the state-owned power utility. His five children were now grown up. Two had moved to the capital, but three remained on Ifutalo's home island of Makira, along with his wife. For work, Ifutalo had spent much of his adult life in Honiara, far away from his family, and far away from the world in which he wanted to live. One year earlier, he had tried to retire, but the company still needed him. He had returned to work, but was unhappy. So he had put a plan into action.

Throughout 2022, the electrical repairman had been squirrelling away some money to create the life he'd always wanted. As a boy, he had inherited a small parcel of land well away from the coast, deep in the bush. He had never known what to do with it. After a life in the grime of the capital and years on the road, travelling town to town, sleeping in cheap concrete motels, this small sliver of land took on a new appeal.

'I used to remember, as a boy, playing in the grass, listening to the birds', he reminisces. 'Then I had to come to study, then to work.'

After a few months working as a semi-retired contractor for Solomon Power, Ifutalo decided enough was enough. In late 2023, he will finally put down his tools. By then, the small new home he has started building on his inherited plot of land will be complete.

'The nearest neighbour won't be for three or four kilometres. I want to re-learn how I cooked as a child. I won't need any refrigerators, no TV, no internet.'

When he arrives home in Makira, Ifutalo will spend a few weeks in town with his adult children. Then, after some time, he will move to his own private oasis, on land passed down to him through generations. He will spend his days tending to the fruits and vegetables he plans to grow. There will be no surplus to sell, no profits to be made. He will have just enough to feed himself and his wife. As he toils in his gardens and rests in his humble thatched-roof hut, he will hear the birds again. Each dawn, he will be awoken by the sounds of his childhood – the rustling of the leaves, the subtle flaps of a nearby wing, the familiar laughter of innocent youth, carried on a stiff sea breeze.

Only then, Roger Ifutalo said, 'I will be free.'

NOTES

1: 'AFUERA!'

1 Lord Amherst of Hackney and Basil Thomson (eds), *The Discovery of the Solomon Islands by Alvaro de Mendaña in 1568, Translated from the Original Spanish Manuscripts*. London: The Hakluyt Society, 1901.
2 Amherst and Thomson.
3 A *teredo* is a type of mollusc known for eating through the hulls of ships, also known as a 'shipworm'.
4 Amherst and Thomson.
5 Amherst and Thomson, p. 22.
6 Amherst and Thomson, p. 23.

2: JUNGLE ROAD

1 Clive Moore, *Tulagi: Pacific Outpost of the British Empire*. Canberra: ANU Press, 2019.
2 William Davenport, 'The Moro Movement of Guadalcanal, British Solomon Islands Protectorate', *The Journal of the Polynesian Society* 76:2 (1967), pp. 123–75.
3 Paul Theroux, *The Happy Isles of Oceania: Paddling the Pacific*. New York: Ballantine Books, 1993, p. 169.
4 Davenport, 'The Moro Movement of Guadalcanal, British Solomon Islands Protectorate'.
5 'The Tensions', www.ramsi.org/the-tensions
6 Theroux, *The Happy Isles of Oceania*, p. 160.

3: RUNNING AGROUND

1 'Captain Oliver Kruess', *Ships Monthly*, 10 March 2011, shipsmonthly.com
2 Jon Fraenkel, Matthew Allen and Harry Brock, 'The Resumption of Palm-oil Production on Guadalcanal's Northern Plains', *Pacific Economic Bulletin* 25:1 (2010), pp. 64–75.
3 Ibid.
4 Alexander Downer, 'Neighbours Cannot Be Recolonised', *The Australian*, 8 January 2003, p. 11.
5 John Howard, address to the Sydney Institute, 1 July 2003, https://pmtranscripts.pmc.gov.au/release/transcript-20769

4: MANASSEH OF EAST CHOISEUL

1 Maritza Brunt, 'Adventists Recognised for Service in Papua New Guinea', *Adventist Record*, 9 January 2017.

2   Radio New Zealand, 'Solomons' PM Wants to Apply for PNG Citizenship', 19 September 2017.

3   Solomon Islands Factfile, Facebook post, 11 April 2019, https://www.facebook.com/Solfafile/photos/a.4576136285749037/26325708967722623

4   Christopher Chevalier, *Understanding 'Solo': A Biography of Solomon Mamaloni*, self-published, 2022, http://hdl.handle.net/1885/262993, p. 79.

5   Chevalier, *Understanding 'Solo'*, p. 133.

6   Chevalier, *Understanding 'Solo'*, p. 136.

7   Mamaloni quoted in Chevalier, *Understanding 'Solo'*, p. 53.

8   Alexis Elizabeth Tucker Sade, 'Incorporating the Archipelago: The Imposition and Acculturation of the Solomon Islands State', PhD thesis, University of California, San Diego, 2017, https://escholarship.org/uc/item/3j3731v1

9   In 2007, Alfred Sasako, a Solomon Islands journalist and former member of parliament, claimed that Sogavare had told him and other MPs about spiritual interactions with Mamaloni. See 'Sogavare "Spoke to Dead Solomons PM"', *The Sydney Morning Herald*, 2 August 2007.

10   Rowan Callick, 'Manasseh Sogavare Wins Third Stint as Solomons PM', *The Australian*, 10 December 2014.

11   'Solomon Islands: New Political Party Challanges Country's Leadership' (interview with Manasseh Sogavare), *Pacific Beat*, ABC Radio Australia, 13 July 2005.

12   A 'debt-free money system' would be the full realisation of Douglas' social credit ideas, and would in theory see money provided to Solomon Islanders through a central bank, without attaching repayable debt to that money.

13   Sam Alasia, 'Rainbows Across the Mountains', *Journal of Pacific History* 42:2 (2007): pp. 165–86.

14   Alasia, 'Rainbows Across the Mountains'.

15   Moore, 'Uncharted Pacific Waters', p. 498.

16   'Solomons Accuse Downer of Interference', *The Sydney Morning Herald*, 9 May 2006.

17   'Taiwan Pulls Solomons Police Training', *The Sydney Morning Herald*, 19 January 2007.

18   'Julian Moti and the Raid on the Prime Minister's Office', Nautilus Institute, 19 December 2011, https://nautilus.org

19   *R v Moti* (2009), QSC 407, austlii.edu.au

5: MAASINA MEN

1   Clive Moore, *Making Mala: Malaita in Solomon Islands, 1870s–1930s*. Canberra: Australian National University Press, 2017, p. 47.

2   Moore, *Making Mala*, p. 96.

3   Moore, *Making Mala*, p. 126.

4   Moore, *Making Mala*.

5   Davenport, 'The Moro Movement of Guadalcanal'.

6: DEVIL'S NIGHT

1   Charlotte Greenfield and Tom Westbrook, 'Solomon Islands Look Beyond Taiwan as Election Looms', Reuters, 21 March 2019.

2   'Solomon Islands Considering Recognising China over Taiwan', *The Fiji Times*, 3 April 2019.

3   'Sogavare Pressured to Switch Recognition', *Solomon Times*, 20 May 2019.

4   'Taskforce Leaves for China via PNG', *Solomon Times*, 5 August 2019.

5   Alfred Sasako, 'Prime Minister's Taskforce on China Heads to Vanuatu', *The Island Sun News*, Facebook post, 25 June 2019.

6   Interview with head of Transparency Solomons.

7   Larry Diamond and Orville Schell (eds), *China's Influence and American Interests: Promoting Constructive Vigilance*. Stanford, CA: Hoover Institute Press, 2019.

8   Edward Cavanough, 'In Mongolia, Climate Crisis Threatens Herding Traditions', *Al Jazeera*, 29 November 2022.

9   'China's Pacific Investment a "Trap"', Radio New Zealand, 26 August 2019.

10 Andrew Fanasia, 'To Switch or Not to Switch', *Solomon Star*, 16 September 2019.

11 'The R.O.C. (Taiwan) Government Terminates Diplomatic Relations with Solomon Islands with Immediate Effect to Uphold National Dignity', Media statement, Ministry of Foreign Affairs of the Republic of China (Taiwan), 16 September 2019, https://en.mofa.gov.tw

12 Analysis of the Lowy Institute's *Pacific Aid Map*: https://pacificaidmap.lowyinstitute.org/

13 'First-time MP Vokia Lose Seat in Petition', *Solomon Times*, 17 February 2020; 'Two Solomons MPs Found Guilty of Bribing Voters', Radio New Zealand, 17 February 2020.

7: ESCAPE FROM ADELIUA

1   Alan Tidwell, 'The Tulagi Turning Point', *The Strategist*, Australian Strategic Policy Institute, 28 October 2019.

8: THE GAMES

1   Liam Morgan, 'Solomon Islands to Challenge Tahiti for Right to Host 2023 Pacific Games', *Inside the Games*, 6 May 2016.

2   Evan Wasuka and Bang Xiao, 'China Bankrolls Solomon Islands Stadium Ahead of Pacific Summit', ABC News (Australia), 17 October 2019.

3   Michael Pavitt, 'Solomon Islands Holds Ground-breaking Ceremony for Pacific Games Stadium Project', *Inside the Games*, 15 May 2021.

9: RIVERS OF GOLD

1   Amherst and Thomson, p. 202.

2   Amherst et al., p. 34.

3   'Gold Ridge' project overview, International Finance Corporation, https://disclosures.ifc.org/project-detail/SPI/27766/gold-ridge

4   'Gold Ridge' project overview, International Finance Corporation, https://disclosures.ifc.org/project-detail/SPI/27766/gold-ridge

5   'Our History', https://stbarbara.com.au/our-company/our-history/

6   'Chinese Redevelopment of Solomon Islands' Gold Ridge Mine Dubbed "Way Over the Top"', ABC News (Australia), 30 October 2019.

7   Fredrick Kusu, 'PS Viulu Says 2023 CDF Should Be Used in Constituencies', Solomon Islands Broadcasting Corporation, 13 December 2022.

8   'China to Continue with CDF Funding; "Not in Cash!"', Solomon Islands Broadcasting Corporation, 15 October 2019.

9   Jonathan Barrett, 'China Pays into Solomons Fund as Part of Diplomatic Switch', Reuters, 6 April 2021.

10 'Chinese Redevelopment of Solomon Islands' Gold Ridge Mine Dubbed "Way Over the Top"', ABC News (Australia), 30 October 2019.
11 Jimmy Nolan, 'Exploiting Desperate People Applying for Seasonal Work', *Solomon Times*, 19 August 2021.

10: 'NO NEED CHINA!'

1 Clive Moore, 'No More Walkabout Long Chinatown', in *Politics and State Building in Solomon Islands*, Sinclair Dinnen and Stuart Firth (eds). Canberra: ANU Press, 2008. DOI 10.22459/PSBS.05.2008.03
2 Moore, 'No More Walkabout Long Chinatown', p. 81.

11: WUHAN WINDOW

1 Edward Cavanough, 'How a Medical Evacuation Exposed Solomon Islands' China Challenge', *Al Jazeera*, 8 June 2021.
2 Interview with a cabinet minister on condition of anonymity.
3 Around US$65,000, or SBD$550,000.
4 Premier Suidani confirmed Nalapat's involvement in an interview with the ABC after returning to Australia from Taiwan, in July 2021: Samuel Seke, 'Malaita Province Premier Says Taiwan for Medical Treatment Was Not Political', ABC News (Australia), 16 July 2021.
5 Robert Iroga, 'Suidani Heads Home After Successful Medical Treatment in Taiwan', *Solomon Business Magazine Online*, 12 July 2021.

12: HONIARA BURNING

1 Charles Kadamana, 'Leave It to Us', *The Island Sun*, 15 August 2021.
2 'Solomon Islands PM Blames Violent Anti-government Protests on Foreign Interference', *The Guardian*, 26 November 2021.
3 Charley Piringi, 'Solomon Islands Unrest: Three Bodies Found in Burnt-out Building', *The Guardian*, 27 November 2021.

13: SEEKING PROTECTION

1 Royal Solomon Islands Police Force, Facebook post, 'RSIPF', 2 May 2023, https://www.facebook.com/RSIPF
2 'Sogavare "Spoke to Dead Solomons PM"', *The Sydney Morning Herald*, 2 August 2007.
3 DCGA refers to the Sogavare-led Democratic Coalition Government for Advancement ruling bloc.
4 'Former Solomon Islands MP Backs Switching Allegiance from Taiwan to China', Radio New Zealand, 6 July 2006.
5 Alfred Sasako, 'Armed Group "Plotting" to Take Down Government', *Solomon Star*, 23 July 2021.

14: RED LINE

1 Celsus Irokwato Talifilu, 'Solomon Islands in Danger of Becoming a Puppet State of China', *The Sydney Morning Herald*, 30 March 2022.
2 Jano Gibson, 'Why Did the Northern Territory Lease Darwin Port to Chinese-owned Company Landbridge?', ABC News (Australia), 7 May 2022.

3   Daniel Hurst and Paul Karp, 'Scott Morrison Denies Solomon Islands "Red Lines"
      Rhetoric Puts Australia More at Risk', *The Guardian*, 6 May 2022.

15: ARC OF ANXIETY
1   Cleo Paskal and Anthony Bergin, 'Sogavare Staging a Coup with Chinese
      Characteristics', *The Australian*, 16 August 2022.
2   Interview with Wendy Sherman, *7.30*, ABC-TV, 9 August 2022,
      https://www.youtube.com/watch?v=2vwbid9ZXc0
3   Stefan Armbruster, 'Who's Responsible When You're Blown Up by a World War Two
      Bomb Today?', SBS News, 20 August 2022.
4   Georgina Kekea, 'Another Life Lost from WWII Bomb', *Solomon Times*, 17 May 2021.
5   Stefan Armbruster, 'Who's Responsible When You're Blown Up by a World War Two
      Bomb Today?', SBS News, 20 August 2022.
6   Dave Sharma, 'Beijing-backed Autocracy in Our Backyard with "Cuba in the Pacific"',
      The Australian, 3 September 2022.
7   'What Sogavare Must Tell Albanese Today' (editorial), *The Australian*, 6 October 2022.
8   Julian Spencer-Churchill, 'Don't Rule Out Intervention in the Solomon Islands',
      The National Interest, 13 August 2022.
9   Blake Johnson, *Supressing the Truth and Spreading Lies: How the CCP Is Influencing
      Solomon Islands' Information Environment*. Canberra: Australian Strategic Policy
      Institute, 2002.
10   Jonathan Kearsley, Twitter, 18 November 2020,
      https://twitter.com/jekearsley/status/1328986579629613057
11   'Chinese Propaganda Against Australia Is Working, Says ASPI Boss', Sky News,
      5 October 2022.
12   Waleed Aly, 'Australia Perhaps Isn't the Big Deal It Thinks It Is to Solomon Islands',
      The Sydney Morning Herald, 7 October 2022.

17: EAST TO FATALEKA
1   Fredrick Kusu, '"Welcome, You Are One of Us", Malaita Provincial Govt Told Prime
      Minister', Solomon Islands Broadcasting Corporation, 24 October 2022.

18: MUSTAFA RISING
1   Robert Iroga, 'Police Confirms Operation to Arrest Atu and They Use Less Lethal
      Ammunition for Tactical Withdrawal', *Solomon Business Magazine Online*, 18 March 2022.

19: MAKING A MARTYR
1   'Symbol of Pacific Resistance to China Garners Support from US Lawmakers After His
      Visa Is Denied', *Samoa News*, 4 March 2023.
2   'Suidani Speaks Out on Planned Motion of No Confidence', Solomon Islands
      Broadcasting Corporation, 7 October 2021.
3   'Swearing-in of Malaita Ministers Unlawful', Solomon Islands Broadcasting Corporation,
      22 October 2021.
4   Fredrick Kusu, 'Suidani Disqualified from Provincial Assembly', Solomon Islands
      Broadcasting Corporation, 5 April 2023.
5   Cleo Paskal, 'Former Malaita Premier (and Noted China Critic) Gets Bipartisan Support
      for US Visa', *The Diplomat*, 1 April 2023.

6   Terry Nguyen, 'The Challenge of Combating Fake News in Asian American Communities', *Vox*, 27 November 2020.
7   Kevin Roose, 'How *The Epoch Times* Created a Giant Influence Machine', *The New York Times*, 24 October 2020.
8   'YOU Can Strike a Blow to the CCP!', *China Uncensored*, 16 April 2023, https://www.youtube.com/watch?v=DRVZMPBErjc

EPILOGUE: IFUTALO'S EDEN

1   Clive Moore, 'No More Walk About Long Chinatown: Asian Involvement in the Economic and Political Process', in *Politics and State Building in Solomon Islands*, Sinclair Dinnen and Stewart Firth (eds). Canberra: ANU Press, 2008.
2   Huiyuan Liu, 'An Overview of Australia's Aid Program Procurement', *Devpolicy Blog*, 14 December 2022.
3   Lisa Visentin, 'Australia Chips in $17 million to Help Solomon Islands Host Pacific Games', *The Sydney Morning Herald*, 9 August 2022.
4   Stephen Howes, 'Questions about Australian Aid to Fund the Pacific Games', *The Interpreter*, 20 April 2023.